Gainsharing and Productivity

A Guide to Planning, Implementation, and Development

ROBERT J. DOYLE

American Management Associations

Library of Congress Cataloging in Publication Data

Doyle, Robert J., 1931–
    Gainsharing and productivity.

    Bibliography: p.
    Includes index.
    1. Gain sharing.   I. Title.
HD4928.G34D69   1983   658.3'225   82-73515
ISBN 0-8144-5764-9

First Printing

A.M.D.G.

Preface

I first heard about gainsharing 25 years ago while conducting an exit interview with Jack Henriksen at Ford Motor Company. Jack was leaving a very promising career in finance at Ford to become vice-president and treasurer for Atwood Vacuum Machine Company. "What," I asked, "could a little company in Rockford, Illinois, have to offer that is better than your opportunities here at Ford?" "Several things," he said, "but the most important one is their Scanlon Plan." This aroused my curiosity, and I began reading about the Scanlon Plan. Within two years I, too, was working for a Scanlon Plan company: Wolverine World Wide in Rockford, Michigan. A few years later, I had the good fortune to join Donnelly Mirrors, Inc. in Holland, Michigan.

What began as curiosity developed into intrigue. How could any program so simple and straightforward generate such enthusiasm? Over the years, I have never seen this kind of organizationwide enthusiasm for MBO, Grid®, job enrichment, or Quality Circles. People who have experienced a successful gainsharing program are not at all shy about it. Without a doubt, gainsharing has some special kind of magic. I have come to realize, however, that the gainsharing magic is white magic for those who have experienced gainsharing at work and black magic for those who are looking at it from the outside. I am convinced that gainsharing has universal applicability, and I am at a loss to explain why it is not being used by more organizations. I believe that gainsharing is good management, good business, and good employee relations. It is a very rational and sound solution to the fundamental causes of low productivity and worker alienation in our organizations. My hope is that this book will enable a few more to see the possibilities in this excellent program.

Having had some great teachers over the years, I am now sharing what they have taught me. Although I could not possibly name everyone who has contributed to this book, I must acknowledge some of them.

At the top of the list, of course, is John F. Donnelly, who has taken the Scanlon idea farther than anyone in his drive to create an industrial organization fit for human habitation. John has inspired many of us to keep searching for ways to make organizations more responsive to the needs of the people they serve: employees, owners, customers, suppliers, and the community. Jim Knister, my first gainsharing teacher, also taught me how to cut through all the mumbo jumbo of finance and accounting. Bob Benningfield first showed me how powerful compensation is in the organizational scheme of things and how very inadequate are many of our current compensation programs. Lew Beem, who invented Quality Motivation, showed me how really simple it is to change a nonproductive organization into a highly productive one. Rensis Likert, the world's first organizational scientist, taught me that the way to successful gainsharing is rational and scientific, not emotional or faddish. Over the years, many others have been a source of ideas and encouragement, such as Bob Keeler, the Cherry Hill Gainsharing Task Group, Ed Lawler, the Scanlon Plan Associates, Carl Frost, Jack Wakeley, Tim Ross, and my partners in the American Productivity Center seminar series: R. J. Bullock, Pete Scontrino, and Carla O'Dell.

Writing this book has been an interesting first experience made truly delightful because it was a family project. I've read in so many other prefaces how books could not have been written without the help of family and staff. I'm not sure I always believed that, but I certainly do now. My wife, Mary, has been my chief counselor and, in many ways, deserves more of the credit for the existence of this book than I do. My daughters Ellen and Marie ripped the first draft to shreds and then helped put it all back together. The other children—Paul, Pat, Barb, Tom, and especially Moira—have been a very supportive cheering section. I am also very grateful to Rob Kaplan and Janet Frick for their very professional help.

Many thanks to all of you.

Robert J. Doyle

Contents

Part I
HISTORY AND DEFINITION

Gainsharing has been available for 100 years in the form of profit sharing, 40 years in the form of the Scanlon Plan® and the Rucker Plan®, and for almost 10 years in the form of Improshare®.

Organizations today have available the combined experience of the four major gainsharing programs and 30 or more years of management and organization development to use in planning and designing a gainsharing program.

This first section of the book will review the history of these past programs and present a comprehensive definition of gainsharing as it has evolved from this wealth of experience.

Chapter 1

Four Major Programs: Scanlon, Rucker, Improshare, Profit Sharing

Gainsharing, as it is known today, has evolved from the experience of four specific gainsharing programs:

Scanlon Plans
Rucker Plans
Improshare
Profit sharing

With the exception of profit sharing, which has a longer history and different origins, these programs are all recent developments that grew out of experience with more traditional incentive programs. Incentive plans such as piece rates, time payments, bonuses, merit pay, and suggestion plans have been around for hundreds of years. Everyone has had some experience with incentives, whether at home, school, factory, or farm. Work measurement, as developed by Frederick Taylor and others, gave rise to extensive use of individual incentive systems in manufacturing companies during the first half of this century.

As more and more companies used individual incentives, and as experience accumulated, problems began to develop. Disputes over rates led to labor/management conflict. Too much emphasis on output led to a deterioration in quality. Unhealthy competition between workers developed. Grievances over improper administration became more frequent. Since the 1940s, automation has eliminated many individual operations and replaced them with crew-served operations. Due to administrative difficulties and changing technology, many companies simply eliminated their incentive plans as being more trouble than they were worth. Others, convinced that the problems lay in the method and not the concept, searched for better ways to reward productivity. This search led some creative pioneers to gainsharing. (Frances Torbert has provided an excellent description of this transition from individual incentives to gainsharing in her article "Making Incentives Work," listed in the Bibliography.)

Gainsharing is not the product of research or academic study. It evolved out of experience as a solution to the constant problem of how to manage an organization to high levels of productivity and performance. This evolution accounts for the development of the Scanlon, Rucker, and Improshare plans. Profit sharing has a slightly different background, which will be discussed later in this chapter.

Gainsharing is an innovative way to manage productivity in an organization while avoiding past incentive problems. Gainsharing has also incorporated new information about organizational effectiveness from the fields of organizational and industrial psychology, organization and management development, and compensation. As we know it today, gainsharing has three basic elements:

1. *Management practices*—leadership and practices in the organization that create a positive climate for excellence and encourage a high degree of employee commitment and participation.
2. *Employee participation*—a system and structure that enables all employees to become more involved in solving problems of productivity, quality, and service.
3. *Shared reward*—a reward system that shares productivity gains above a predetermined base between owners and employees.

These three gainsharing elements are applied differently according to the needs, circumstances, and preferences of each organization. No two gainsharing programs are, or ever will be, identical. To get the most from gainsharing, each of the elements must be designed specifically for a particular organization and its people. Early gainsharing programs were developed to deal with the unique problems and circumstances facing the people who designed them. Copying these original programs has not been highly successful, but *adapting* the three basic elements to the needs of an individual company has been more than successful in numerous cases.

To fully understand the state of the art in gainsharing requires some knowledge of its origins. The following is a summary of the history and major features of each of the four specific gainsharing plans.

Scanlon Plans

Joseph N. Scanlon was a local union president (formerly a cost accountant) who invented his plan when the steel company where he was employed was forced to close due to competition from more efficient firms. Led by Scanlon, extensive discussions were held between the Steelworkers Union and company management. A new spirit of cooperation emerged, and a plan was developed that enabled the firm to reopen and compete with the larger, better-equipped steel companies. The principal feature of this original Scanlon Plan was to tie wages directly to productivity. As productivity increased, wages were to be increased. Later, a formal suggestion committee was included to encourage and process employee productivity suggestions. The suggestion-committee system, proposed by Steelworkers vice-president Clinton Golden, was modeled after a program that had been successful in the railroad industry.

Foremen and employee representatives made up floor-level production committees to consider all suggestions from departmental employees. A senior group, the screening committee, made up of top management and employee representatives, administered the plan and approved or disapproved suggestions submitted by the production committees. The screening committee also provided productivity information for all employees to encourage and direct productivity-improvement efforts.

This original plan was successful, and the idea began to spread. Scanlon accepted a position as research director for the Steelworkers and began to install plans in other companies with Steelworkers contracts. Immediately following World War II, Scanlon was invited by Douglas McGregor to join the industrial relations department at the Massachusetts Institute of Technology, where the plan was further developed, refined, and publicized. Scanlon died in 1956. However, his work has been carried on by Fred Lesieur, now a consultant, who continues his affiliation with MIT. In the early fifties, Dr. Carl Frost, a colleague of Scanlon, moved from MIT to Michigan State University and introduced the Scanlon Plan to several companies in that area. The Michigan companies formed the Scanlon Plan Associates for mutual assistance and to promote the plan to other companies. Today, both the Scanlon Plan Associates and MIT sponsor conferences for users and other interested companies.

It has been estimated that as many as 500 companies have tried the Scanlon Plan with varying degrees of success. There are perhaps 200 to 300 plans in operation today. The great majority of these have been in small to medium-size manufacturing firms, which has given rise to the erroneous notion that Scanlon Plans work only in small manufacturing firms. Dana Corporation is currently the largest firm to use the Scanlon Plan as a gainsharing strategy. Dana has Scanlon Plans in more than 20 individual plants, including one in Venezuela.

There has been very little formal research about Scanlon Plans. However, several leading management experts have made very strong statements supporting this gainsharing approach. A brochure prepared by the Scanlon Plan Associates in 1970 contained the following:

WHAT IS THE SCANLON PLAN?

The Scanlon Plan is an innovative strategy for managing an organization. It is innovative in philosophy—participative. It is innovative in structure—formal committees to involve all employees in the decision-making process. It is innovative in compensation—a productivity sharing bonus.

The Scanlon Plan puts it all together. It combines the leverage of capital, the skill of managers, the creativity and competence of all employees, and the opportunities of technology into a system supported by participation and an equitable sharing of productivity to meet the needs of customer, owner, and employee. In so doing, a company also fulfills its proper role in the larger economic system: worthwhile employment, worthwhile goods and services, worthwhile investments.

In the company the system is a series of interlocked committees to process ideas and suggestions reinforced by an equitable sharing of the increased productivity. In a Scanlon Plan, employees typically contribute better suggestions more frequently and receive a monthly bonus based on the savings realized by these suggestions. There are many variations of the suggestions committees and bonus formula according to the situation and needs of the organization. Cooperation and participation can take many forms as well, but regardless of form, these are the essential ingredients.

The excellence of the Scanlon Plan has been recognized by many. Douglas McGregor wrote:

Management by integration and self-control (Theory Y) can take many forms. One of the most unusual of these is the Scanlon Plan. Out of his deep interest in union management cooperation, the late Joseph Scanlon evolved a collaborative strategy which has achieved solid results, in both economic and human terms, in a number of industrial companies.

Rensis Likert observed:

All too often the Scanlon Plan—like all profit-sharing plans—is thought of only as a device for increasing the motivational forces arising from the economic needs of the members of an organization. As Scanlon emphasized, however, the plan requires the development of an interaction-influence system in which ideas for developing better products and processes and for reducing costs and waste can flow readily, be assessed, improved, and expeditiously applied. Such an interaction-influence system is appreciably more characteristic of System 4 than of the other management systems.

Robert T. Golembiewski noted:

> Curiously, the principle of group decision making has had few full-fledged applications. Various bastardized "participation plans" do exist. Often they attempt to get without giving and must take their place in the storehouse of gimmicks that might (or might not) work in the short run and are likely to fail in the longer run. The Scanlon Plan, in contrast, attempts to exploit the possibilities of participation and distributes the benefits among all. It does not pussyfoot. . . . Basically, the Plan's purpose is to heighten cooperation between labor and management, to sustain it by mutual participation in decision making, and to nourish it by mutual sharing of the fruits of the cooperation.

Clinton Golden, a vice-president of United Steelworkers of America, said about the Scanlon Plan:

> It is ironic that Americans—the most advanced people technically, mechanically, and industrially—should have waited until a comparatively recent period to inquire into the most promising single source of productivity: namely, the human will to work. It is hopeful, on the other hand, that the search is now under way.

An editorial in *Life* magazine in 1952 opined that the Scanlon Plan, while no panacea, was one of the most hopeful developments in recent labor/management relations, and that when Scanlon Plans were no longer news, we should have licked one of the great problems of the industrial age: how to tame the machine for liberty and democracy.

MANAGEMENT PRACTICES

Scanlon Plans place great stress on an employee-centered, or participative, leadership style that has been identified by McGregor as Theory Y, by Likert as System 4, by Blake and Mouton as 9,9, and by others with other names. A successful Scanlon Plan begins with a leadership or management style that acknowledges that employees have a good deal more to contribute to the organization than just their sweat and also understands that employees need much more from their jobs than just a weekly pay check.

The participative management style leads to practices that create a climate for excellence. Information is shared widely throughout the organization, so all know what the goals are and where the problems lie. Ideas for improvement or the elimination of waste are actively solicited by management and used by the organization. Managers encourage people to learn, grow, and contribute. They stress and achieve cooperation between people, departments, and shifts.

In early applications, Joe Scanlon interviewed the managers of interested companies to see whether they had the right management practices. If satisfied, he would continue to help the company develop its plan. If dissatisfied, he declined to work with the company and told management it was not ready for his gainsharing plan. Today there are more sophisticated and objective ways of determining the readiness of management, and there are training programs to help prepare a management group to use gainsharing.

EMPLOYEE PARTICIPATION

Most Scanlon Plans employ a two-level system of suggestion committees. At the shop or office level, the first-line supervisor and two or three employees make up the first-level productivity committee. Suggestions are brought before this committee by the employee representatives. In the committee, the ideas are discussed and either adopted, rejected, or referred. If adopted, an idea is put into effect as soon as possible. If rejected, the suggester is told why and encouraged to "keep thinking." If the suggestion is favored by the productivity committee but is beyond its authority, it is referred to the second-level screening committee for approval. Ideas requiring coordination with another department or shift are referred, as well as ideas that cost more to implement than the supervisor can approve.

The screening committee is made up of representatives from each of the first-level productivity committees, senior managers, and, where applicable, union officials. In addition to approving or rejecting all suggestions referred to it from productivity committees, the screening committee also handles any administrative matters associated with the plan; this includes screening the financial and business results each month and announcing the bonus to all employees. Figure 1 shows a typical Scanlon Plan committee organization.

SHARED REWARD

The reward, in most Scanlon Plans, is based on labor productivity only. A productivity base is determined by examining the actual labor costs from two to five years of normal or near-normal operations. This base is expressed as a percentage of labor costs to sales and established as the "ratio." Gains occur and are shared when actual labor costs are less than what is allowed by the ratio. Each month, results are measured against the ratio. When a gain occurs, the savings are shared between the company and the employees. The company share increases income, and

Figure 1. Organization of a Scanlon Plan committee.

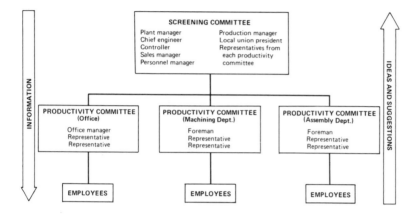

the employee share is paid in the form of a cash bonus. Employee bonuses of 10 percent to 15 percent are common in successful Scanlon Plans. Although monthly bonuses are the most common, other time periods more suitable to the needs of a particular business have been used.

In plans measuring only labor, 75 percent of the savings is paid to the employees and 25 percent to the company. The company receives the full benefit of savings other than labor. For example, as labor productivity improves, there is usually less scrap and better use of supplies and equipment. These additional benefits to the company tend to equalize the shares. Figure 2 is an example of a typical Scanlon Plan monthly bonus statement.

Productivity usually fluctuates from month to month, and year-end figures usually turn up inventory adjustments, so it is necessary to hold back a portion of each month's savings in a reserve fund to cover future deficits. The size of this reserve varies from 10 percent to 35 percent, depending on how much productivity is expected to fluctuate from month to month. The reserve account builds up each month or is used to cover a monthly deficit and is closed out at the end of each year. A surplus in the reserve fund is paid out as a year-end bonus on the same basis as the monthly bonus. A deficit in the reserve is usually absorbed by the company to enable the plan to start the new year without having to overcome a loss.

Scanlon Plan practice recommends that all employees, both management and labor, participate in the same bonus. Not all Scanlon companies

Figure 2. Typical Scanlon Plan monthly bonus statement.

Sales	$ 92,000
Inventory increase or decrease	10,000
Production at sales value	$102,000
Less returns and allowances	2,000
Adjusted production	$100,000
Allowed labor per ratio	$30,000
Less actual labor	25,000
Savings or gain	$ 5,000
Less reserve for deficit—10%	500
For distribution	$ 4,500
Company share—25%	$1,125
Employee share—75%	$3,375
Participating payroll (adjusted for new employees, vacation pay, etc.)	$22,500

Bonus: $\dfrac{\$3,375}{\$22,500} = $ 15% paid to each employee as a percentage of monthly wages

do this, however. In some companies, managers are not included. Others exclude outside commissioned salespeople. These exclusions usually occur because the company uses other performance bonuses for management and salespeople. There are no data to support either the inclusion or exclusion of managers, but Scanlon literature strongly recommends that everyone be included to encourage and reward teamwork among employees at all levels.

The preceding material represents the most typical features of Scanlon Plans; however, many companies using Scanlon Plans today have been innovative in modifying the original Scanlon concepts to meet changing conditions and specific needs. Some have borrowed heavily from recent developments in management theory and have improved in the area of management practices. Others have modified their bonus formulas to include materials and other costs in the productivity measurement, in addition to labor. Some have expanded their participation systems to include new structures such as work teams and new techniques such as Quality Circles.

Scanlon Plans are definitely the flagship of the gainsharing fleet. They have provided most of the innovation, and therefore most of the experience, to our fund of gainsharing knowledge.

Rucker Plans

Allan W. Rucker, an economist, developed a gainsharing program from research in the manufacturing sector that showed that labor cost, as a percentage of value added, remains quite stable over long periods. His research also showed that while industry patterns differ from the national economic trends, they are stable within the same industry. Variations range from very high productivity levels for highly capitalized industries to very low productivity levels for companies with low capital investment. This stable relationship of labor to value added continues through the peaks and troughs of the business cycle.

Finding similar patterns in individual companies led to the practical application of this economic research: the Rucker Plan. In more than 90 percent of the companies studied, there has been found a stable ratio of labor to value added, which forms the basis for measuring productivity changes. Rucker experience has been exclusively with manufacturing firms where the ratio of labor cost to value added has been well researched and developed. It would seem that similar measures could be developed for nonmanufacturing businesses, but, thus far, it has not been done.

In the late 1930s, Rucker's research was first used by some companies as a guide for wages and salaries, and to control labor costs as the economy emerged from the Great Depression. Following this, a few companies used the information as a basis for productivity bonuses while prices and wages were frozen during World War II, the Korean conflict, and during the 1971–72 wage-price controls. In each of the freezes, legitimate noninflationary productivity bonuses were exempt from the freeze. The Rucker Plan provided the data to identify productivity improvements. Gradually the idea was picked up by companies that saw the value of gainsharing regardless of government wage freezes.

There are between 200 and 300 Rucker Plans in operation today. One consulting firm, The Eddy-Rucker-Nickels Company, has registered the Rucker Plan and title. It helps companies determine their productivity ratio (Rucker standard) and install and maintain the plan.

The following material is from an Eddy-Rucker-Nickels Company brochure:

ABOUT THE RUCKER·PLAN

WHY   To maximize operating profit by obtaining the active cooperation
           of all employees in meeting the company's goals.

WHERE   In plants with 50–800 hourly people; at least a three-year history
           of profitable operations; good human relations between plant peo-
           ple and management; and where the manufacturing process is such
           that the plant people can actually make a substantial contribution
           to improved productivity if they are motivated to do so.

WHAT   A "broad spectrum" incentive for all direct and indirect plant
           people, their supervisors and others—providing opportunities for
           gains in both profit and pay from:
             Improved use of materials
             Improved use of supplies
             Improved output per man-hour
             Improved product quality
             Improved production methods
             Improved machinery
             Improved service to customers

HOW   Of every 100 competitive and profitable manufacturing concerns
           about 95 will show a stable relationship between the input of
           Plant Employment Costs and the output as measured by Produc-
           tion Value (essentially equivalent to the U.S. census "Value
           Added by Manufacture"—that is, Sales Income less Material and
           Supply Costs).

WHEN   The program should be introduced when there will be sufficient
           work for the current people so that improved efficiency should
           not result in layoffs. These can be avoided by actual volume gains
           or by normal attrition of the workforce.

MANAGEMENT PRACTICES

Participative management style and practices have not been stressed as
heavily in Rucker Plans as in Scanlon Plans but are considered important
to a successful plan. Management is encouraged to communicate with,
listen to, and solicit ideas from all employees. Managers in successful
Rucker Plan companies express a strong belief in effective communications and employee involvement. Rucker Plan literature also lists "good
human relations between plant people and management" as one of the
prerequisites to success.

EMPLOYEE PARTICIPATION

In early Rucker Plans, participation was of the suggestion-box or campaign variety. Employee ideas for improvement and elimination of waste
were solicited and used. With experience, some companies have added
Rucker committees. These are usually single plantwide committees that

process suggestions. Larger Rucker Plan organizations use multilevel committees similar to the Scanlon structure. Rucker committees include ex officio management and, where applicable, union official members, along with elected or appointed employee representatives. Rucker Plans stress heavily the idea that bonuses are created by employees who find new ways to eliminate waste, reduce costs, and improve methods.

SHARED REWARD

The method for measuring productivity and determining the gain is unique to Rucker Plans. It is based on Rucker's research that showed that the labor portion of value added tends to remain constant over time despite changes in selling price and labor costs. A careful analysis is made of three to five years of company financial experience in obtaining the ratio of labor costs to value added. (Value added is the difference between the selling price of the company's products and the purchase price of materials, supplies, and services.)

Where it is found that labor costs, as a percentage of value added, are stable or consistent over several years, the Rucker standard can be determined and the Rucker Plan can be used. Figure 3 shows how the Rucker standard is determined. (All figures represent an average of three to five years of actual experience.)

Bonuses are earned in a Rucker Plan, as in all gainsharing programs, by improving productivity. Some Rucker suggestions for improving productivity are:

Material and supply savings.
Lower scrap and less rework.
Fewer customer rejects and returns.
Increased prices.
Higher output.
Better use of people's skills and time.

All savings, regardless of type, increase the company's value added, and employees receive the difference between the actual labor cost and the Rucker standard as a bonus. Bonuses are usually paid monthly as a percentage of total monthly earnings. Other time periods—such as four weeks, bimonthly, or quarterly—can be used for bonus periods. Figure 4 is an example of a monthly Rucker Plan bonus statement.

Under the Rucker Plan, the employee bonus is the labor savings effect of any improvement in value added. The company's share is the effect of the improvements in the "other" costs. If the Rucker standard is 37.4 percent, labor receives 37.4 percent of value added, either as wages and benefits or as a bonus.

Figure 3. How the Rucker standard is determined.

Sales	$100,000
Less materials, supplies, services	50,000
Value added	$ 50,000
Labor costs	$18,700
Other costs	$31,300

Rucker standard: $\dfrac{\text{Labor costs}}{\text{Value added}} = \dfrac{\$18,700}{\$50,000} = 37.4\%$

Labor costs include:

Straight-time pay	Family emergency pay
Overtime premium	Workers compensation insurance
Shift premium	Medical insurance
Vacation pay	Life insurance
Holiday pay	Unemployment insurance
Jury duty pay	Social Security taxes
Sick pay	Pensions

Other costs include:

Executive and management pay	Rent
Profit (dividends and reinvestment)	Advertising
Property taxes	Contributions
Property insurance	Travel costs
Sales expenses	Legal costs
Cost of equipment (depreciation)	Income tax
Telephone and telegraph	Bad debts

A portion of each monthly savings is put into a balancing account to offset the deficits of negative months or to cover year-end adjustment. This account is closed at the end of each year. Funds, if any, are paid out as a year-end bonus, and losses are absorbed by the company. The amount set aside in this account is generally 25 percent to 30 percent of the gain, depending on what is needed to cover monthly fluctuations and year-end adjustments.

Rucker Plans include at least all direct and indirect factory personnel. Other employees can be included in either of two ways:

1. *Direct*—the labor costs of supervision, staff, and/or managers can be included in the Rucker standard, and those employees can participate directly in the bonus.

Figure 4. Sample Rucker Plan monthly bonus statement.

Sales	$100,000
Less purchases	50,000
Value added by production	$ 50,000
Rucker standard—37.4%	$18,700
Less actual labor cost	16,700
Gain	$ 2,000
Balancing account	500
For distribution	$ 1,500
Participating payroll	$15,500

Bonus: $\dfrac{\$1,500}{\$15,500} = 9.7\%$ paid to participating employees on the basis of monthly earnings

2. *Matching*—for those employees not directly covered, the company can pay a matching bonus from its share of the savings.

In general, there tends to be more uniformity among Rucker Plans than among Scanlon Plans. Recently, however, as experience has grown and become more public, it would appear that Rucker companies are learning some new approaches from Scanlon companies and vice versa. We are beginning to see the emergence of a universal gainsharing concept with common features.

Improshare

More recently, an innovative plan by Mitchell Fein has been introduced in the gainsharing field as Improshare (*Im*proved *Pro*ductivity *Shar*ing). Introduced in 1974, Improshare emerged from traditional industrial engineering experience. The rather common industrial engineering wage-incentive plans have been plagued with problems such as not including indirect labor, resistance to new processes and equipment, artificial ceilings on production, and unwanted competition between workers. Improshare provides a fairly simple and effective solution to these problems.

In effect, Improshare is an adaptation of the older forms to the realities of today's workplace. Automation has changed work structures from individuals to groups and has increased the ratio of indirect to direct workers. Technology has increased the rate of change in machines and processes. Today's organizations need a plan that:

Rewards group performance.

Includes indirect workers in measuring and rewarding productivity.

Facilitates the introduction of new equipment.

Avoids negative attitudes toward the system.

Improshare meets all of these current needs. It has a group bonus system that includes all hourly employees. The productivity measurement is the labor hours, direct and indirect, it takes to produce one unit of product. Gains are recorded as hours saved, which are divided 50/50 between the producing employees and the company. The employees' share of hours saved is converted to a cash bonus based on actual time worked during the period.

The plan includes a provision for adjusting the base when a new method or new equipment is introduced, which also provides an incentive for workers to help install and use the new method or equipment.

The plan also includes a buy-back provision whereby the company adjusts the base productivity factor and pays each employee one year's worth of the savings reflected in the changed rates. These one-time payments prevent the negative reaction to rate changes characteristic of traditional incentive plans.

MANAGEMENT PRACTICES

Improshare literature stresses that management can gain greater employee commitment and involvement, and improved productivity, without giving up any traditional management prerogatives. The plan does not encourage the adoption of new management styles or practices but does encourage management and labor to recognize that their interests are the same. Improshare theory stresses that the goals of management and labor are congruent and can be met by encouraging the workers' will to work. The group gainsharing bonus is regarded as the principal method of encouragement. The key elements in the Improshare plan are that rewards are tied to improved performance and that practices that penalize workers as productivity improves are stopped.

EMPLOYEE PARTICIPATION

Improshare does not include a formal employee-involvement system like those in Scanlon Plans or Rucker Plans. The plan suggests that as workers realize that bonuses come from better (cost-saving) methods, the ideas will flow. Management should be quick to respond to these ideas. If management does a good job of responding to new ideas when they are proposed, a formal structure is said to be unnecessary. In actual practice, many successful Improshare companies have added formal structures, similar to Scanlon Plans and Rucker Plans.

SHARED REWARD

Improshare plans, unlike other plans, calculate savings in hours required to make a unit of product. Only in the final step are the hours converted to dollars for bonus purposes. Using historical or measured standards, all of the time needed to produce one unit of product is calculated and becomes the base productivity factor (BPF). As an example, a BPF might be 1.80 hours, composed of 1.00 hour of direct labor and .80 hour of indirect labor required to produce one unit of product. (If direct labor were 1.50 hours and indirect labor .80 hour, the BPF would be 2.30 hours, and so on.) Weekly output is counted and multiplied by the BPF, yielding an allowed number of Improshare hours. If actual hours worked are less than the allowed Improshare hours, there is a savings, which is split 50/50 between the company and the workers. The workers' share is calculated as a percentage of total hours worked, and each employee receives a bonus of hours multiplied by his or her rate of pay. Figure 5 is an example of a weekly Improshare calculation.

Figure 5. Sample Improshare calculation.

Base productivity factor = 1.80

Production	20,000 units

Improshare hours earned:
20,000 × 1.80 =	36,000
Actual hours worked	30,000 hours
Savings	6,000 hours
Company share—50%	3,000 hours
Employee share—50%	3,000 hours

Bonus hours: $\dfrac{3,000}{30,000} = 10\%$

Sample bonus calculation for one worker:
Hours worked	40
Pay rate	$8.12 per hour
Bonus hours (10%)	4.0 hours

Bonus: 4.0 hours × $8.12 = $32.48

Improshare bonuses are paid weekly and included in the employee's regular pay check. To avoid the problem of fluctuating weekly bonuses, a moving average is maintained for four or six weeks, and bonuses are paid at the average. There is no provision for a reserve fund, since the moving average adds savings, subtracts losses, and pays only when the cumulative amount is a savings.

Bonuses are not paid in excess of 30 percent. When the bonus exceeds this level, the excess is banked and carried forward to a future lower week and then added back. Because of the 50/50 split, the 30 percent bonus ceiling level is reached only when savings reach 60 percent.

There are two provisions for changing the BPF. When introducing new technology, the rates are adjusted by only 80 percent. If a new process saves ten hours, only eight hours are taken out of the rates. When the level of productivity surpasses 60 percent permanently, there is a provision to "buy" a permanent rate change by paying a full year's worth of the savings to all employees. When, for instance, the savings has reached the 70 percent level, there is a 30 percent bonus and 5 percent banked each week. At this point, the plan provides that the company can change the rates (lower the BPF, for example, from 1.80 to 1.75) to a point where the savings represents a 40 percent gain. The employee share of this change is equal to 15 percent of the hours saved. For an employee earning $8 per hour, a 15% bonus would amount to $48 per week, or $2,496 per year. The calculation is shown in Figure 6.

When the change is made, all employees receive a check for the one-year savings, a new BPF goes into effect, and the new rates are used to calculate further savings. Improshare plans are new, and few companies have had actual experience with the buy back, but the provision is very appealing to most employees at the time of installation.

Figure 6. Sample buy-back calculation.

Savings level at old BPF	70%
Savings level at new BPF	40%
Change	30%
Company share—50%	15%
Employee share—50%	15%
Employee buy-back bonus:	
40 hours × 15% = 6 hours	
6 hours × $8 = $48	
$48 × 52 weeks = $2,496	

The 50/50 split is common to all Improshare plans and tends to be accepted by the employees as fair. In addition to its 50 percent share, the company also benefits from savings in materials and other costs, which improve as labor becomes more productive.

Improshare is designed for nonexempt operating personnel and excludes executives, managers, supervisors, or professional staff personnel. To provide a bonus for these employees, it is recommended that they be paid a matching bonus from the company's 50 percent share of the gain.

As a form of gainsharing, Improshare has special appeal for manufacturing firms accustomed to dealing with individual incentives, work measurement, and other industrial engineering concepts. The plan also has strong support from the American Institute of Industrial Engineers. Service sector organizations, such as banks, are beginning to try the concept. As with other gainsharing plans, the myth that these programs work only in manufacturing will not be dispelled until a few farsighted pioneers in the service sector sit down and figure how to apply them to their situation.

Profit Sharing

Profit sharing is reportedly used in over 350,000 U.S. companies today. It is said to have started in Paris in 1835, giving it about 100 years of seniority over the other three gainsharing plans. Le Claire, a Parisian painting contractor, began sharing profits with his painters, much to their delight and to the consternation of his competitors. It is reported that, due to increased productivity of the profit-sharing painter, Le Claire virtually cornered the house-painting market in Paris. In 1850, a German, Von Thunen, began a system whereby his tenant farmers earned credit during each working year toward a small plot of land, which became theirs upon retirement. This is the first record we have of a deferred-benefit profit-sharing plan so common among U.S. companies today.

Procter & Gamble pioneered profit sharing in the United States as early as 1887 and in the 1920s was joined by other major corporations such as Kodak, Sears Roebuck, Johnson Wax, and Harris Trust. Despite the leadership of these companies, profit sharing enjoyed only limited success in the United States until 1939, when Congress passed a law allowing tax deferments for qualified plans. This legislation led to the widespread use of profit sharing as a deferred retirement benefit. It is estimated that over 90 percent of today's plans began as a result of this tax law.

Profit-sharing plans are relatively easy to understand, implement, and administer. Most plans include the following principal features:

° A once-a-year profit-sharing bonus that can be taken as cash, deferred for retirement, or split between the two options.

° Regular communications from management to employees concerning profits, costs, and productivity. Small to medium-size companies use employee meetings for communicating this information. Larger companies use written materials such as letters and the company's annual report. Often, in these communications, employees are encouraged to find ways to reduce waste and improve productivity.

MANAGEMENT PRACTICES

Profit sharing promotes the idea of employee involvement in reducing costs and improving profits. The literature encourages managers to communicate and to listen to employee ideas. There are, of course, wide variations in how this is done in 350,000 companies. Most tend to view their profit-sharing plans as another fringe benefit and do very little to encourage a high level of employee involvement. Due to the efforts of consultants, and organizations such as The Profit Sharing Research Foundation, more attention is being given to management practices that facilitate greater employee involvement. There is evidence to show that such efforts produce good results, but, so far, only a few companies have adopted this change.

EMPLOYEE PARTICIPATION

Profit-sharing plans generally provide for only a minimum level of employee participation. There are usually nonmanagement employees in addition to managers on a committee that administers the profit-sharing plan and trust. This group makes administrative policy, such as establishing methods for disbursement and withdrawal; audits the plan's books; and decides where and how to invest the plan's funds. In some companies, profit-sharing meetings are held with all employees to discuss the progress or results of profit sharing and the business. Employees are encouraged to be cost- and waste-conscious to improve the profit share. These meetings are effective as pep talks but seldom result in any direct action. Some profit-sharing companies are beginning to explore employee involvement techniques such as Quality Circles and profit-improvement teams.

SHARED REWARD

The term *bonus* is not used in profit-sharing plans. The reward is called the *profit share*.

The great majority of the plans in the United States today are deferred plans, where the share is invested in a retirement account. This share is

Figure 7. Principal features of four specific gainsharing programs.

	Scanlon	Rucker	Improshare	Profit Sharing
Management practices	Participative system highly stressed	Participative system recommended	Reduction in conflict between labor and management recommended	Better education and communications recommended
Employee participation	Suggestion committees or work teams	Rucker committees	Good ideas used when they occur	None specified
Productivity target	Reduction in cost and/or labor	Cost reduction with emphasis on labor	Reduction in labor time, direct and indirect	Improved profit
Bonus basis	Ratio of costs to sales value of production	Labor: percentage of value added	Hours saved compared to standard	Share of profit
Bonus frequency	Monthly to quarterly	Monthly to quarterly	Weekly	Annually— usually deferred
Participants	All employees	Hourly employees— others optional	Hourly employees only	All employees

determined and paid into the employee's account once a year when the company's books are closed and audited. There are some "cash" plans, where an annual or more frequent cash bonus is paid. A few are combination plans, which pay some of the share in cash and defer the rest. Where the plan is used as a retirement program, the company tries to put an amount equal to 8 percent to 10 percent of pay into each employee's account. There are several ways to accomplish this. Most plans provide that a fixed percentage (15 percent to 25 percent) of profit, before taxes, goes to the profit-share fund. In other plans, the board of directors decides at the end of the year how much can be contributed to the fund. Still other plans use a combination of a fixed percentage of profit plus a discretionary and optional amount as decided by the board.

Some plans allow employee contributions to increase the size of their individual retirement accounts. Due to the 1939 tax law, money contributed by the company to an employee's fund is not taxed until it is withdrawn. This provides a savings in federal taxes, since withdrawal is intended to occur when the employee is retired and in a lower tax bracket. There are tax regulations and laws, such as the Employee Retirement Income Security Act (ERISA), that apply to deferred-income plans. These are beyond the scope of this book but should be studied carefully by any company planning to install a profit-sharing plan.

Profit-sharing literature claims employee motivation and productivity improvement as potential benefits of profit sharing. However, these plans are viewed by management and labor in most organizations as retirement plans, not productivity-improvement plans. Profit-sharing programs have considerable potential to improve productivity, but, so far, this has not been realized to any great extent.

Summary

Among the four plans, there are similarities and differences. Figure 7 presents a comparison of the major features of the four plans. Though each plan has its advocates, a definite trend is emerging to use the best features from any of the plans to design a gainsharing program just right for "our" organization.

Chapter 2

Experiences from Successful Programs

After "What is it?" the most frequently asked question about gainsharing is "Does it work?" Some people are skeptical—they have heard it all before. Others ask about it enthusiastically—they believe in the concept and are eager to find a program that works.

A problem we face in answering this question is that there has been very little systematic research in the field of gainsharing, such as before-and-after studies, studies among comparable groups, or studies of the causes of success and failure. Although systematic research is lacking, field reports of success and failure are beginning to accumulate. There are positive reports from many companies, which show what is possible with a gainsharing program. The following represents the kind of successes that have occurred.

Profit

All successful companies report an improvement in profit. Gainsharing programs are designed to increase the income of the company as well as that of the workers. The company's share goes directly to increased profit as shown on the profit and loss statement. Profits do not show an increase every month or even every year, just as bonuses are not paid every month or every year, but a properly designed plan will show a profit improvement any time an employee bonus is paid.

Experience varies considerably from company to company. One firm with low profit may show a tremendous increase in earnings. Another, starting gainsharing during a good profit period, may have a relatively smaller increase. There are no data to suggest how much of an increase in profit a company can expect from a gainsharing program. However, any company could prepare a simple model to show the effect on profits of certain assumed increases in productivity. For instance, if $100,000 were saved in labor cost and this amount were shared 75 percent to workers, 25 percent to the company, the company's pretax profit would increase by $25,000. Assuming a similar savings in materials, in supplies, and in the use of capital, the pretax profit increase could be as high as $125,000 ($25,000 in labor and $100,000 in other cost savings).

Bonuses

Everything pertaining to profit applies similarly to bonuses. Successful gainsharing programs pay bonuses as part of the design. One purpose of gainsharing is to increase productivity. When productivity increases, new dollars are available for sharing between the company and the workers.

Bonuses vary greatly from plan to plan. Successful programs tend to pay bonuses that average from 5 percent to 15 percent of pay. There will be months when no bonuses are paid and some where the bonus may be 25 percent or more. Sustained bonuses in excess of 20 percent are rare, but they have happened.

In one very unusual case at Company M, a Scanlon Plan company, the employees decided to discontinue annual pay increases. After several years of no wage increases, their bonuses increased to over 100 percent of pay. These employees did not receive any more money by this method, but they did seem to enjoy the high bonus percentage. Whether money is taken in the form of wages or bonuses, the amount is determined by the level of productivity and the price structure in those markets where the company does business.

In addition to increasing employee income, the bonus serves as a scorecard. High bonuses (15 percent or more) generally show that the organization has performed very well, and a high-bonus announcement is often a time of great satisfaction to everyone.

What happens when the inevitable low-bonus month, or months, occur? Periods of low productivity are a crisis for any organization, but they have a particular significance for gainsharing companies. How the organization reacts to low bonuses is a measure of the health of a gainsharing program. If the program is weak, groups tend to blame each other for low productivity. Management blames employees for not trying hard enough. Employees blame management for poor decisions or lack of support. And everybody blames sales.

In organizations where the program has been properly implemented, people react to low-bonus periods by rolling up their sleeves. They go to work looking for new ways to improve productivity. In periods of depressed sales, people tighten their collective belts, do the best they can, and wait for the business cycle to become favorable again.

Several years ago at an MIT Scanlon conference, a group of union officials who were complaining about low bonuses appeared to reach a consensus that management should get all the blame for the problem, when a new voice was heard. A union president stood up and told the group that his company, Company K, had introduced a Scanlon Plan two years previously and had yet to pay a bonus. During those two years, its industry had been through a very difficult period of excess capacity, price cutting, layoffs, and plant closures. In his plant, there had been no lay-offs, and he reported that the employees felt that having their jobs was an adequate bonus. The increased productivity resulting from their Scanlon Plan had enabled the company to stay healthy through the difficult competitive struggle.

Only a few gainsharing companies have reached the level of maturity where there is a positive let's-do-something-about-it response to adversity. This ideal is an achievement, and not an automatic benefit of gainsharing.

Use of Capital

Gainsharing savings are recorded each year in the profit and loss statement, and there is a tendency to see this as the only impact on business results. Over several years, however, an equally important additional impact will be observed in the amount of return on investment (ROI). Suggestions that improve methods result in more product per machine or other piece of capital equipment. Employees quickly learn that production or output helps to create savings and that production is possible only when the machines are running. Down time decreases as people take better care of the equipment. When breakdowns occur, repairs are more carefully made. All of this reduces the need for additional equipment and results in longer useful life of machines and equipment.

Company M workers bragged about a pre-World War II production lathe that ran more parts and with closer tolerance in the 1970s than when it was purchased new in 1938.

Company W, which had 13 production plants, calculated that it had saved one complete, 200-employee plant due to productivity increases over a six-year period. This savings included land, building, machines, and other equipment. Better use of capital is a significant, though longer-term, benefit of gainsharing.

The company's share of the productivity gain increases the return portion of ROI, and over time, the extended life of machines and equipment reduces the investment portion. The cumulative effect is such that if profits were to increase by 10 percent over a five-year period, ROI might increase by as much as 15 percent.

Scheduling and Delivery

Because smooth and efficient scheduling is more productive, people find ways to improve scheduling. "Getting it out" becomes important to everyone, and "keeping it moving" is the best way to "get it out." Batches or orders don't get lost, because customers don't pay for lost orders. Work-in-process inventories tend to decline, which improves cash flow, reduces interest expense, and increases ROI.

Suggestions begin to come from employees about how to schedule more efficiently and how to reduce costs by less frequent setups and longer production runs. People at the machines recognize some of the causes of bottlenecks, which are not apparent to the production control clerk at a computer terminal in the office. And because the production control people share in the bonus, they are more inclined to be attentive to suggestions and feedback from the floor. Unusual scheduling situations can also be handled better.

Company P, a manufacturer of large capital equipment, was asked to accept a large special order to replace equipment lost in a fire. Normal production time to complete such an order was nine weeks. Through a series of meetings, the employees agreed to produce the order in the seven weeks required by the customer. The order was completed on time and with no disruption to normal production schedules. The company maintained one good customer and added to its reputation for being the best in its field. Gainsharing companies typically report a higher rate of on-time deliveries and fewer delinquencies.

Quality

Quality of products and services is a critical factor in productivity. One major problem with past incentive plans has been that quality deteriorated as volume was emphasized. Special care is taken to prevent this from happening in a gainsharing program. First of all, only good product is counted as production. Second, customer returns and adjustments are deducted from subsequent bonuses. Third, employees quickly learn that they can increase the bonus by reducing the cost of inspection necessary to insure product quality. Doing it right the first time is rewarded. Therefore, it happens.

Almost all gainsharing companies report that quality improves and the cost of producing a quality product goes down. Company D replaced 14 line inspectors with 3 auditors and reduced customer returns by 75 percent. The gainsharing program accomplished what much preaching and many posters could not. Quality improved because production personnel had a real stake in producing a quality product.

Scrap

In every gainsharing productivity measurement, only good production is counted as output. Scrap does not contribute to the bonus, and field returns are deducted from subsequent monthly bonuses. The organization learns to scrap doomed parts early to avoid more cost and to salvage parts when it can be done economically. Scrap reductions occur in every gainsharing program, saving labor, material, and other manufacturing costs. The president of a food-processing company was lukewarm toward gainsharing because he felt the plan applied only to labor-intensive operations. When asked what the potential savings might be if scrap were reduced, his interest picked up dramatically. "We could double our profit if we could reduce scrap losses by 20 percent," he said. At Company G, a small glass-door manufacturer, the president announced there was to be no Scanlon bonus for the month. "Why not?" asked the disappointed employees at the monthly bonus meeting. "Come with me," replied the president. He then led all of the employees to the back of the plant and, pointing to a larger-than-normal pile of broken glass, said: "There is our bonus." This story also wins an award for effective communication, since there was a sudden and substantial reduction in scrap at Company G.

Market Share

Many companies report an improvement in market share resulting from the gainsharing program. Better quality and delivery contributes to this, and cost improvements add even more. In markets where price competition is intense, companies have been able to price their products and services more competitively and obtain a larger share of the available business.

The long-term success of any organization depends on keeping its customers or clients. They want value for their dollars. To a customer, value is a combination of price, quality, and delivery. An improvement in any of these gives customers greater value, which is their share of productivity improvement. Company D, over a 20-year period, reduced prices by 25 percent and secured 90 percent of the market for a specialty part. A substantial portion of the increased share came when one major customer stopped producing a portion of the product itself because it was receiving better value from Company D.

Survival

The first Scanlon Plan, and many of the early gainsharing plans, were installed to cope with or prevent a serious crisis. Desperate companies are more likely to experiment with a new idea; they feel they have nothing to lose. Several organization studies show that a crisis or threat to the organization tends to rally the energy it takes to make a major change such as gainsharing. Necessity sometimes is the mother of invention. As a result, gainsharing has established a track record for saving companies in trouble. As experience grows, other companies will approach gainsharing as a proven strategy for preventing crises, and the ''salvage'' reputation will diminish. However, in one way, gainsharing will remain a survival strategy. As far as we know, there will always be ups and downs in economic or business cycles. Each time we go through a recession, organizations that don't perform are forced out of competition, and the fittest survive. By providing value and reliability to its customers, who will keep the company in business, a successful gainsharing company provides survivability and security to shareholders and employees alike.

Understanding the Business

Over time, and as a result of joint effort to improve productivity, all employees, even managers, develop a greater awareness of what it takes for the organization to be successful. The opportunities to do this already exist in every business, but in a company with an active gainsharing program, people tend to learn more from their daily lessons. More employees become aware of the importance of cost, quality, and delivery performance. They become aware of the value of cooperation and coordination within work groups, between shifts, and between line and staff groups. They also become aware that having a strong, competent, and effective organization is one of the greatest assets of all and is the principal source of employment security. Company B, seeing the importance of this feature, named its gainsharing program "The Facts of Life Plan."

Successful gainsharing companies typically report that employees and managers alike have a much better understanding of how productivity is necessary to the immediate and long-range stability and growth of the business. This, of course, does not happen automatically or by magic. Administering a gainsharing program effectively requires that financial information be shared with and explained to employees. Each month there is the business of announcing and explaining the bonus. As bonuses go up and down, and the causes are explained, people develop a better understanding of the business and what it takes to be productive.

For several months, Company D paid low bonuses when high bonuses were expected. People complained that costs in an aerospace division had not been reduced in proportion to its declining sales volume. Managers then explained that four highly paid skilled workers who could not be replaced if laid off were being kept on in the hope of future business, even though there was presently no work in their specialty. This decision lowered overall productivity, which reduced everyone's bonus. Once explained, the decision was supported by all as being in their mutual long-range interest.

The bonus gives everyone a stake in decisions of this type, and employees will ask that such decisions be explained. Good decisions are supported; poor decisions bring additional complaints. Leaders learn to make better decisions, and everyone learns more about what it takes to make the business succeed.

Managing Change Effectively

Change becomes part of the culture in successful gainsharing companies. Through the participation system, people are encouraged to innovate. The bonus rewards changes that improve productivity. People suggest changes more frequently and support changes suggested by others.

This does not mean, however, that the organization begins to make changes indiscriminately or without careful study. On the contrary, the organization becomes more sophisticated and discriminating about change while increasing its acceptance of change. The productivity measurement and the bonus provide the means to make a more accurate evaluation of a proposed change.

The participation system insures that all who will be affected by a change have the opportunity to review and approve it. People want to be more involved in changes and will support and help implement changes when they have been allowed to influence the decisions. At the same time, people in gainsharing organizations will resist, with greater resolve, changes forced upon them or those that have not been properly studied.

The following is a classic example of how successful changes occur in a gainsharing company. There is a correct way and an incorrect way, as this example illustrates. A glass-manufacturing company needed a machine to cut glass faster and with less scrap. The engineering department was asked to design a new machine. True to the participative nature of the company's gainsharing program, the engineers met with production workers to "solicit" their ideas—to involve them in the change. Ideas were collected, and the engineers disappeared to the drawing board. In a few months, the new machine was delivered and installed. The operators were stunned. None of their ideas were incorporated in the machine design. They felt betrayed and angry.

Once the machine was installed, everyone—engineers, supervision, and employees—struggled mightily with it to get it to produce to expectations. But, try as they might, the machine would not produce. It would run properly for a while and then suddenly get out of adjustment or break down. Engineering and maintenance were constantly working with the machine to try to get it to produce. The engineers began to accuse the production workers of not trying or even of deliberately tampering with the machine to prevent it from functioning properly. Production workers blamed the faulty design. After almost a year, it was decided to scrap the machine and look for a better one.

A better one was located already designed and ready for delivery. Normally the project engineer alone would take a pallet of glass to the manufacturer, try the machine, and make recommendations based on the trial. From the previous experience, everyone realized that involvement and participation required a different approach. A team of engineer, foreman, and production worker was therefore sent to conduct the trial. The engineer went as the engineer. The production foreman went as the person who would supervise the machine once it was turned over to production. And one operator was selected by his peers to run the machine during the trial.

After the trial was conducted by the team of three specialists, they returned with the recommendation that the machine be purchased. Most importantly, the operator gave a very positive report to his fellow operators. This new machine was installed and within two months was operating 140 percent faster and better than the manufacturer had said it would. Several jigs and fixtures suggested by the operators were added by the engineers to facilitate loading and unloading. The machine rarely broke down or got out of adjustment. This example, albeit a dramatic one, is illustrative of how changes do happen in successful gainsharing programs.

Cooperation

Organizations of all types have become incredibly complex in the past 50 years, because of greater size, new technologies, and new specialities. Success in more complex organizations requires the ability to achieve coordination, cooperation, and integration of the various elements. Since gainsharing rewards teamwork, cooperation, and coordination, these qualities do appear in successful gainsharing companies. In Company P, the entire engineering department postponed their vacations to complete design of a new product in time to prevent the layoff of production employees.

Production departments on three shifts at Company D decided to stop the unhealthy intershift competition and cooperate to increase production. One shift agreed to do all the maintenance and clean-up work, enabling the other two shifts to run production full time and thereby achieve greater overall production results. In Company H, one wood finisher had developed some shortcuts, which he kept secret while the company used piece rates. When the company put in its gainsharing program, he quickly shared his secret processes with his fellow workers, and department productivity increased substantially.

From other gainsharing companies, there are many reports of improved cooperation between labor and management, between production and engineering, between sales and engineering, and between individual workers. Because gainsharing rewards teamwork, it happens.

Employment

Gainsharing companies tend to increase their employment while eliminating work. Productive companies grow faster. Growth provides more work, which offsets work eliminated due to improved productivity. A study done several years ago by The Profit Sharing Research Foundation showed that ten major retailers with profit sharing grew faster in volume and profit than a similar group of companies without profit sharing.

Another aspect of employment is the matter of job security. Asking people to be more productive is asking them to partially or wholly work themselves out of a job. The issue is how to make it possible for a worker to suggest the elimination of his or her own job. The answer is quite simple, but many companies balk at it. The more successful gainsharing companies guarantee employees that they will not lose their employment due to productivity improvements from the gainsharing program. They commit to using attrition to absorb workers displaced by suggestions. This does not mean that the companies guarantee there will be no layoffs. Layoffs may still occur due to a lack of sales or from a major product or technology change. But they will not occur due to the employees' own suggestions or suggestions from their fellow workers.

At Company D, after a very successful cost-reduction drive, 33 workers out of 200 were without jobs. It took about six months to absorb the 33 workers. Carrying the extra people was viewed as a postponement of the full effect of the savings. As a cost, this represented only 25 percent of the actual first-year savings, which this company saw as reasonable. Moreover, the extra people were used effectively on maintenance projects and in training programs.

In another gainsharing program, Company J had been steadily moving jobs to the South, where labor costs were more favorable. In time, thanks to the gainsharing program, the hometown plant improved productivity to a point where unit labor costs were lower despite a higher wage level. Work and jobs were then brought back to the hometown.

Supervision

Gainsharing makes a big impact on supervision. Initially, the supervisor's job changes from production pusher to production facilitator, with the workers becoming the production pushers. The supervisors then begin to do more planning, training, and problem solving. As a rule, they need help and training to make this transition. Some will not make the change successfully, but most do and become very effective and more valuable in their new role. Workers will demand better supervision. At Company C, an Improshare company, workers complained to management that their supervisor was not assigning the proper people to jobs, hurting both quality and quantity. They demanded management action to solve this problem. The shared reward gives workers a greater stake in how well the plant or office is managed. Upward pressure such as this can be intense. The president of one gainsharing company was heard to say: "Because of gainsharing, I have to deal with a much tougher board of directors [that is, the employees] than ever before."

Another aspect of the supervisory question concerns the amount of supervision needed. Under gainsharing, workers become better producers, turning out more work at a higher quality level. Once properly trained, they need less supervision. Over time, it is common to see the elimination of some supervisory positions. Experiments that involve eliminating supervisors entirely or even partially, such as having one supervisor for two or three shifts, have generally not been successful. On the other hand, expanding the supervisor's area of responsibility has been successful. A ratio of 20 workers to one supervisor is average in U.S. manufacturing. In a mature gainsharing company, this ratio can increase to 30 or 40 workers to one supervisor.

Grievances

It is quite common to hear from gainsharing companies that the frequency of grievances has declined and that they are handled more quickly and satisfactorily when they occur. The reason for the reduced frequency is that, as cooperation becomes more important, people stop doing the things that cause grievances. As supervisors and others focus their attention on increasing productivity, they become more sensitive to—and avoid— actions that might interfere with the output or disrupt productivity.

The better handling of grievances results from an awareness that grievances, while unsolved, take energy away from the primary goal. When the two parties are sincere in their efforts to cooperate, both become interested in reaching a just decision quickly and getting back to business. For this reason, more grievances are resolved at earlier steps in the process.

It is also very important to keep the grievance procedure separate from any suggestion system. This is required by the union contract, where one exists. But even without a contract, productivity committee meetings should not process grievances. Where this has happened, meetings have turned into gripe sessions. Though every organization needs effective policies and methods to deal with legitimate employee grievances and to protect the rights of workers, successful companies separate such grievance procedures from the productivity-improvement system.

Wages and Benefits

Gainsharing bonuses cannot be used to replace competitive base wages and benefits. A bonus plan has impact only to the extent that employees see it as an extra reward for above-average productivity. The most successful gainsharing programs are those where base wages and benefits are average to above-average, with the bonus providing an opportunity for even greater earnings.

In one very successful gainsharing company, the policy is to keep base wages and benefits in the top 10 percent of the community. Even when bonuses are small, the employees of this company earn well above the area average. This company also has very high earnings for its industry. This is the ideal in gainsharing: Everyone wins—employees and shareholders alike.

Turnover

Employees don't want to leave a company that provides good income, good working conditions, and the opportunity to contribute talent and effort in concert with others toward a desired goal. As a result, turnover tends to be lower in successful gainsharing companies. Furthermore, these companies are very attractive to job applicants. Gainsharing companies often attract more applicants and therefore have greater choice in the selection of new people.

In one small town, gainsharing has spread from two pioneering firms to several others. Due to the attraction of gainsharing, managers in other companies realized they were losing some of their best people to the gainsharing companies. As a defense, several managers started exploring gainsharing for their own companies. It cannot be said for certain whether any of them installed gainsharing programs for defensive reasons, but the turnover problems started the search.

Absenteeism

For a number of reasons, attendance improves with gainsharing. First, the cost of absenteeism is greater. Bonuses are only earned and paid when people are at work, producing. Second, greater involvement enriches jobs and adds to satisfaction. People like their work more. Third, the increase in cooperation and teamwork brings with it a greater sense of responsibility toward one's job and the part one plays in the success of the whole business. Finally, employees are less tolerant of unnecessary absenteeism and put pressure on each other about good attendance as well as about other aspects of good workmanship.

In one Scanlon company, absenteeism dropped from 5 percent to 0.5 percent, which led to a new concern. The company's managers are now asking themselves if there is so much pressure on employees for attendance that they come to work sick when they should stay home or seek medical attention.

Job Satisfaction

Workers at all levels in successful gainsharing companies indicate high levels of job satisfaction, some instances of which we have already cited. In addition to the added reward provided by the bonus, they report better relationships with supervisors and co-workers, more involvement, the opportunity to learn and to use more of their skills, a greater sense of accomplishment, and more influence over matters that affect them. As an employee in one gainsharing company expressed it: "They make you feel important, like a person should, and best of all, they listen."

Summary

Does it work? It would be nice if we could point to one study that neatly answers this question to the satisfaction of all, but such is not the case. The reports in this chapter are not from formal research; not every gainsharing company has experienced all of these successes. But these are some of the good things that have happened in gainsharing companies. They will happen again.

Chapter 3

Experiences from Unsuccessful Programs

A very common question from those exploring gainsharing for the first time is "Why do gainsharing programs fail?" They know from experience with incentive plans that plans do fail. News of failures tends to travel fast, so anyone who has not experienced a failure has probably heard of one. For those new to gainsharing, the impact of failure is seen as a fairly high risk.

People ask about failures both as a way to determine the risks of trying a new plan and as a way to learn about the problems of installing and maintaining a gainsharing program. The question cannot be answered easily. Due to the same lack of good research mentioned in the last chapter, even less is known about the failures than about the successes. This is to be expected for two reasons: First, those who fail are not as willing to discuss their experiences as those who succeed, and second, the cause of failure is not always known by those who failed. We must assume, at least in some cases, that organizations would have fixed the problem and prevented a failure if they had understood what was going wrong.

Again, with the caution that we do not have as much information as we would like, we can examine some of the failures and their apparent causes. In doing this, we will draw on the experience of programs that have failed and were discontinued and of programs that developed problems that were corrected. In the latter examples, the assumption is that the trouble would have led to failure had it not been corrected.

When gainsharing programs fail, they tend to do so quietly. They do not crash and burn, leaving wreckage to sift and analyze. Instead, they fade away. Company X installed a gainsharing program in one of its units as a trial. During the program's first year, nothing of consequence happened. Productivity did not improve, and no bonuses were earned. At the end of the year, the company sent a memo to all employees announcing its decision to discontinue the gainsharing program. Most of the employees responded: "What gainsharing program?" The program was dead long before the memo was issued. More often than not, there is little resistance to discontinuing a failing gainsharing program. The experience is similar to what happens when other programs such as management by objectives, performance appraisal, and Quality Circles fail. Despite the original promise, the program never really gets off the ground, so no one misses it when it is gone.

Despite the limitations of the data, we can explore some of the known problems and learn from them. Here, then, is some information we have about failures, near misses, and their causes.

Mergers

One famous and very successful Scanlon Plan was dropped when Company L was bought by another company. The new owners simply didn't believe in gainsharing and discontinued the program. It is difficult to understand why the new owners would drop a successful program. The more probable reasons are:

- They were philosophically opposed to the idea of sharing productivity gains. Although still fairly common, this form of opposition to gainsharing seems to be diminishing.
- They saw a potential conflict with other operations if they allowed the newly acquired company to retain a bonus program. Large organizations find the need for interunit consistency to be a serious obstacle when considering gainsharing.

Loss of a Strong Leader

At Company S, a manufacturer of electrical appliances, an otherwise successful gainsharing program was abandoned shortly after the death of one of the company founders, who had been the main force behind the program. His other managers did not support the concept and dropped the program when they could. A gainsharing program dependent on one strong leader is on thin ice. Support must be broadly based in the organization.

Gainsharing as a Fad

Too often, organizations implement programs such as gainsharing, management by objectives, and Quality Circles because others have done it successfully; it becomes the thing to do. The management of XYZ Company asks for failure if its sole reason for installing a gainsharing program is because ABC Company did it. The scene is all too familiar: Send two or three staff people over to ABC to find out what they are doing. The staff people return with a full report giving all the details of ABC's meetings and bonuses. XYZ initiates a program. It does all the things being done at ABC, and everyone anxiously awaits results, such as bonuses and better profits. When nothing happens, everyone gets frustrated. Management throws out the program, deletes the expletives, and vows never to do that again.

This problem is the failure to ask the important first questions: What is gainsharing, and what can or must it do for our company? Without answers to these questions, the planning that must precede a successful installation does not occur. The lack of proper planning is the cause of most failures. Following fads prevents proper planning.

Gainsharing as a Super Carrot

Higher income is an incentive for employees and company alike. But to view the gainsharing program as a new, fresh, or bigger carrot is a mistake. The bonus is the most visible aspect of gainsharing to outsiders. But to those who have worked in companies with successful gainsharing programs, the bonus is not seen as the best feature. The best features are the gainsharing management practices and employee involvement: "They treat us like persons," as one participant put it.

When gainsharing is seen primarily as an incentive, people will be pleased with the program as long as there are bonuses. Such plans lack real vitality, and as soon as a slow period occurs and bonuses dry up, employees become dissatisfied. Managers then drop the plan and complain about ungrateful employees. Gainsharing has much more to offer both to organizations and to their people than just a bonus.

Dishonesty

No matter how hard a company tries to communicate and educate, there are aspects of the program that some employees never understand and must accept on faith. This is especially true of the productivity measurement and bonus. Honesty is therefore an essential ingredient. Even in the most successful programs, there always seem to be a few employees who harbor lingering doubts about management's honesty.

In Company D, even after 25 successful years, an employee stated that he did not believe the monthly financial reports. He was convinced that each month top management decided what the bonus would be. Cynically he said: "They figure what they think it will take to keep us happy this month." Fortunately, this cynic lacked influence, so he did not affect other employees.

In Company W, several employees were discussing the gainsharing program, generally agreeing that it was great and the owners were good managers for putting in such a program. In the course of this discussion, a sour note was sounded by one employee, who said: "Look, I've worked for these people for 25 years, and they've never done anything for anybody but themselves. If they're giving us a bonus, you can bet that they're keeping plenty for themselves." In this case, management was not trusted, and the speaker was able to influence his listeners. The gainsharing program was not strong and eventually failed for reasons of trust. It is important that managers do nothing to add credibility to such cynicism. Everything pertaining to the program must be open, honest, and aboveboard.

A tragic case of dishonesty concerns a company with several manufacturing plants, each with its own gainsharing program. The business required the frequent introduction of new models of standard products. Productivity gains were calculated separately for each product and were earned by employees over the life of the product. Plant I had proved to be more consistently productive, so most of the new models were started there. The product entered production with an engineered standard, and bonuses were earned as productivity increased over this base. After a time, new models were moved to one of the other plants. There was some grumbling among the employees at Plant I that as soon as they started earning bonuses on a new model, it was given to another plant. After several years, the employees discovered that the standards were raised when a product was moved, thus eliminating the productivity increases and the earned bonuses. The employees realized that this management maneuver was intended to deny them their productivity gains. In the ensuing uproar, several major modifications were made in an effort to salvage the programs, but too much damage had been done, and within a couple of years, the gainsharing programs were abandoned.

Low-Wage Supplement

Some companies have opted for gainsharing as a way to supplement low wages. This is not the path to gainsharing success. Employees have an expectation of what an adequate wage/benefit package should be. They know from friends and from their own job shopping what other companies pay and, from this, develop their basic expectations. The accuracy of these expectations is sometimes uncanny. At Company G, where the average employee wage was $5.61 per hour, a group of production workers was asked whether they felt this to be low, average, or high for the area. They responded without hestitation that it was high; they quickly added that it was low compared to a nearby major electronics firm but high for the type of work they did. Their information and evaluation agreed completely with local wage surveys conducted by the personnel department. Consideration of this point must start with the understanding that employees know what a fair wage is.

Some companies set their wage rates below the labor market and explain to employees that the gainsharing bonus will more than make it up. In such situations, the bonus never functions as a reward for additional productivity, no matter how high the bonuses go. Once the bonus has been defined as making up for low wages, it is always seen as a supplement and nothing more. Then, for all practical purposes, there is no bonus, and the gainsharing program is without one of its principal elements. Lacking a real bonus, such mediocre programs limp along, never achieving their full potential, and in time, everyone loses interest.

Antiunion

The only data available on this issue come from companies that are exploring gainsharing as a way to prevent unionization of their employees. Such a preoccupation causes them to examine gainsharing superficially. Some will ask "How much of a bonus is necessary?" This comes from viewing the bonus as a bribe, which is not the gainsharing ideal. Or they ask "How much information must we communicate?" The implication here is "What is the least we must do?" Gainsharing cannot succeed when management looks for the minimum needed to get by. To succeed, gainsharing must be approached positively and wholeheartedly. Union prevention is not an appropriate reason or goal for a gainsharing program. One started for this reason will be on a shaky foundation and its future doubtful.

Unsolved Problems

Even the best-designed program will develop problems sooner or later. Measurements become obsolete due to new products or processes. Suggestion systems break down, and ideas don't get action. A supervisor gets frustrated and cancels the suggestion-committee meeting. Low bonuses occur for several months, and people do not get good information about why. Someone makes an indiscrete remark as a meeting is breaking up, and a rumor races through the plant or office that the company is fudging the monthly bonus figures. A new engineering manager is hired, and suddenly there is a rash of rejected suggestions. The general manager, who was a key figure in starting the plan, leaves and is replaced by a manager reputed to be opposed to gainsharing. Any of these problems, and more, do happen to the best of programs.

No amount of planning can prevent problems from occurring. It is what happens when problems do occur that determines the future of the gainsharing program. The organization that confronts problems and works through them with dispatch not only will maintain the gainsharing program but will strengthen it. The organization that procrastinates when problems arise will find it more and more difficult to maintain an effective program. The gainsharing program contains the structure and process to solve problems when they occur, but it is the responsibility of the leadership to see that the processes are used quickly and effectively.

Poor Preparation of Supervisors and Other Key Employees

Until recently, the focus in gainsharing programs has been exclusively on the production and office worker. These employees have been, and still are, seriously underutilized in many organizations. Much effort has gone into finding ways to communicate more to and with, and receive more communication from, the blue collar and white collar workers. Suggestion systems have been designed to let hourly workers recommend ways to improve operations and productivity. In our rush to motivate hourly workers, we have inadvertently downgraded the supervisors and their contribution. This is also true of other professionals, especially engineers. The statement "No one knows more about the operation than the operator" has become a slogan for all manner of employee-participation programs, but it simply is not true. Full knowledge of the operation resides, at the very minimum, in a trio: supervisor, engineer, and operator. In some situations, the maintenance mechanic and set-up person and others must be added to the "expert" group as well.

The problem of inadequate preparation of supervisors and others came to light in two different companies in the following ways. At Company W, an employee turned a written suggestion in to her supervisor to be processed at an upcoming productivity-committee meeting. The supervisor flew into a rage, tore up the suggestion, and told the worker to get back to work. When cooler heads reviewed this problem, it became clear that nothing had really been done to prepare supervisors for their important role in the gainsharing program. For the supervisors, processing employees' suggestions was an added burden on top of an already busy work schedule. The extra workload plus all the talk about operators knowing more about the process than anybody else caused this supervisor to come apart at the seams.

In Company D, which used employee surveys extensively, the data about the impact of a gainsharing program on supervisors are more complete and conclusive. Over a three-year period, all indicators of satisfaction and organization climate among hourly employees rose to very high levels. At the same time, the survey scores of the first-line supervisors and engineers declined significantly. Examination showed that the supervisors, engineers, and other salaried employees felt that their expertise and experience had been downgraded by placing so much emphasis on hourly employees. The supervisors said: "If the hourly workers are going to do all these new things, what remains for us to do?" Some engineers left the company during this period, complaining that they had too little influence and were not appreciated.

These cases demonstrate two basic gainsharing problems. First, the role of the supervisor changes. In traditional situations, the supervisor is primarily a production pusher and quality policeman. As workers become more motivated, there is no need for the supervisor to push and police. People begin to do this for themselves. This is what Douglas McGregor meant by Theory Y: management by integration and self-control. When this change happens in an organization, supervisors can and must do different things. Supervisors must plan, train, help people perform, build their work groups into effective teams, and they must solve problems or facilitate problem solving when needed. Supervisors need training and coaching to perform these new roles. Some gainsharing programs have failed because of resistance and opposition from the supervisors.

The second problem is directly related to employee involvement and participation. Organizations have been designed around the idea that there is a small core of professional experts and a larger group of unskilled and semiskilled workers. These professionals are in engineering, quality control, accounting, production control, information systems, maintenance, and other areas. Being the expert is part of the reward package for professional employees. (Titles and credentials are very important.) Their status in the organization depends on their expertise. When an "unskilled" worker discovers a better way, an improved process, a simple solution to a complex problem, the status of the "expert" is threatened. First of all, the expert's ego is bruised because he or she didn't think of it first. Secondly, it is fairly common for professionals to be criticized by their superiors because of something they missed.

Compounding this problem, all suggestion systems provide for review and approval by the experts in whatever department the suggestion pertains to. Besides the ego bruising, suggestions represent an additional workload. Some gainsharing companies find that suggestions tend to be bottlenecked in engineering and other departments where there is little time and less motivation to process them. Any unexplained delay in processing ideas is interpreted by the employees as a lack of sincerity on the part of the company. In time, this will lead to a lack of interest and the possible demise of the plan.

Summary

Gainsharing is not a toy to be played with by gamesmen or amateurs. It is a powerful tool that, when used correctly, can produce impressive results in both productivity and quality of work life. With the full understanding and commitment of its leadership, any organization can have a successful plan. Without full understanding and commitment, one or more of the preceding problems will undoubtedly cause a plan to fail.

Chapter 4

Three Basic Elements: Management, Participation, Reward

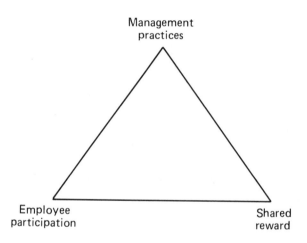

The preceding chapters presented a summary of gainsharing as it has evolved over the past 40 years. The day-to-day successes, failures, and near misses have created the present state of the art. From this experience, three elements emerge as the basis for success in gainsharing programs: (1) management practices, (2) employee participation, and (3) shared reward.

A successful gainsharing program is one in which management practices facilitate a high degree of employee participation resulting in rewards that are shared equitably among those who produced the results.

Individually, there is little about the three elements in a gainsharing program that is unique or innovative. The gainsharing innovation is putting the three elements together into a single program. While each of the elements has a powerful effect on organizational performance, combined in a gainsharing program, they interact and produce even greater performance. Gainsharing provides an integration that has been missing in many organization development efforts thus far.

Organization and Management Development

Beginning with the Hawthorne Studies in 1929, there has been steady growth and progress in efforts to make organizations effective and more human. We have passed through phases called labor relations, human relations, organization development, human resource management, and quality of work life. What began at Hawthorne as a trickle grew to a good-size stream in the fifties, a major river in the sixties, and a veritable flood in the seventies.

We entered a new era in 1960 with the publication of McGregor's thesis that a new theory of management, Theory Y, was needed to replace traditional management, Theory X. New psychological research by Maslow and others had shown that traditional management theories (X) were based on assumptions about people at work that were not correct or at least were no longer correct. McGregor proposed a new theory of management (Y) based on the recent research and new assumptions about people at work.

Theory X assumptions
  People dislike work and tend to avoid it.
  People must be coerced and controlled to get them to work.
  People prefer to be controlled and avoid taking responsibility.
Theory Y assumptions
  Work is as natural as play or rest.
  People are self-directed toward goals to which they are committed.
  Commitment is a function of rewards.
  People will take responsibility.
  Many people are creative and able to solve problems.

McGregor concluded that organizations today use only a small percentage of the human resources available to them and issued a call for new management theories to correct this problem. Likert was the first to respond to McGregor's call. In 1961, he published *New Patterns of Management* and proposed four management theories: In his Systems 1 and 2, he provided a clearer picture of Theory X management; Systems 3 and 4 are prescriptions for Theory Y management. Likert also provided documentation based on careful research to show that organizations at Systems 3 and 4 are considerably more productive than those at Systems 1 and 2.

In 1964, Blake and Mouton presented another Theory Y management program. Their management Grid described as ideal the 9,9, or team-management, style. The river grew.

Try T-groups, said NTL, and eliminate all the hidden conflict that inhibits effective managerial teamwork. Job enrichment and job enlargement were proposed by Herzberg, Walters, Ford, and Hackman as ways to cope with blue collar blues and white collar woes. AT&T provided a spectacular job enrichment success story from its stockholders relations department. Books and brochures arrived daily urging organizations to try a variety of programs, such as behavioral modification, sociotechnical systems, quality of work life, performance planning and review, Quality Circles, autonomous work groups, assessment centers, N'Ach, attitude surveys, industrial democracy, human asset accounting, transactional analysis, team building, assertiveness training, time management, ombudsmen, job sharing, and everything imaginable by objectives.

While not as intense, there has also been some development in methods of rewarding people in organizations. New effort has been put into improving programs such as piece rates, measured-day work, commissions, merit pay, suggestion awards, pay for performance, safety awards, cafeteria fringe benefits, job evaluation, wage surveys, flexible work time, and a variety of special incentives and bonuses. (See Lawler in Bibliography.)

Problems Persist

There is no denying that many of the developments listed above have been useful. Nor can it be denied that many of them have been unsuccessful. Considering all of the effort and the many new programs, there are still too many productivity and people problems. Productivity in the United States began to slow down in 1967 and turned negative in 1980. At the start of the eighties, inflation, unemployment, and foreign competition were visible proof that productivity was a serious national problem and not getting better.

Quality of work life wasn't much different. In 1969, the Institute for Social Research at the University of Michigan began a national quality of working life survey. The study, which was repeated in 1973 and 1977 in an effort to determine changes and trends, shows a slight negative trend from 1969 to 1973 and a more substantial decline from 1973 to 1977. This does not appear to be an isolated problem. The decline in quality of working life is about the same for men and women. It is negative for all workers under 45 years of age but more so for those under 30. While both blacks and whites report declining job satisfaction, black workers show a lower level of satisfaction than do white workers. The decline is uniform across all educational levels. Both the employed and self-employed show declines, but wage and salary employees are much less satisfied. By type of occupation, operatives, laborers, clerical, craft, and service workers (the bulk of the employed workforce) show the lowest level of job satisfaction.

In general, these studies reveal that the blue collar blues are not quite as dark blue as is reported in the popular media, but they are getting darker; the trends are all negative. We begin the 1980s with a situation where productivity and quality of work life are deteriorating at the same time organization and management development programs are proliferating. The Pennsylvania Dutch have an expression for this: "The faster I go, the behinder I get."

Why, given all our good efforts, are we not making better progress? There are two reasons. First, although the programs have been well designed and well planned, their application has not. Too many programs have been tried for the wrong reasons or, worse, for no reason. The operations manager for Company E said he was interested in Quality Circles for his firm. "Why Quality Circles?" he was asked. "Well, they are working effectively at Company T, so they should work effectively here." How many programs have been tried because some other company was using them? How many people would go out and get an appendectomy because the doctor prescribed one for a neighbor? The medical example sounds absurd, but we frequently see the same logic used in organizations. Each and every program has some value, but only when applied in the right situation and for the right reasons.

The second reason for our lackluster performance in this field is that there has been no focusing or integrating force for our many efforts. Organization development, management development, and compensation programs have been fragmented, piecemeal approaches to difficult problems in complex systems. Company D was as committed as any to organizational excellence. In its efforts, it tried Theory Y, Grid, System 4, and the Scanlon Plan. One day a very frustrated foreman blurted out in a training session: "What the hell are we doing now? We've tried Scanlon, Grid, System 4, and Theory Y. Why don't we settle down and do just one of them well?" The organization development staff saw a clear relationship among these efforts. The managers did not. Rather than having the cumulative effect the planners were seeking, these multiple efforts created confusion and frustration. Certainly no one started out to frustrate and confuse people, but that is what happened.

All these theories and programs have been aimed at solving organizational problems but were fragmented because our understanding of the problem was fragmented. Hence, these scattered efforts of the past 50 years had to happen, and in a way, we are fortunate that they did. We have accumulated a great deal of experience from the successes as well as the failures.

The only harm done through this process was in overselling the theories and programs. Too many managers were allowed to believe that each theory, and most of the programs, would solve every problem in the organization. With a psychological wrench, a manager could adjust his style from 9,1 to 9,9, and suddenly everyone would be happy, fulfilled, and highly productive. Those who developed the programs never made any such claims, but they did promote the programs enthusiastically, and many leaped to conclusions they wanted to hear.

One negative side effect of this has been that people who jumped on bandwagons found themselves with a punk rock group rather than the McGregor Philharmonic. They are now against all bandwagons and all music. It is amusing to meet a manager who had a bad experience with a poorly conceived or executed management by objectives program and is unalterably opposed to management by objectives. To be against management by objectives is like being against gravity. By its nature, management, like all human activity, is directed toward objectives. Some managers do it well and some do it poorly, but all manage—systematically or haphazardly—toward some objective, clear or vague, worthwhile or worthless.

Despite the tendency of organizations to be copycats and the piecemeal approach of the past 50 years, we have made progress in our knowledge of management practices, employee participation, and rewards. To be sure, more knowledge is needed, but, more importantly, we need a way to consolidate what we have learned and to use it more effectively.

Gainsharing: A Total System

The one major remaining task is to integrate all of these theories and programs into a single program. An organization is like a living body. Tamper with one part of it and you may get problems in another part. In prescribing medication, doctors must be certain that a medicine that cures one problem will not cause a more serious problem in some other area of the body. We need an approach to improving organizations similar to the technique doctors use in healing the body: a systemic approach.

In gainsharing, as in no other strategy, we see a total system approach. By system we mean viewing the organization as a whole body. Odiorne calls this approach organic as opposed to mechanistic (see Bibliography). There are many individual parts—each with a specific purpose. The parts are intended to work together and help each other to do the job of the whole. Too often, organizations do not function as a whole system. Have you ever bought a car and had the salesman tell you that the service department has 14 mechanics and a service manager whose sole purpose in life is to fix your car? Then, when you go in for service, you have to threaten a court action to get any attention. Some service departments keep you waiting for hours or question whether you bought the car from them. The service manager never heard of the salesman. Don't you wonder whether the salesman and the service department are even working for the same company? In good organizations, the parts work together for a single, overall result. In poor organizations, the parts not only don't work together but sometimes work against each other. Gainsharing improves the way the whole system functions—every part working smoothly together to give the final result, which is a satisfied customer.

When we view the organization as a system and work to improve the whole system, we get a new perspective about each of the points on the gainsharing triangle. While each is important in itself, in gainsharing, all three points work together as a system to serve the organization, which is also a system.

In 1975, Raymond Katzell, Daniel Yankelovich, and others published a study entitled *Work, Productivity, and Job Satisfaction*. The purpose of the study was to determine which of the many programs designed to improve productivity and job satisfaction were succeeding. The study concluded that specialized, single-purpose programs generally have limited and short-term success. It also concluded that longer-term and significant improvements would be most likely to occur from approaches that combined certain features.

The features identified in the study as necessary are grouped here according to the elements of the gainsharing triangle.

Management
    Competent supervision.
    Effective, efficient methods and equipment.
    Good working conditions.
    Good employee and labor relations.
Participation
    Proper placement of workers.
    Worthwhile and challenging jobs with some diversity.
    Worker input into decisions that affect their jobs and lives.
Rewards
    Fair pay.
    Job security.
    Pay for performance.

Each Program Unique

None of the items on the list is new. We have been working on them for years. What *is* new and innovative is combining all of these features into a single program, which is exactly what gainsharing does.

While the elements listed above, and others, are necessary to success, it must be stressed that each element has to be designed to meet the needs of each organization, for each organization has its own requirements for management practices, its own opportunities for employee participation, and its own requirements and opportunities for rewards.

This caution seems to be a stumbling block for many when they first look into gainsharing. People seem to want nice, simple solutions to the very complex problems of how to manage an organization to a high level of excellence. Management is not a simple profession; it is very complex and becoming more so as organizations grow, add new technologies, and try to deal with emerging social issues. Each organization has its own special management needs dictated by market, community, employees, technology, and mission.

Employee participation was simple 100 years ago but not today. In just the past 20 years or so, the average formal education of the workforce in the United States has moved from one year of high school to one year of college. A more educated workforce requires more challenge and more opportunities to participate. Each organization has its own workforce with its own needs. A system that works fine for ABC Company may be a total flop at XYZ Company. Even within the same firm, a participation system that works in a division in Ohio may fail miserably in Oregon.

Compensation and rewards must also be tailored to the needs of the business. A shoe company in Michigan cannot afford to pay automobile-industry wages when its competition is in Missouri or Italy, where labor rates are low. How rewards are earned is also unique to each organization. In some industries, like garment manufacturing or electronic assembly, rewards come mainly from labor efficiency. In a retail store, rewards come mainly from effective inventory management. In some of the newer high-technology industries, quality is rewarded more than any other factor.

Many organizations today are looking for simple, "off-the-shelf" solutions to their productivity and organization problems. There are controllers who want to be given ready-made formulas to use in measuring productivity rather than do the analysis necessary to determine a formula just right for their business. There are executives who want self-administering programs that won't take any of their time. There are managers who want an incentive guaranteed to increase production for less cost but don't want to be bothered with employee suggestions. All these managers want easy, instant fixes to their productivity problems.

It is not surprising that managers want simple solutions, but today's complex organization problems do not lend themselves to simple solutions. This is primarily because we have not yet found them. With more experience, perhaps, we will develop more standard programs; but for now there are few useful "off-the-shelf" gainsharing programs. Organizations should plan to develop their own programs out of the three basic elements, and they should consider several options for each.

Management practices can be:
Authoritarian
Paternalistic
Consultative
Participative
Employee participation can be accomplished through:
Suggestion boxes
Suggestion committees
Work teams or Quality Circles
Shared reward can be based on:
Labor only
A multicost productivity base
Value added
Financial plans
Labor hours
Profit (ROI)

With the exception of authoritarian management, a successful program can be made of almost any combination of these options. However, very careful work must be done to select the right combination for a particular organization. The chapters that follow present the many options and guidelines to help each organization build its own unique gainsharing program.

Chapter 5
Management Practices

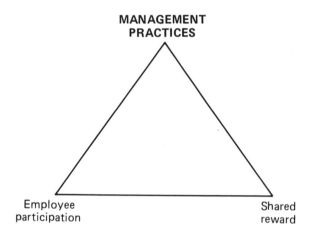

MANAGEMENT
PRACTICES

Employee
participation

Shared
reward

All three points of the gainsharing triangle are indispensable, but each has a special purpose in the success of the program. Management is the head, which provides leadership for the program, just as it is the head of the organization. Management is that function in any organization that plans, gets things moving, leads the way, removes obstacles, provides resources, and solves the inevitable problems. Gainsharing is a strategy to use in doing the work of an organization, and strategy is the province of management. For anything to start in an organization, management must act, and in this sense, the role of management is primary.

While it is primary, the management role is not exclusive. Management is no more exclusively responsible for making the gainsharing program work than it is for making gismos at General Gismo, Inc. Everyone must contribute to the success of the gainsharing program, just as everyone must contribute to making gismos. The point is that while competent and effective management is no guarantee that a gainsharing program will work, poor management is a guarantee that it will not.

It is generally agreed that management, as currently practiced in American organizations, can be significantly improved. Business schools and business journals constantly remind us of the deficiencies. (See Judson in Bibliography.) Criticism of management in the United States has become especially acute since the beginning of this decade because of the economic decline. With great regularity, newspapers and journals tell us that the American economic problem is a management problem. Some of the criticism says that our economic difficulties are due to poor marketing decisions, as in the automobile industry, where we failed to see the need for more fuel-efficient cars. However, most of the criticism is directed at the way of managing work and workers. While American management blames high labor costs and low worker motivation for the productivity and quality problems, the experts point to management practices as the cause of low worker motivation.

Because of the success of the Japanese, especially in automobiles and steel, many of the critics contrast the American management style with that of the Japanese. The Japanese use gainsharing as standard practice. Their management style is characterized by consensus and involvement. They have developed one of the best-known employee-participation systems: Quality Circles. Quarterly or semiannual bonuses based on a share of profits represent up to 30 percent of the workers' pay. In his book *Theory Z,* William Ouchi provides a description of what American managers can learn about human resource management from the successes of the Japanese. Pascale and Athos provide a comprehensive model that they call the 7S Model. It was derived from a comparative study of Japanese and American companies and is described in their book *The Art of Japanese Management.* American managers should not attempt to copy Japanese management methods but should take advantage of the new knowledge about management practices emerging from the Japanese experience. (See Bibliography for both these books.)

Management Problems

It is not our purpose here to enumerate a long list of problems facing U.S. management today, but it might be helpful to point out two that pertain to gainsharing: low priority given to management of employees, and short-term focus for results.

"NONMANAGEMENT" OF EMPLOYEES
Some have criticized managers for *mis*management of people, but it may be more accurate to identify the problem as *non*management. Granted, some managers do incorrect things to and with people, but more do nothing at all. Managers, especially at the upper-middle and senior levels,

give the highest priority to functions such as marketing, finance, and technology and a lower priority to the management and development of the human organization. Lower-level managers and supervisors give their priority to the cost, quality, and delivery of widgets and see people concerns as a distraction from the real business issues. It is very common to see a statement in job descriptions to the effect that the right person for the job will be a self-starter who needs very little supervision. There is nothing wrong with a manager wanting employees who are self-starters, unless it means that the manager doesn't want to be bothered supervising.

Perhaps we can learn more about this from the way managers work with people other than employees. How do managers deal with shareholders and customers? Shareholders and customers are people, just as employees are. Do managers think about, react to, and treat these other people the same as they do employees? In at least one significant way, they do not.

To a great extent with customers and to a lesser extent with shareholders, managers listen very carefully and respond to their needs. We go to great lengths to find out what customers want. Surveys, panels, questionnaires, test marketing, and samples are used regularly and at great expense. We also spend tons of money telling people that our soap, beer, or big green pleasure machine is what they really want. Management's attitude toward customers is to be responsive to their needs. To be sure, managers try to influence those needs, but in the final analysis, the customer's needs determine what will be made and sold. In a similar way, managers are responsive to the shareholders' needs, and while they may grumble about demanding shareholders, they grumble under their breaths and listen very carefully.

Now back to our first group of people—the employees. Employees, as a group, are not treated as other people are. Management tends not to be as responsive to their needs. Nothing of the magnitude of consumer surveys is used to determine employees' current thinking. Communications to employees do not come near the volume and quality of communications to consumers or shareholders. And there is a great need—perhaps a greater need—for managers to communicate with and listen to their employees.

Over the past 50 years, there has been a decided change in employee needs and attitudes about work, to which management has been very slow to respond. Some of this slowness is a state of mind that says employees are here to do the managers' bidding. Is this management attitude contributing to the low level of motivation in our organizations? Is management projecting an attitude that says, "We don't care what you want"? And are employees returning the favor? The so-called blue collar blues could be changed if managers changed their attitudes toward employees. To have an excellent organization requires people committed to the organization. Committed people are those who have their needs met by working in the organization.

Effective gainsharing management must start from the position that a committed organization is important and that it is management's job to do the things necessary to create commitment among the people who work in the organization. To do this, management must give a much higher priority to the management of people.

SHORT-TERM FOCUS FOR RESULTS

The second management problem has to do with long-term versus short-term results. Whereas management needs to think and plan strategically, it is preoccupied with short-term performance. The annual profit and loss statement has been the primary cause of this. Success has come to mean success *this year,* as measured by the P&L. In addition, there is an alarming trend toward a quarterly reckoning. Managers, especially senior managers, are being distracted by short-term results from their real job, which is to plan and make decisions that move the organization to strategic objectives.

One result of this short-term focus has been that managers begin to do the work of others. This process starts at the top and works its way through an entire organization. Presidents do marketing and finance work. At Company N, despite a 20-person accounting department, the president still opens the mail every day, collects the checks, and personally makes the bank deposit. Middle managers engineer, schedule, buy, and sell rather than manage. In most manufacturing firms, the manager of engineering carries the job title of chief engineer. The top technical executive in an automobile plant is referred to as the master mechanic. Even first-level supervisors are not immune. Foremen running around after tools and materials and operating machines are a common sight. Managers who do the work of their subordinates in order to obtain short-term performance have no time for real management work: planning, organizing, and developing an effective work group and organization.

The second result of the short-term focus is that the organization does not receive strategic direction. Some firms feel they have a strategic plan when they prepare a five-year sales forecast. This is self-deception. A sales forecast is not a strategic plan; it is only a projection of past activity. A strategic business plan sets goals and plans for every aspect of the organization: marketing, technology, capital equipment, management, human resource utilization, productivity, and others, depending on what the business of the organization is or will be. When the organization focuses most of its attention on short-term results, the future is left to chance. But good management means that the organization's direction is well planned. Good management is not a gamble.

Compounding these and other management problems are the rapid changes that have occurred over the past 50 years. Population growth and urbanization have led to bigger, more complex organizations. New knowledge and technology have increased the sophistication and complexity of organizations. A rising standard of living, better education, and greater mobility have led to much different worker aspirations and expectations. Just when we think we have an organization problem solved, the situation changes, and we must start again to find the correct solution.

These are only some of the problems in the area of management practices to be addressed and resolved as part of a successful gainsharing program.

Effective Management for Gainsharing

Much has been written about effective management in the past 20 years. Several excellent books on the subject are listed in the Bibliography for those who wish to study the issue in more depth. The remainder of this chapter will present several key factors for effective management in a gainsharing program, including values, policies, goals, climate, technology, leadership, and teamwork.

VALUES

Values are deeply held beliefs that evolve from our experience and influence everything we do. They are often cultural, broadly held, and slow to change. Values influence what we strive for, how we act, and our choice of goals. They not only determine our commitment to one set of goals and our rejection of another but also cause us to decide how to reach the goals to which we are committed. Some behavior will be judged to be the proper way to achieve goals; other behavior will be seen as improper, or unethical. There are values about justice and fairness in our dealing with customers, shareholders, and employees; there are values about service and quality; there are values about private ownership, freedom of choice, use of natural resources, environmental protection, worker safety, and equal employment.

The values upon which the organization is founded and by which it will be governed should be clearly stated, for the guidance of everyone in and associated with the organization.

Perhaps the best-known value statements are the Declaration of Independence and the Preamble to the Constitution, which state the values upon which the United States government is founded (for example, that we all have unalienable rights to life, liberty, and the pursuit of happiness). In just the last few years, several innovative organizations have also published value statements or corporate philosophies to guide their organizations. Several examples of corporate value statements appear in *Theory Z* by William Ouchi.

Likewise, the gainsharing program needs an introduction or preamble to express why gainsharing is important and what value the organization places on participation, involvement, quality, service, security, and equity. One value of particular importance to gainsharing is that of partnership between labor and management. The organization that is serious about gainsharing must state clearly the value that labor and management not only are *not* adversaries but *are, of necessity,* partners in the enterprise.

POLICIES

Policies flow directly from, and express the values of, the organization. They are the rules or laws by which the organization will be governed. The Constitution of the United States expresses our national policies, the basis for the laws of the land. Policies need to be clearly stated to be understood and to insure that they are congruent with the organization's values. Policies are more subject to change than values. When conditions change, new or modified policies must be prepared to keep the organization moving in a proper manner toward its goals.

Personnel policies are especially important to gainsharing, because they communicate the attitude of the organization toward its people. To be successful, an organization needs to have people committed to its goals. For this to happen, the organization must, in turn, be committed to its people. Personnel policies define the organization's commitment to its people.

GOALS

Management must prepare a strategic plan that defines specific long-range goals for the organization. When we say that people are committed to an organization, we mean that they agree with its values and goals and will work to support those values and achieve those goals. For this commitment to occur, the goals must first be set and then clearly communicated to everyone in the organization.

A gainsharing organization needs to set and communicate goals in the following categories:

○ *Marketing.* What, where, and who will be the market? How will the organization serve customers? What products? What services? At what quality, price, and delivery level?

○ *Human organization.* What size? What level of expertise? How economically secure? How physically safe? What employment and career opportunities? What levels of performance, productivity, quality, and innovation? What rewards?

○ *Resources.* What resources (capital, materials) are needed? How will they be obtained? How will they be used? At what level of productivity?

○ *Social responsibility.* To whom do we have a social responsibility? How will it be discharged?

○ *Profit.* How much profit does the organization require to achieve its strategic goals? How will it be gained?

This list may be excessive for some organizations and incomplete for others. Each must determine its own organizational goals and strategic plans. These plans must be kept current, which means they must change over time, as circumstances and opportunities change. An organization new to this process will find it difficult at first, but skill will improve with practice.

One of the keys to successful gainsharing is clearly defined goals that are thoroughly communicated and accepted by the organization. Effective employee participation is possible only when there is something worthwhile in which to participate.

CLIMATE

One of the dictionary definitions of climate is "any prevailing conditions affecting life, activity, and so forth." Management establishes a climate that affects the life of the gainsharing program. A favorable organization climate for gainsharing includes some or all of the following:

Communications. Information, ideas, and other communications move with ease up, down, and sideways throughout the organization: People who need and can use information get it. Early gainsharing efforts emphasized only the upward communication of employee ideas. Experience has shown that it is equally important to get information downward to people to start them thinking about things that need to be improved. Coordination between groups is also important and can never be any better than the horizontal communications between the groups.

Decision making. Decisions are made promptly at appropriate levels by those with the best information. Those affected by decisions are consulted before decisions are made. Prompt and effective decision making is one of the most important elements for the success of the suggestion system. Procrastination sends out the message that the organization is not serious about new ideas and better methods. Poor decisions are interpreted by the organization as a lack of management competence or an abuse of power and position.

Influence. For people to feel as though they are a part of an organization, they must be able to influence its values, policies, goals, and activities. The decision-making process established by management either restricts or facilitates the influence of people at all levels. This is a serious stumbling block for many managers as they first consider gainsharing. They fear that once the system is opened to influence from below, management will lose control. Experience indicates that this does not happen to managers who are strong and competent. However, weak or incompetent managers will have difficulty controlling a strong, enthusiastic workforce.

Organization. Management must organize people and resources for efficiency and effectiveness. Resources to be organized include jobs, work groups, schedules, systems, and controls, as well as performance standards for people and systems. In a climate of efficiency and high performance expectations, people rise to the occasion. In organizations where administration is sloppy and performance standards are mediocre, people are less motivated to perform.

TECHNOLOGY

Management also controls the quality of technology available to the workers. Inadequate or poorly maintained tools, equipment, and systems send the message that excellence and quality are unimportant. Management must see that people have good equipment to work with and that it is properly maintained. There must be systems and processes that facilitate excellent performance. There is always the question of economy; there will be some technology that would be nice but that the organization cannot afford. People will tolerate this up to a point, but they will expect management to obtain the technology necessary for the organization to achieve its established goals. People consider it unfair when they are asked for superior results from mediocre resources.

LEADERSHIP

Managers in a gainsharing company are leaders, not drivers. They show respect for and are supportive of their workers. They provide help by training, coaching, and problem solving where and as needed. They encourage people to strive for excellence for both personal and organizational benefit. They are attentive and responsive to workers. In a successful gainsharing program, leadership is of a tough, no-nonsense type, and at the same time, it is very human and personal.

This ideal style of leadership produces an enthusiastic response from everyone in the organization. The success of the organization becomes the source of motivation. People work well because they want the organization to succeed, not because of fear or threat.

TEAMWORK

The importance of teamwork and cooperation to gainsharing is obvious. Any and all friction in the organization is wasted energy that hurts productivity and employee satisfaction. In any successful gainsharing program, competition is seen as something that belongs outside, not inside, the organization. Managers work hard to build each department and unit into a strong team and to create positive, cooperative working relationships between teams. Each unit develops pride in its ability to contribute and respect for the contribution of other groups. In an effective gainsharing program, there is no place for interdepartment and intershift conflicts or for the traditional adversarial relationship between engineering and production, between sales and engineering, or between labor and management. This does not mean that disagreements and conflicts never occur. They do, but when normal conflict arises, it is considered a source of innovation. A disagreement guarantees that an issue will be examined closely and, from that, often come new insights and creative solutions. Conflict is not resolved by compromise but rather by a careful and respectful exploration of differences until a fully acceptable solution is found.

How to Develop Gainsharing Management Practices

The preceding pages describe an ideal model for gainsharing. To suggest that all of those conditions must be met for gainsharing to succeed would be to place gainsharing out of reach for most organizations. Gainsharing can work under less than ideal conditions. However, the closer to the ideal the company's management practices are, the better the gainsharing program will work.

It is stated in the definition of gainsharing that management facilitates a high degree of employee participation. Clear values, good policies, challenging goals, a motivating climate, effective leadership, and teamwork determine the degree of employee participation. To the extent that any of these management practices are deficient, employee response will be deficient. To the extent that management wants a high degree of employee participation and commitment, it will have to improve the practice

Figure 8. Characteristics of four systems of management as they relate to gainsharing.

	System 1	System 2	System 3	System 4
Style	Authoritarian	Paternalistic	Consultative	Participative
Communication:				
Direction of	Down	Mostly down	Down and up	Down, up, and sideways
Reaction to	Considerable suspicion	Some suspicion	Some acceptance, some suspicion, some questioning	Acceptance, open questioning
Effective teamwork	None	Little	Some	Much
Decision making	Only at the top	Policy at the top, some discretion delegated	Policy at the top, considerable delegation	Extensive delegation—initiative encouraged
Employee attitudes and commitment	From hostile to apathetic	From apathetic to mildly favorable	Favorable and supportive	Enthusiastic and supportive
Productivity	Poor	Fair	Good	Excellent
Labor/management relations	Competition	Arbitration	Sharing	Full cooperation
Prospects for gainsharing	Poor	Good	Better	Best

of management in the organization. Rensis Likert, in his books *New Patterns of Management* and *The Human Organization,* provides a useful model to assess management practices. It describes four systems of management and the strengths and weaknesses of each. The model can show a management group how it is managing and what changes may be necessary to insure the success of the gainsharing program. Figure 8 provides a brief summary of Likert's four management systems as they relate to gainsharing.

SURVEY OF ORGANIZATIONS

The Survey of Organizations (SOO) is a questionnaire especially designed to measure management practices according to the four-system Likert model. This questionnaire, effectively administered to an organization, provides good data to assess management practices and a baseline from which to measure improvements over time.

Management practices are not easy to change, so it is important to have a good assessment of the current management practices as the organization begins to develop the gainsharing program. The assessment will suggest priorities for training and development. (See Bowers and Franklin in Bibliography.)

Summary

Management practices are important; they are complex; they are difficult to learn; and they are hard to change. However, it must be stated emphatically that management practices will determine the success of any gainsharing program. The process of developing effective management practices for gainsharing starts with an ideal model: What do we want our management practices to be? The next step is to determine how effective the current management practices are. A good diagnostic survey such as the Survey of Organizations will provide these answers. Current practices are then compared to the ideal model, and plans are made to correct any deficiencies. The organization must be just as committed to improving management practices as it is to improving productivity, since improved productivity is one of the results of effective management practices.

Chapter 6
Employee Participation

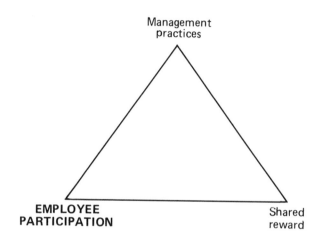

As management practices are the head of the gainsharing program, employee participation is the body. Scanlon Plans promote participation with production committees and screening committees. Rucker Plans encourage employee ideas by using a single plantwide productivity committee. Many other techniques are being used to enable workers to suggest ideas for improvement or to solve problems. Suggestion programs, Quality Circles, and work simplification are popular. Major campaigns are used to promote specific short-term results, such as zero-defects, cost-reduction, and safety-improvement campaigns. In and out of gainsharing, there is a good deal of experience in the area of employee participation. This chapter describes several employee-participation systems and techniques appropriate to gainsharing.

Before we look at the techniques, we need to explore the purpose and nature of employee participation. There is much more to participation than techniques. Participation in gainsharing has both a human and an economic dimension, for it is concerned both with the quality of work life and with the business results. Of the two dimensions, the quality of work life is the more important, for two reasons. First, human needs, goals, and objectives are more important than economic results, and second, strategic or long-range economic results can be achieved only when and as human needs are met. On the other hand, standard of living and economic security are major human needs, and they cannot be met unless the business is successful. So although human needs are primary, the two are inseparable.

An interesting example of this inseparability of human and economic needs is a program started in the 1960s in Sri Lanka to help the poor rural villages. The Sarvodaya Shramandama movement has Buddhist spiritual values as its primary focus. However, the first order of business is to secure an adequate and nutritious food supply for the villages in the movement. The organizing principle is total participation of all the villagers—men, women, youth, and children—in a cooperative effort. In this program, participation and cooperation are activities. The results are economic (more rice) and human (as defined by Buddhist spiritual values). Similarly, the gainsharing program must produce results that are economic (business performance) and human (as defined by the organization's values).

The Human Side

Participation in a gainsharing program appeals to the several human needs of workers. Workers must know that they are involved in an important and worthwhile pursuit; this is why it is so important for management to establish and communicate meaningful goals. The system must be open to worker influence. An oppressive system does damage to the human spirit; an open system appeals to man's basic needs to contribute and grow. In actual practice, experience has shown that few employees attempt to exert influence beyond their immediate job or work group. Even though it is not used extensively, the open door or opportunity to influence is a source of security and satisfaction that builds trust and commitment.

The participation system allows workers to use a wide range of personal skills. In the process of industrialization, job design has tended to use a narrow range of employee skills. Workers today have more education and more skills than ever before, and they want to use these skills in their work. Participation provides the opportunity to employ these additional skills. It enables workers to suggest job designs that make better use of their skills as well.

The system must also provide an opportunity to learn new skills. For many employees, work is the major source of personal growth. When new skills can be learned on the job, growth occurs. This is another example of the close relationship between personal and organizational goals. An increase in skills satisfies a personal need of the worker, and more highly skilled workers are more versatile, productive, and useful to the organization.

Achieving worthwhile goals appeals to the human side. People know without being told that achieving their personal goals of providing for themselves and their families, or developing their personal skills and expertise, is worthwhile. But they do need help in understanding that working for the Acme Widget Company is worthwhile and that their personal contribution to the effort is meaningful. They say that in the old days at Ford Motor Company, Henry Ford would sometimes take a worker outside the River Rouge Plant and, pointing to a Model T going down the street, would tell the worker: "That car wouldn't be there except for the carburetor you put in it." Not every company has such opportunities for employee communications, but this exemplifies what must be done.

A participation system with a strong human dimension holds the greatest potential for a successful gainsharing program. However, it can be very difficult for managers and workers alike to achieve. Managers hesitate because they fear they will have to give up power and authority and that they will lose control. For their part, workers are cynical about management efforts to tap the human will to work; they feel that such efforts are just designed to get more widgets. In organizations where managers are hesitant and workers are cynical, it will take time and require a good deal of hard, creative work by managers and employees to fully develop the human dimension of participation. However, its achievement is both possible and very important to the success of the gainsharing program.

The Business Side

The second dimension of employee participation is to tap the unused creativity and energy of the workforce and apply it to raising the productivity and performance of the organization. Attention should be given to involving the employees more fully, first, with their assigned jobs; second, with other workers in their immediate work group; and finally, with the work of the entire organization.

Job Participation
○ Employees should know and understand how their jobs relate to other jobs and to productivity, quality, delivery, sales, internal efficiency,

and other important business results. Some jobs have only an indirect or remote impact on important end results and require special efforts by supervisors to help employees see their impact and contribution.

○ Each employee should know, understand, and accept the performance standards that apply to his or her work.

○ Employees must be given regular and meaningful data about how well their work is being performed, such as feedback about quality, quantity, scrap, and costs.

○ Employees should be consulted about methods and techniques for doing their jobs. The employee performing a job has specific knowledge and a perspective about the job that no one else has, which can be used to solve problems, eliminate waste, and otherwise improve performance and productivity.

○ Employees must be encouraged and expected to find better ways to do their jobs and contribute to overall performance. This encouragement can take many forms, from avoiding discouraging statements such as "We have always done it this way," to formal training in methods improvement and problem solving such as work simplification and Quality Circles.

○ Employees should be consulted about changes that will affect their jobs.

○ Employees should be encouraged to learn additional job skills and use them in the performance of their work.

○ Employee suggestions for job improvement should be processed and decided quickly and effectively.

Work-Group Participation

○ Employees should be organized into meaningful work groups to promote cooperation and productivity.

○ Work groups must be given information, performance feedback, and other data for them to function as a team with direction and purpose.

○ Work groups should be taught to analyze and diagnose their performance and identify problems and opportunities for improvement.

○ Regularly scheduled meetings should be held to enable employees to communicate, to analyze and solve problems, to plan, and to build teamwork.

Total Organization Participation

○ Employees should know and understand the relationship and contribution of their jobs and their work team to other jobs and other work teams in the organization.

○ Employees and teams must be given information about the organization's goals, objectives, and plans.
○ Employees and teams must be given information about the progress and performance of the organization.
○ Employees and teams should be encouraged to suggest ideas beyond their own jobs and work groups that will help the entire organization. Suggestions should be processed and decided on expeditiously.

Achieving Participation

The above elements, the human side and the business side, represent an ideal model of participation. It is also a general model and, as such, can be used as a checklist. Each organization considering gainsharing must prepare its own ideal model, which may be more or less extensive than the one presented. Each organization must also think through how much time and effort it will take to reach an ideal level of participation. A gainsharing program can be started with a level of participation less than that of the ideal model presented above. However, if this is the case, there must be a plan to increase participation as experience accumulates.

The degree of employee involvement will vary depending on how much is necessary to insure the success of the gainsharing program. This may or may not represent a major change for the organization. Assume that we can describe employee involvement on a scale of from 1 (very little involvement) to 10 (very much involvement). The degree of change for any single company will depend on how much employee involvement there is at the beginning and how much is needed to sustain a successful gainsharing program. For example:

Company A		
Necessary involvement level	6	
Current level	4	
Increase	2	minor change
Company B		
Necessary involvement level	7	
Current level	3	
Increase	4	moderate change
Company C		
Necessary involvement level	8	
Current level	2	
Increase	6	major change

How Much Participation?

Much of the management literature of the past 20 years has emphasized the need for more employee participation and involvement. Many books and articles published in the 1960s and 1970s led to a belief that every single employee in every single organization was dying for greater involvement. In organizations that attempted to achieve a 100 percent level of participation, the results were disappointing. Given the opportunity, not everyone jumped to take advantage of it. Many managers were surprised that their good intentions and efforts were ignored or even rebuffed. Some became angry and disappointed by this apparent lack of response: "The ungrateful wretches!"

Experience, as usual, has been the great teacher. Now we know that some employees want to be more involved, and others do not. In a 1980 survey conducted by the United States Chamber of Commerce, this experience has been confirmed. The survey results, summarized below, show that many, but not all, employees want to be more involved.

In your company or organization, would you like to be more involved in efforts to get people to do their best on the job or would you rather not be involved in this kind of effort?

Would like to be more involved	60%
Rather not be involved	24%
Would like to be less involved	2%
O.K. as is	8%
Don't know	5% *

The 60 percent who desire greater participation still represent a huge, unused resource that should be tapped. But to avoid disappointment, an organization should begin its gainsharing effort with an understanding that about 60 percent of the people, not 100 percent, are eager for the opportunity to participate. That is, the system should be structured for 100 percent participation with the expectation that only 60 percent will take advantage of the opportunity.

Who Is the Expert?

Before exploring participation techniques, we should, for the sake of perspective, examine the myth of the expert, one of the most pervasive er-

* Reprinted with the permission of the Chamber of Commerce of the United States of America, from *Worker's Attitudes Toward Productivity: A New Survey* (1980).

rors in gainsharing literature. One constantly encounters statements similar to these: "No one knows the job as well as the person performing it," or "The expert on a job is the person who does it eight hours a day." However inaccurate the statement, this idea continues to be heard and has done a good deal of mischief in some gainsharing companies. The statement is a deliberate exaggeration intended to convey the idea that the person on the job has a great deal of useful information about the job that has been ignored in the past. Nevertheless, the statement per se is inaccurate.

First, to clarify the record, the person on the job knows some things about the job that no one else knows but does not know everything about the job. He or she is not *the* expert. In fact, due to the way jobs are structured in today's complex organizations, there is no single expert for any one job, not even the CEO. Expertise regarding a machining operation in a factory requires the combined input of the operator, the supervisor, the engineer(s) who designed the job and the machine, the maintenance mechanic who repairs the machine, and possibly the set-up person and the quality inspector. Expertise regarding an office job includes the job holder, the supervisor, a systems analyst, and several others who give or receive information from the person in the job.

While the exaggeration that the person in the job is *the* expert can be excused as a noble effort to give needed status to the job holder, the statement has caused some undesirable side effects, and its use should be discontinued. Efforts to raise the status of factory and office workers have inadvertently lowered the status of the others who also have valuable expertise. Due to the attention lavished on the operators, we have seen resentment and dissatisfaction increase among engineers, first-line supervisors, maintenance personnel, and others. No one ever intended to put down their valuable contribution, but that is what has happened.

At worst, supervisors and engineers have become openly hostile toward employee participation and have resisted the company programs. Supervisors have been known to tear up employee suggestions with a stern warning to return to work. Engineers have been known to falsify dates on drawings to claim that an idea had been considered previously. Engineers and others have left companies over what they feel to be a personal and professional put-down. In less severe situations, these mid-level employees resist the participation system, but not openly. They do not participate actively, and they put a low priority on cooperation. Suggestions are criticized, and approvals are delayed. These unfortunate situations can be avoided by resisting the temptation to oversell the program and by focusing attention on the proper use of everyone's expertise in innovation and problem solving. The support of first-line supervisors, engineers, and other staff specialists is necessary to the success of any program. Their role is important and must be properly recognized in the program's design and operation.

Employee-Participation Systems

Many organizations have experimented with employee-participation systems, and from this a great variety of methods and techniques has evolved. For the purposes of gainsharing, the different systems can be categorized into three degrees of participation, with each higher degree representing greater participation and involvement. The three degrees and their identifying characteristics are:

First degree—the suggestion box
Second degree—the suggestion committee
Third degree—work teams

There are significant differences in technique at each level and also significant differences in results. The material that follows will present, for each level, a general description, the structure (forms, committees, special roles), the steps to process an employee suggestion, and the management or leadership role.

Again, caution is advised. This information should not be used mechanically. The concepts should be employed to design the correct program for each organization. Company D had a second-degree suggestion-committee system but was not satisfied with the number of suggestions being made. One small group of inspectors was asked why there had been so few suggestions from them. They explained that neither of the two representatives on the productivity committee really understood the inspectors' work and that their suggestions were seldom well processed. When it was suggested that the committee have a third representative from the inspectors or that the inspectors attend the committee meeting to present their suggestions in person, the inspectors were surprised. "Are we allowed to do that?" they asked.

For several years, this company had operated its Scanlon Plan under the assumption that there could only be two representatives on the productivity committee and that only the representatives could attend the meeting. Mechanical thinking like this is not the way to success in gainsharing. The techniques presented throughout this book must be made to work for the organization just as with any other system or procedure. In this case, the company quickly changed the makeup of this and other committees and also started to look for other situations where mechanical thinking was inhibiting the success of its program.

Every organization must study the different participation techniques and design a system that will facilitate the desired level of involvement. With that warning, the following information is presented.

First-Degree Participation: The Suggestion Box

The suggestion box is the first and least complex of the participation techniques. It is characterized by the familiar system in which employees write out suggestions and deposit them in a suggestion box for processing. Participation is limited under these systems and only involves the employee in the preparation of suggestions. All processing and decision making is done by managers or staff specialists. A company can expect about 10 percent to 25 percent of the employees to participate in the program, although a few companies with very well managed programs have reached levels of participation in excess of 50 percent. Most companies use forms and boxes to give the program structure, but a word-of-mouth system could be used. Improshare literature recommends an informal first-degree participation system. It states that no formal system is necessary but stresses that supervisors and managers should listen carefully, be open to workers' suggestions, and implement good ones quickly to improve productivity.

STRUCTURE

An informal suggestion system has no structure other than what is already present in the organization. There are no forms, coordinators, or committees. Employees' suggestions are given informally and usually verbally to their supervisor, who processes the ideas informally. A formal suggestion system has at least a suggestion form and a designated collection point, usually a box marked "Suggestions." Larger organizations employ a part-time or full-time coordinator whose job it is to collect, process, and expedite the disposition of the suggestions.

STEPS IN PROCESSING SUGGESTIONS

The steps in processing a suggestion in an informal system are quite simple. When an employee has an idea or a suggestion, he or she communicates the idea to the supervisor, who implements it if possible. If the supervisor believes the idea to have merit but cannot approve it, he or she forwards it through channels for approval. If the supervisor does not believe the idea or suggestion to be practical or feasible, it is not forwarded, and the matter is dropped unless the employee decides to argue or appeal. At any point in the decision-making chain, a suggestion can be dropped for lack of an interested sponsor.

In a formal suggestion system, the suggester completes a suggestion form and puts it in the designated box. Where boxes are not used, the suggestions are turned in to a designated person or office.

After collecting the suggestions from the box or other collection point, a suggestion coordinator studies each suggestion and routes it to appropriate staff specialists or managers (safety suggestions to the safety department, equipment suggestions to engineering, scheduling suggestions to production control, and so forth). These specialists analyze each suggestion and recommend approval or rejection to managers, who decide its disposition. The coordinator usually follows through and expedites each suggestion until it is implemented or rejected. In the case of a rejected suggestion, the coordinator notifies the suggester that the idea was rejected and explains why it could not be used. This notification is usually in writing but is sometimes done by speaking with the suggester.

MANAGEMENT ROLE

At this degree of participation, management's role is passive and reactive. Other than an occasional promotional letter or bulletin-board notice, management waits for employee ideas to occur. There is no special effort to focus attention on operational or administrative problems. Once an idea gets into the system, management decides if it will be used or not. This degree of participation carries the message that management is aware that workers will occasionally have useful ideas and that managers are open to these ideas if and when they occur. Management hires and pays staff specialists and supervisors to solve problems and does not expect innovation and problem solving from other workers. The suggestion system is intended to catch things that are overlooked or are just more visible to the worker. The success of a first-degree system depends on how well management reacts to ideas that are suggested. When ideas are processed quickly and fairly, these systems work well. Delays, unfair disposition, or poor communications discourage suggestions, and participation does not develop.

No special training is required for managers or employees at this degree. Those who have responsibilities for processing suggestions should be given clear instructions about what priority to give to suggestions and how they are expected to process a suggestion.

Second-Degree Participation:
The Suggestion Committee

The second-degree participation system is commonly found in Scanlon Plans and Rucker Plans. There can be a single plantwide committee, or there can be multiple committees of two or even three tiers. Committees, which vary in size from 3 to 30 people, are often named to reflect their function, such as department productivity committee, plant productivity committee, screening committee, or Rucker committee. Committee members are appointed or elected, and their job is to solicit, collect, and process employee ideas and suggestions. The overall system is designed to accomplish the same result as the first-degree suggestion-box system but is much more effective because it is more personal and because the very structure promotes more active participation.

There is in fact considerably more employee participation with a second-degree than with a first-degree effort. The level of active participation under second-degree systems runs between 50 percent and 75 percent, and the percentage of suggestions directly related to improving productivity is often several times greater than with a first-degree system. What accounts for this greater involvement? First, there is the more active solicitation of suggestions by both management and committee members. Second, committee membership is a form of participation that does not occur with a suggestion-box approach. Third, the discussion of suggestions between workers and supervisors at committee meetings represents additional involvement. And, finally, the feedback process is person-to-person and not just by letter.

STRUCTURE

There is considerable structure in a suggestion-committee participation system. There are management communications, suggestion forms, committees, election or appointment of representatives, scheduling, and meetings.

Management communications. To stimulate more active and meaningful participation, second-degree systems begin with communications from management. Information is provided to everyone in the organization to insure that all know where the organization is going and what progress is being made. More specifically, the following information is provided:

○ Strategic or long-range plans, such as market standing, growth objectives, new products or services, quality and service levels, organization objectives, resource objectives, and profit requirements.

○ Progress reports to enable everyone to enjoy success as it is achieved. Variance reports that show everyone where the problems are and how to contribute ideas and suggestions to improve performance and productivity.

Of particular value is information about productivity. An excellent system is one that predicts bonuses at the beginning of the month based on production schedules and current productivity levels and then posts progress and variance information weekly. The prediction tells the organization where it will be at the end of the month if everything goes according to plan. If this is satisfactory, no special action is needed except to stay on plan. If the predicted bonus seems too low, there may be some actions the organization can take to change the outcome. The weekly progress report gives quick feedback so people can evaluate their progress and, if necessary, take corrective action. These reports are useful for discussion and to stimulate better suggestions.

Another approach is a productivity-problem list, like the FBI's most-wanted list. Each month, a list of the five to ten major productivity problems is posted. Experience has shown that employees will take action to raise productivity (and bonuses) when given good data to direct them to areas needing attention.

A common deficiency in many early gainsharing programs was the failure to provide information about problems and areas where improvements were needed. The absence of important business information is one cause of worker apathy in organizations. When workers do not know what the organization is trying to achieve, there is no way for them to become interested in the organization's goals. Also, without knowledge of problems, they are unable to suggest appropriate solutions. Effective communications is the first step in meaningful participation. Management has the necessary information and is solely responsible for communicating it to the organization.

Suggestion forms. Second-degree systems have been tried with and without forms, and experience shows that suggestion forms do serve a useful purpose. There is some resistance to the use of forms because it represents a new cost in a situation where everyone is trying to reduce costs. There is also a general aversion to new paperwork in almost every organization. Despite the cost and inconvenience, the use of forms is recommended. Suggestion-form examples are shown in Appendix A.

The form requires the employee to make a succinct statement of his or her idea or suggestion. Occasionally an employee will need help in describing an idea and completing the form. Supervisors, staff specialists, suggestion-committee members, and other employees can and should provide help when it is needed. Not only does this insure that the idea will not be lost, but the idea may be enhanced by the helper. Two heads are often better than one.

Suggestion forms can be recorded, counted, and tracked. Appendix A also presents a suggestion log and status report. An organization may want to analyze its suggestion experience to see how many suggestions are being made and by whom. An abundance of suggestions from production and a lack of suggestions from the office or maintenance department may indicate a problem that should be solved. A sudden increase or decrease in the frequency of suggestions may show that the gainsharing program is working well or having problems. Suggestion forms can be tracked to determine how long it takes to process a suggestion. Excessive delays can and should be corrected. A fairly common occurrence is a bottleneck in the engineering department. Most productivity suggestions require an engineering evaluation, which increases the workload for engineers. When other projects have priority, suggestions go to the bottom of the pile. By tracking suggestions, such problems can be identified and acted upon before they cause trouble. Suggestions are usually summarized in committee meeting minutes, which are posted or circulated to provide recognition for the suggesters and to publicize the program.

Committees. Second-degree systems use productivity committees to solicit, collect, and process employee suggestions. In organizations where employees are represented by a labor union, a union official usually sits on the productivity committee (or senior productivity committee if there is one), ex officio, to participate in policy decisions and to prevent any conflict between the gainsharing program and the labor contract. Union members and officers participate in other committees as well but generally not in an official capacity.

The number and type of committees will depend on the size of the organization and the organization's preferences and/or need for participation. Three basic models, from simple to complex, are presented below to aid in planning. Membership and committee functions for the three models will be discussed.

Single Productivity Committee Structure

The single productivity committee can be used in organizations of up to 200 people. Normally there are 15 to 20 committee members. Ex officio members include the top general manager, the controller, the chief engineer, the personnel manager, the operations manager, and the local union official. Employees representing major departments, functions, or areas are elected or appointed to the committee. The principal functions of this committee are to:

1. Establish policy and make all administrative decisions regarding operation of the gainsharing program.
2. Analyze bonus results, past and future productivity, and other business information.
3. Review all employee suggestions and decide disposition of each.
4. Publish minutes of meetings to communicate bonus results, details of important business information, and disposition of all suggestions.

Bi-Level Productivity Committee Structure
The two-level productivity committee (Figure 9) is appropriate for an organization of 100 to 500 people.

Senior Productivity Committee   In Scanlon Plans, this committee is referred to as the screening committee, because it screens the monthly bonus figures. Companies often give the group a descriptive name. However, the term *senior productivity committee* is generic and will be used here. The ideal size for this committee is about 15 people; the maximum is 30. Ex officio members include, as in the single-committee structure, the top general manager, the controller, the chief engineer, the personnel manager, the operations manager(s), and local union official(s). Elected or appointed members include employee representatives from each department productivity committee.

Figure 9. Structure of a two-level productivity committee.

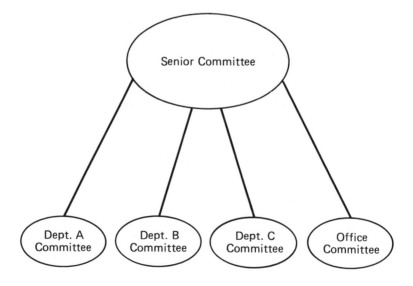

Principal functions are the same as those of the single committee, except that the suggestions reviewed by the senior committee are referred by department committees rather than received directly from employees.

Department Productivity Committees   The sole ex officio member of each is the department supervisor. Two or more employees representing all department personnel are elected or appointed. The principal functions are to:

1. Relay information from the senior committee to all department employees. Each department committee appoints a representative who sits on the senior committee and serves as the primary communications link to take suggestions forward and bring information back. When there are two or more employee members, they are usually elected or appointed for staggered terms, in which case the senior member is usually the representative to the senior committee.

2. Review all suggestions from department employees. Depending on the committee's authority, it may approve and implement a suggestion immediately or after additional study for feasibility and cost-effectiveness. If the suggestion is considered good but is beyond the authority of the committee, it is forwarded to the senior committee with a recommendation to accept and implement. If the suggestion is not considered feasible or cost-effective, it is forwarded with a recommendation to reject. Usually all rejected suggestions are reviewed by the senior committee to insure that no useful ideas are missed. If the senior committee concurs in the rejection, the suggestion is returned to the department committee, which then notifies the suggester of the rejection and the reasons why.

3. Publish meeting minutes providing a summary and disposition of all suggestions.

Tri-Level Productivity Committee Structure

The three-level committee (Figure 10) is appropriate for organizations in excess of 500 employees.

Senior Productivity Committee   The membership, size, and function of this senior committee is identical to that of the senior committee in the bi-level model, except that the employee representatives come from the area committees rather than from the department committees.

Area Productivity Committees   These intermediate committees are necessary in larger organizations to prevent the senior committee from becoming so large as to be ineffective. The ideal size of this committee is 15; maximum size is 30. The senior area manager and staff are ex officio members, and employee representatives from each department productivity committee are appointed from department committees.

Figure 10. Structure of a three-level productivity committee.

The area committee's principal functions are to:

1. Relay productivity information from the senior committee to the departments. Also communicates to the departments information such as past performance, future plans, schedules, and anticipated problems and/or opportunities specific to the area.
2. Review all employee suggestions referred from department productivity committees and decide disposition of each. Suggestions within the authority of this level are approved and implemented or rejected and forwarded to the senior committee. Suggestions beyond the authority or spending limits of this committee are forwarded to the senior committee with recommendations.
3. Publish meeting minutes to include area information and a summary of the disposition of all suggestions referred from the department committees.

Department Productivity Committees   These committees are the same as those in the bi-level model, except that they send representatives to the area committee who form the two-way communications link between the department committees and the area committee.

A department committee member may represent the department at the area committee and may, in turn, be sent from the area committee as a representative to the senior committee. When this occurs, the two representative roles must be seen as separate jobs and performed independently. When this person sits with the senior committee, he or she is not a department representative but an area representative and should represent the interests of the entire area, not just those of the home department.

Election of representatives. Each organization must decide how representatives will be selected: by election or by appointment. In Chapter 8 are suggestions for the election of representatives to the feasibility task force. The process and issues outlined there apply equally to the election or appointment of productivity-committee representatives. A formal process tends to add status to the position of representative. A casual approach to the selection of representatives diminishes the importance of the job in the eyes of employees and has led to the selection of unqualified or unwilling representatives who then fail to perform the job adequately. In Company W, a practice developed of electing the newest employees to the suggestion committees as a form of hazing. The bewildered new employees had no idea what to do and were unable to perform the representative tasks well. An election process such as the one presented in Chapter 8 will prevent problems of this nature.

Turnover of representatives is another issue to be decided. Some companies encourage turnover to enable many employees to have experience as a representative. These companies feel that service on such a committee is a valuable learning experience that should be shared by as many people as possible. This turnover is accomplished by limiting the term of office for a representative to one to two years and prohibiting a person from being reelected until all others have had their turn.

Those who favor the selection of the most qualified, regardless of turnover, do so because they feel that not every employee will be effective in a representative role, and above all, they want the job done well. These organizations also use a term of office of from one to two years but do not restrict a person from being elected to additional terms. This process allows the employees to decide who is competent and who will represent them. Those who perform are reelected. Those who don't are replaced.

There are advantages and disadvantages to each position, and both have their advocates. The arguments for selecting the most qualified candidate do appear to be somewhat stronger, and therefore, this approach is recommended. Rotating the representative position as a learning experience means that the job is always being performed by inexperienced people. The role of the representative is much too important for this. A strong corps of employee representatives can be a most valuable resource for the organization and the gainsharing program.

Scheduling. All productivity committees in second-degree systems meet once each month on a fixed schedule. Monthly meetings are generally adequate for single-level, bi-level or tri-level structures. Special meetings may be needed occasionally, but most of the business can be handled in one monthly meeting.

The senior committee is always the key to scheduling. Its members schedule themselves to meet when the bonus figures from the preceding month are available. This should occur within five to ten days after the end of the month. Lower-level committees are scheduled to meet in advance of the senior committee to prepare suggestions for consideration at the senior committee meeting. A three-level committee might be scheduled this way:

- Department productivity committees meet two weeks prior to senior committee meeting (second last week of the month).
- Area productivity committees meet one week prior to senior committee meeting (last week of the month).
- Senior committee meets first or second week of the following month.

Scheduling should be designed to speed the processing of suggestions or upward communications. The bonus announcement following the senior committee meeting is generally made by public address, special bulletin-board announcement, or other speedy method. People become anxious to know the bonus percentage and should be told as soon as the senior committee has reviewed and approved the monthly productivity statement.

Meetings. A regular schedule of meetings is recommended to keep the suggestion and information processes moving in second-degree systems. Without a regular schedule, there is a constant danger of allowing the urgent to interfere with the important. In active organizations, there are, at any one time, at least 17 good reasons to postpone a meeting until tomorrow or next week. Habits are easy to form, and soon tomorrow never comes. Company D had progressed so well with its participation system that some departments decided to eliminate regularly scheduled meetings and hold formal meetings only when there was an agenda. In the meantime, they held informal, on-the-floor meetings to handle problems and suggestions. In time, the departments learned that some employees were waiting for more formal meetings to bring up suggestions.

These employees needed the structure of the regular meetings to help them participate. The company also found that it was missing the value of the team communications that occur in the meetings.

Further study of this experience in Company D showed that regular meetings were also very helpful to the supervisor. With no schedule, employees often approached the supervisor at inopportune times when he or she was busy with some other important matter. When this happened, the supervisor was not able to give employees the undivided attention they deserved. The supervisor might cut the employee off with "I'll get back to you later." Sometimes the supervisor forgot the incident and failed to return to the employee. Some employees felt ignored and disappointed, and participation declined. When this was recognized, the departments resumed regular meetings, and the problems were corrected. Thus, a simple structure of regular meetings can help both the supervisor and the employee.

With scheduled meetings, the employee can decide to hold an idea until the meeting, where it will be given a proper hearing. Sometimes, though, an idea occurs that should be acted upon immediately and not held for the meeting, which may be two or three weeks in the future. An employee with an urgent idea can decide to approach the supervisor immediately and not wait. Then, when the supervisor is approached, he or she will know that the issue must be too important to wait and will give the person a more careful hearing. This is an example of a structure that facilitates and does not restrict. Such structures are important to the success of the gainsharing program.

STEPS IN PROCESSING SUGGESTIONS

In the second-degree participation system, all employee suggestions are processed through the committee structure. The usual procedure begins with the employee writing the idea on a suggestion form as previously described. The completed form is given to a member of the suggestion committee, who enters it into the committee process.

Useful suggestions should be implemented as quickly as possible. Many suggestions can and should be implemented immediately. Some require approval by or coordination with another department or shift. The department supervisor or area manager is responsible for obtaining the needed approval or arranging the necessary coordination. With experience, these and other tasks associated with suggestion processing may be delegated to other committee members at the manager's discretion. Delegation of this sort increases the opportunities for employee participation and is highly desirable.

Most suggestions require buying materials or supplies or incurring some other expense for implementation. To speed the process of implementing suggestions, gainsharing companies sometimes provide special spending authority for department and area committees. For instance, supervisors might be given authorization to spend up to $500 or $1,000 to implement a cost-saving suggestion. For "convenience" suggestions—that is, those that are desirable but do not result in a cost savings—the spending authorization is usually lower. When the expenditure is within the supervisor's spending authority, a requisition is prepared and taken directly to purchasing, and the necessary part, equipment, or material is promptly ordered. Suggestions that are beyond the supervisor's authority to implement are taken to a higher committee by the representative, and so on through the structure until the suggestion arrives at that level where it can be authorized.

Suggestions that are turned down at any level are usually taken through the process to the senior committee. This is an extra effort to insure that a potentially useful idea is not turned down due to lack of perspective or information. An idea that seems impractical to the department committee may be seen by the chief engineer or other members of the senior committee to have merit. This review also encourages the department supervisor to examine every idea carefully and from a positive point of view. When under pressure, the supervisor may be tempted to rush the review and reject an idea prematurely. The senior management review helps the supervisor to withstand this temptation.

Some suggestions must be processed through certain staff departments, such as engineering, systems, quality control, and so forth. Referral to the staff department for technical or procedural approval should be as simple and straightforward as possible; a quick response is needed and should be standard procedure. Special attention should be given to this step in the process, since it is the one most likely to be a bottleneck and cause delay.

Some companies use specially colored forms or interoffice mailing envelopes to give suggestions visibility and prevent their being lost in the bottom of someone's basket. Normal channels are adequate as long as they are prepared to give priority to suggestions. An extra precaution may be to have someone from the referring committee—chairperson or member—responsible for expediting each referral to insure a quick response.

Some suggestions can be implemented immediately. Others can be approved immediately but for various reasons must be scheduled for implementation in the future. Some suggestions must be rejected. The important last step is to close the communications loop back to the employee(s) who initiated the suggestion. Whether the idea is approved for immediate or future implementation or rejected, the employee(s) should be told of the decision as soon as it is made. Quick responses to people's ideas and suggestions is a key—perhaps the most critical one—to encouraging employee participation.

MANAGEMENT ROLE

In the second-degree system, management's role is more active and visible. Supervisors and managers chair various committees and, in so doing, participate actively with employees from all departments and levels. Management makes an initial investment of resources, time, and money to operate the system. These actions by management send a clear message of confidence that employees can and will contribute ideas to improve productivity.

Management also provides information about progress and problems that helps employees to focus their attention on areas where improvement will have the greatest benefit. This sharing of information is in itself a type of participation. It shows a respect for the employees' ability to contribute beyond assigned tasks. It tends to involve people in the business in a very fundamental way. The lack of information about progress and problems carries the message that people are unimportant because they aren't capable of doing anything to help. The responsibility of providing useful information also requires that management be creative in the way that information is reported. Standard accounting reports using technical terms and symbols are not understandable to most employees. Fuzzy communications lack credibility and sincerity. Technical reports must be translated into terms that everyone can understand.

Though management reserves the right to approve or reject any suggestion, it does, through the committee structure, share some of its decision-making responsibility with other employees. Being open to employee influence is another subtle dimension of participation that enhances the whole process. Influence is reciprocal: As management becomes open to employee influence, employees become more open to management influence, and the total amount of this reciprocal or mutual influence will continue to grow.

Management must set up, operate, and maintain an efficient system for processing employee suggestions. The right system, properly maintained, will stimulate employee participation and the ultimate success of the gainsharing program.

Third-Degree Participation: Work Teams

The third-degree participation system represents the greatest degree of effective employee involvement known today; it is—theoretically—total participation. There are very few examples of this level of participation in organizations in the United States. The work-team concept does not use a separate structure of committees or special representatives to increase participation. Rather, existing organization structure is redefined and strengthened to stimulate greater participation and more effective communications.

Participation and meaningful involvement are viewed as essential ingredients in every job rather than an extra feature, as is the case in the first- and second-degree systems. The best theory supporting third-degree participation is the overlapping group form of organization developed by Rensis Likert and described in his book *New Patterns of Management*. Likert states that to achieve the full potential from human resources, employees must be organized into high-performing teams to which they feel a loyalty and from which they get support and strength. Most organizations have been divided into functions, departments, and individual jobs, which isolate members and groups from each other. A third-degree participation system puts the parts back together into a productive whole.

While Adam Smith's division of labor is a sound principle, it can be applied incorrectly. In a classic chapter of his book *The Practice of Management*, Peter Drucker asks: "Is Personnel Management Bankrupt?" Drucker points out that in applying the principle of the division of labor, we made an unfortunate wrong turn. We have divided work into thinking work and sweating work. By so doing, we have designed our organizations and our jobs in ways that prevent a large majority of employees from using their creativity and problem-solving abilities in the service of the organization. A third-degree participation effort goes to the heart of this participation problem. It creates effective teams of people at work, and it facilitates the use of all of the skills and capabilities people bring to their jobs. It is a more ambitious undertaking and therefore requires greater management effort and skill to sustain it.

STRUCTURE

The basic unit in a third-degree participation system is the work team, and every employee in the organization is a member of one or more teams. Work teams usually consist of five to ten workers who share responsibility for an important task. At the first level, there are production teams, assembly teams, and a variety of service teams. Above the first level are supervisory teams, staff teams, and management teams. At the top of the organization is the executive team. Figure 11 shows a model of overlapping teams.

When companies adopt this organization model, they find that some realignment of the organization is required. Generally, the upper levels are already organized into teams and need only to redefine relationships

Figure 11. Model of overlapping work teams.

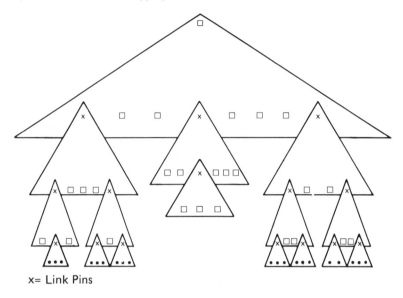

x= Link Pins

among team members. At the production-team and service-team level, however, change is often required. Traditional production departments usually consist of 15 to 30 workers. An analysis of tasks and relationships often shows that within the traditional department, there are two or three distinct work teams.

In Company D, it was found that three workers from Department A constituted a team with two workers from Department B. To implement the new team structure, the Department B personnel were transferred to Department A to form a team. Once the team was properly organized, ideas began to flow, equipment was moved, and a major cost savings resulted. At Company C, materials handling personnel had been organized into a single centralized department. As a third-degree participation system was installed, the materials handlers were reassigned to the teams they served, and an unnecessary department was eliminated. The materials handling supervisor was reassigned, resulting in a significant cost savings.

An important feature of this organization structure is a new role for supervisors and managers (shown by the Xs in Figure 11). Supervisors and managers are leaders of the teams they supervise and also members of the next higher team. As members of both teams, they are linking pins uniting two work teams. The cumulative effect of this is that all teams are united into one productive organization.

This linking-pin concept, pioneered by Likert, goes further than the traditional notions about linkage. It includes the traditional organization role (chain of command and communications link), but beyond this, it is a unifying principle that enables a complex organization to synchronize a bewildering array of separate tasks into a single output. Through these linking pins, information, ideas, and suggestions flow up, down, and sideways, to and from all parts of the organization. It is this synchronizing and free flow of information that enables the third-degree organization to be highly productive. Information about goals, progress, and problems flows to where it is needed. Ideas and suggestions for innovation and problem solving flow to where they can be used. And it all happens through the basic organization, without the need for an additional structure.

Forms. Special suggestion forms are not as essential in this system but may be useful and should be included where necessary. Suggestions that must go to other work teams for approval can be processed more easily when written. Forms can be read, signed, logged, counted, and traced with ease. The requirement for rapid processing and feedback is just as important in a third-degree system as it is in the first- and second-degree systems. With forms, the process can be checked to be sure it is working efficiently. Forms, when used, can be the same as those for the second-degree system. See Appendix A for examples of such forms.

Meetings. Meetings are an essential element of the work-team system. All work teams meet regularly to communicate, analyze their own performance, plan, and solve problems. There are two types of work-team meetings: formal and informal.

Each work team holds formal, regularly scheduled meetings once a month, in a sequence like this one:

Week 1—production and service work teams
Week 2—supervisory work teams
Week 3—management and staff work teams
Week 4—executive work team

The schedule is designed to facilitate upward communications and the rapid processing of ideas and suggestions. Suggestions move up from level to level and are implemented or approved at the level where the necessary coordination and authority occur.

In the beginning, these meetings may take up to two hours, but, as experience is gained, a work team can learn to complete its agenda in one hour, except in unusual circumstances. Teams should have a quiet place in which they can hold an effective meeting. Company T, famous for its team-management approach, constructed meeting rooms in each production area of a new plant to facilitate these meetings. Special facilities are not required, but adequate facilities are.

In addition, supervisors generally require some specialized training in meeting leadership, such as the interaction method described by Doyle and Straus in their book *How to Make Meetings Work*. Additional training in problem-solving techniques, such as work simplification and Quality Circles, is valuable for the entire work team. Trained facilitators may be used to start this process, but care must be taken not to weaken the position of the supervisor or team leader. If the supervisors use facilitators as a crutch, their leadership role becomes progressively weaker, which ultimately harms the entire organization. If the supervisor's role in the organization is important, it should be well performed. If the position is not important, it should be eliminated.

STEPS IN PROCESSING SUGGESTIONS

Suggestion-processing steps follow the structure of the organization. They involve no additional committee structures or a coordinator. Suggestions can occur anywhere in the organization, and when they do, they go first to the suggester's work team.

What happens to a suggestion in a work-team meeting is quite a bit different from what happens in a suggestion committee. In the work team, there are several other workers who have the same information and perspective as the suggester. They are the ones most likely to use the new idea if it is approved. The other members of the work team can add to or otherwise modify an original idea and make it better.

The work team can show enthusiasm for a good idea and commit to making it work. This is reward for the suggester and insurance for the organization that good ideas will be adopted. In other systems, many good ideas have failed due to lack of support from others in the organization. The work team can also reject an impractical idea before it develops momentum and wastes time. A mature work team will do this in a way that is not harmful to the person proposing the idea. Its members will give the idea a fair hearing and then show the suggester why it cannot be used. More often than not, however, they will work with an idea until it is made practical and usable.

Second-degree suggestion committees generally are not able to provide this same level of support for suggestions. Representatives may try to sell the idea of a fellow employee but don't have the knowledge or perspective to enhance it to the extent that the work team does. Complaints that an idea was misunderstood or not given a fair hearing are fairly common in first- and second-degree suggestion systems but rare in a third-degree system.

Suggestions should be implemented as quickly as possible, which means that no unnecessary additional processing is done. It also means that any necessary additional processing must be done expeditiously. Consider the case of a first-shift production work team suggesting a new or changed inspection procedure. First, the initiating work team discusses and decides to support the new method. But before the change can be implemented, it is necessary to obtain the support and approval of the others who will be affected by the change.

The work team then decides how best to obtain the support of the second and third shifts and the approval of quality control. In some cases, the supervisor meets with the other shift supervisors and the quality control manager to facilitate the adoption of the idea. In other cases, a work-team member, usually the person who originated the idea, is assigned to the task. Teams develop good skills in selecting the most effective and efficient tactics and personnel to use in promoting an idea. To obtain the support of the second and third shifts in this example, one or more team members from the originating team may be assigned to meet with the second- and third-shift teams to explain and discuss the idea thoroughly. This generally results in obtaining the support needed from the other shifts, but it is just as likely that further improvements will be made as the other shift personnel discuss the idea.

The quality control manager is responsible for all inspection methods and has the authority to approve or reject the idea. He or she may decide the matter or may refer it to the quality control work team before deciding it. The purpose of all of these meetings and discussions is threefold: First, the organization uses all of its resources in developing the *best* method; second, all of the people whose work will be affected by the change are brought into the analysis and decision making; third, the support of all of the people who must use the new method is obtained in advance.

More time is spent in this process discussing, analyzing, and selecting new methods, but this cost in time and effort is more than offset by the organization's ability to innovate and make improvements successfully. The additional time is, of course, an added cost. It is a worthwhile cost to the extent that it results in reducing other costs and increasing productivity. In one year, Company D budgeted $14,000 for work-team meetings, and the work teams generated ideas that reduced costs by more than $500,000. The company considered this a satisfactory return on the cost of the work-team meetings.

When to hold meetings. In both second- and third-degree systems, meetings must be held. Thus, there is a need to decide whether the meetings will be held during the regular work shift or outside of the normal workday (before or after the shift). There are two issues to be considered in making this decision: cost and attendance. When meetings are held before or after the regular work shift, nonexempt employees must be paid overtime, which is an additional cost. The cost of holding the meetings during the regular shift should be compared to the cost of overtime meetings and the least expensive time selected. Since on-shift meetings can result in lost production, production departments will probably find it less costly to meet on overtime, despite the additional pay (except when production is not running full). Service and staff departments can usually meet during the regular work shift without delaying production. A good general rule is to hold all meetings during normal working hours except where overtime meetings are less expensive.

The second issue is attendance. Attendance is always 100 percent when meetings are held during regular work time but drops off when meetings are held before or after the normal shift. People have other things to do, and the overtime premium is not an incentive to everyone. As with other aspects of the gainsharing program, this issue must be decided according to the needs of the company and the preferences of the people. There is no single approach that will work best for every organization.

MANAGEMENT ROLE

In a third-degree system, management has a most important role. It is in this type of participative system that the ideal of McGregor's Theory Y and Likert's System 4 becomes reality. Management develops an organization of people who know, are committed to, and are motivated to achieve the goals of the organization. Excellence is a hallmark of management in this system. Managers provide models of excellence and expect excellence in every aspect of the business. They provide excellent leadership, communications, planning, and resources for the organization. They insist on excellent quality and value for the customers, and they expect excellent performance from all the people in the organization. They know and understand the value of highly motivated people and provide the structure and the opportunity for individual motivation and excellence. They expect new ideas and welcome them. They expect change and encourage it. They expect creativity and manage it. This is a difficult and challenging style of management, but it is the most productive.

Summary

Employee participation is what makes a gainsharing program go. The idea is to get people more involved; to allow their ideas to be heard, thereby increasing productivity; and to enable people to use more of their skills and know-how on the job. In deciding which system to use, an organization may start at any of the three degrees. As the organization develops skill and experience with participation, it will inevitably move toward a third-degree system, and someday perhaps a fourth degree will be discovered.

Chapter 7
Shared Reward

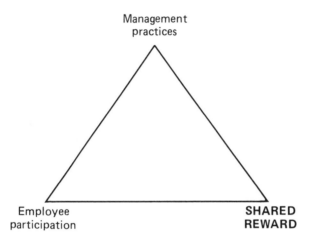

Management practices

Employee participation

SHARED REWARD

The reward is the food for the gainsharing program. As management practices stimulate employee participation and improved performance, productivity increases. The increased productivity generates a financial reward: the gain. Because these improvements result from cooperation between employees, managers, and owners, the reward is shared among them; hence, gainsharing. The employee's share is usually paid as a cash bonus, while the company's share is retained as additional earnings or profit. This is the most innovative and unique feature of gainsharing.

Compensation and Reward Problems

For years, the whole field of compensation has been one long dogfight characterized by acrimony, adversary relationships, and considerably more dissatisfaction than satisfaction. Periodically a new program emerges that reduces the dogfight to a tug-of-war. For instance, the Hay Job Evaluation System puts a portion of the problem on a more rational basis, and cafeteria fringe benefits are more desirable from the employees' point of view, but no program other than gainsharing attempts to go to the very root cause of the problem: the conflict.

There is no logical basis for a compensation tug-of-war between management and employees. Neither management nor labor provides the money over which they fight; customers provide the money. As Drucker has stated very clearly: "The purpose of a business (or any organization) is to create a customer." This requires a joint effort by capital and labor. Buildings and machines alone cannot produce products or services. Workers without tools are very limited in the type of products and services they can produce. When labor and owners of capital join their efforts to create customers, they are rewarded according to how well they perform. If they perform well, the customers will pay them for it. This pay then goes for wages, profits, dividends, and reinvestments. This is the fundamental premise of our economic system and the basis for the gainsharing reward system.

The gainsharing reward system begins with a productivity base point at which customers are being served and owners and employees are being properly rewarded for their performance. If the producing organization can raise performance above the established base, it will have *earned* an additional reward. Because gainsharing provides in advance for the sharing of the reward, when the gain occurs, there is no tug-of-war. Everyone receives his or her agreed-upon share. This experience further reinforces the cooperation and teamwork that create the reward, which, in time, results in a new culture in the organization. The win-lose battle of labor and management as adversaries is replaced by a system in which everybody wins. This is innovative. This goes right to the root of the problem. This is the unique feature of gainsharing.

In starting a gainsharing program, the shared reward causes the most difficulty for both managers and employees. Managers ask ten times more questions and show much more hesitation and skepticism about the reward than about any other element. Employees, in general, and labor unions, in particular, also show great concern about the bonus. In new installations, it is necessary to remind the parties frequently that there are three important elements to a successful gainsharing program. Concern about the bonus tends to block proper consideration of the other two elements: management practices and employee participation. Once a plan is in place and operating successfully, managers and employees report that the most important aspects of the program are improved communication, more participation, positive attitudes, and a better climate for results. Rarely do experienced companies report the bonus as the most important element in their plan. It might be well to consider briefly some of the reasons why people new to gainsharing tend to be so cautious about the bonus.

Sharing productivity gains equitably depends, first of all, on our ability to accurately measure those gains. To measure gains, there needs to be a sound productivity base. Management's hesitation to pay a bonus based on improved productivity is due, in part, to its lack of confidence in productivity measures. We have many ways to measure performance, but few of them are true productivity measures. Traditional measurement systems focus attention on costs and profits, neither of which measures productivity. In measuring productivity, costs are irrelevant except as they relate to output. It is unimportant whether the widget maker got $4 or $8 or $16 per hour (except, of course, to the widget maker and his or her family). What is important is the labor cost per widget (unit labor cost). Consider the following example:

Hourly wage	Widgets per hour	Unit labor cost
$ 4	100	.04
8	250	.032
16	600	.0267

All other things being equal, the $16-per-hour widget maker is the least expensive and most productive. The cost that counts is not the hourly wage but the unit labor cost. Yet most managers complain about the hourly wage and ignore the unit labor cost. When first discussing gainsharing, the manager who is accustomed to focusing on the hourly wage sees the bonus as an increased cost. The manager who feels that wages are already too high gets white knuckles over the idea of even higher pay in the form of a bonus. The manager who looks at costs and not productivity is hesitant about any bonus program. This is also true of the manager whose boss looks only at cost levels and not at productivity. Lack of adequate productivity measures is a fairly serious problem, and it is all too common.

For employees, the source of hesitation is a matter of trust. Few employees are genuinely satisfied with their pay. They see themselves in the tug-of-war with managers over pay issues, and as a result, they view management as always trying to get more for less. When gainsharing is first proposed, it is usually seen as just another incentive plan. When employees don't trust management, the questions in the back of their minds are "What are they up to this time?" and "What will I have to give up for this gainsharing business?" This situation is also far too common.

So we find that almost everyone who first looks at gainsharing is preoccupied with the bonus. In time, and with good communications, people learn the proper role of the bonus: a reward for increased productivity. With experience, the organization also develops a more balanced view of all three of the principal gainsharing elements.

Figure 12. Typical multicost ratio calculation for a manufacturing division.

Sales	$ 90,000	*Monthly—shipped and billed*
Inventory Increase	12,000	*Produced but not sold*
Production	$102,000	*At sales value*
Less Returns and Allowances	2,000	*Unacceptable prior production*
Adjusted Production	$100,000	*Basis for productivity computation*
Allowed Expenses	$50,000	*From the base productivity measure*
Less Actual Expenses	45,000	*Actual cost of allowed expense items*
Savings Pool—Gain	$ 5,000	*Allowed minus actual*
Less Reserve—10%	500	*To reserve for deficit months*
Sharing Pool	$ 4,500	*Net available for sharing*
Company Share—50%	$2,250	*To profit*
Employee Share—50%	$2,250	*Paid out as gainshare bonus*
Total Payroll	$23,000	*Actual pay of all employees*
Less Ineligible Payroll	500	*New employees, vacations, holidays*
Participating Payroll	$22,500	*Payroll of employees eligible for share*
Gainshare Bonus	10%	*Paid immediately to all eligible employees; 10% of actual monthly pay for all time worked, including overtime*

This chapter will present examples of the more common gainsharing bonus formulas and the principles common to all of them. There are two major components to the bonus: measuring the gain and sharing the gain. Each is important and must be properly designed and well understood for the bonus to have its intended impact.

Figure 12 presents a typical monthly bonus statement that the reader may find useful for reference throughout this chapter. Presented are all of the elements as they might appear in an actual statement. Other examples in the chapter show only partial statements.

Measuring the Gain

Because the purpose of gainsharing is to increase productivity, there is no reward unless there is a gain in productivity. Some kind of productivity base must be used in order to determine whether a gain has occurred.

Simply stated, a gain is a measured improvement over the established base. Therefore, this productivity base is the key element in determining the gain, and establishing the base is very important to the success of the gainsharing program. There is no single productivity base that can be applied to every gainsharing program, but all involve a ratio of output to input.

OUTPUT/INPUT

Doug Park, of Boise Cascade, Inc., prepared a model showing five basic ways to improve productivity by increasing output, decreasing input, or a combination of the two:

$$\text{Productivity} = \frac{\text{output}}{\text{input}}$$

1. Cost reduction $\dfrac{\text{Output: no change}}{\text{Input: down}}$

2. Growth plus efficiency $\dfrac{\text{Output: up}}{\text{Input: up less}}$

3. Better utilization of resources $\dfrac{\text{Output: up}}{\text{Input: no change}}$

4. Growth plus cost reduction $\dfrac{\text{Output: up}}{\text{Input: down}}$

5. Recession $\dfrac{\text{Output: down}}{\text{Input: down more}}$

Output can be expressed in units (10,000 widgets, 2,000 tons, or 1 bridge) or in dollars ($100,000 sales, $50,000 billings, or $50,000 value added).

It is also possible to express output indirectly, as is done in Improshare plans. In such measurements, each unit of output represents a certain number of earned or standard labor hours. This method uses hours to represent units, which, in turn, represent dollars of sales. Though indirect, these are valid output measures.

Inputs are the various resources used to produce the output. All inputs are costs, but they can be expressed in other ways. Inputs are unique to each organization and include some or all of the following seven principal categories:

1. Labor (in dollars or hours):
   ○ Direct labor—direct work on product or service.
   ○ Indirect labor—support to direct labor.
   ○ Overhead—management, administration, staff.

2. Materials (in dollars, units, or quantity):
   ○ Direct materials—materials that become part of a finished product, such as the metal or plastic in widgets or the peanuts in peanut butter.
   ○ Indirect materials—materials that are used up in the production process but do not become part of the finished product, such as lubricants, tools, and office supplies.
3. Energy (in dollars, BTUs, tons, or barrels):
   ○ Direct—for industries using large amounts of energy in production, such as aluminum reduction or an airline.
   ○ Indirect—energy for equipment operation, heat, light, and air conditioning.
4. Purchased services (in dollars):
   ○ Services purchased from other companies that directly or indirectly contribute to output, such as maintenance, janitorial, heat treating, printing, consulting, and training.
5. Other expenses, such as interest expense and auditing.
6. Expensed investments, such as research and development.
7. Capital (in dollars) for land, buildings, machines, vehicles, computers.

$$\text{Total factor productivity} = \frac{\text{output (total sales)}}{\text{input (all direct and indirect costs)}}$$

Partial measurements relate some of the inputs to total output.

$$\text{Labor productivity} = \frac{\text{output (total sales)}}{\text{input (labor costs)}}$$

$$\text{Materials productivity} = \frac{\text{output (total sales)}}{\text{input (material costs)}}$$

$$\text{Energy productivity} = \frac{\text{output (total sales)}}{\text{input (energy costs)}}$$

Total versus Partial Base Productivity Measurement

A base productivity measurement can be total or partial. A total measurement relates all inputs to the organization's output. Many other partial productivity measures are possible using different outputs and inputs. It is important to develop a productivity base that provides the best measurement of productivity for the organization. Most Scanlon Plans and all Improshare plans measure only labor productivity. This method has apparently been adequate for the labor-intensive manufacturing companies, where these plans have enjoyed their greatest success. The Rucker value-added method measures total productivity, but so far it has been used only in situations where labor is a major cost.

Labor productivity alone would probably not be an adequate measure for a capital-intensive operation where labor costs are one of the minor inputs. The first rule in selecting inputs for the base productivity measure is to include those that have the greatest impact on productivity. The second rule is to include as many inputs as possible to insure that true productivity is being measured, because inputs are interchangeable.

The interchangeability of input resources is one of the challenges to productivity improvement. Finding the right balance and using inputs efficiently is a key to increasing productivity. For years, industry has been replacing human muscle power (labor) with mechanical horsepower (machines). At the time of our Revolutionary War, one shoemaker could make a single pair of shoes in a 12-hour day. This is one reason why Washington's army was barefoot at Valley Forge. Today, with modern machines, one shoemaker can make more than ten pairs of shoes in an eight-hour day. And this is the reason why most Americans today own several pairs of shoes. As productivity goes up, relative costs come down, and more people can afford to buy.

We have reached the highest standard of living ever achieved by any country as a result of increased mechanization, automation, and other capital investments. By changing materials, it is possible to reduce the cost of materials, energy, and labor, but different and more expensive machines may be required. Purchased services may be used to replace direct and indirect labor costs and vice versa. Managing productivity can be a very complex process of finding the right combination of inputs to get the best output. Putting the right inputs into the productivity base will enable the organization to measure, and therefore manage, its productivity.

The best possible productivity base for gainsharing is the total-factor base, because it alone rewards true productivity increases. If a gainsharing suggestion saved $1,000 in labor but increased energy and material costs by $1,000, there would be no real improvement in productivity. On the other hand, a $1,000 labor savings might also result in an additional savings of $1,000 in materials and energy. In this case, productivity has actually increased by $2,000 as a result of the $1,000 labor savings suggestion. The preferred productivity base is that which reflects the full effect of improved productivity.

Any of the input categories can be divided into smaller and smaller parts. Labor can be divided into direct, indirect, and overhead. Direct labor can be further divided by department and, again, by individual operators. Productivity can be measured hour by hour for every person in the company, as it is in so many piece-rate and time-payment plans. However, such minute measures of productivity run contrary to the gainsharing idea, which is to create unity in the company toward the attainment of total productivity. Partial measures tend to encourage tunnel vision regarding productivity, and the smaller the part, the narrower the tunnel.

Performance versus Productivity

There are, in most organizations, many valid performance measures, such as machine utilization, reject and scrap rates, backlog and delinquencies, absenteeism, efficiencies, sales targets, and many more. These are useful for directing people's attention to areas where improvements can be made. However, they are not measures of productivity as needed for gainsharing. Performance measures usually focus narrowly on a single process or department, which tends to cause improvements in the particular area regardless of the impact on total productivity. The gainsharing productivity base places individual or department performance in its proper perspective: as part of the whole.

Short-Range versus Long-Range

Gainsharing is concerned with total productivity, which includes long-range productivity. In a gainsharing program, people are encouraged to spend $1 today to lubricate a machine and avoid a $1,000 repair 12 months from today. Significant short-range cost reductions can be made by not doing needed preventive maintenance work, but in 6 to 12 months, the true impact of such a cost reduction may be felt in the form of more down time and more costly repairs. Partial bases focus people's attention on short-term gains and prevent them from seeing longer-range, and sometimes greater, opportunities. A broader productivity base will focus people's attention on longer-range productivity management.

Measuring the Productivity of Capital

Conventional accounting practice does not provide measures of capital productivity as it does for the other inputs. Labor, materials, energy, and other costs are referred to as expenses and shown as such on the annual profit and loss statement. Capital investments in land, buildings, and machines are not listed as expenses and are therefore not included on the profit and loss statement. Depreciation allows for a portion of the capital investment to be charged as an expense, but depreciation rates are governed by various tax laws and do not reflect the true annual cost of capital. Profit earned by a capital investment is measured by return on investment and its many variations. Another method for measuring return on capital is the payback study, which shows how long it will take for the savings in labor, materials, and other expenses to equal the cost of a new machine or other capital investment.

The varied accounting methods for expenses (labor, materials, energy) and for capital investments make it difficult to have an ideal total productivity measure. Until new accounting techniques are developed, partial measures will have to be the only option for most organizations. Partial measures have been used in many successful gainsharing programs and can be used in new ones. But we should be aware of their shortcomings and be alert to insure that partial measures do not cause tunnel vision and shortsightedness in our efforts to improve productivity.

Selecting a Measurement

In deciding on a productivity base, a company should look at several alternatives and select the one that best measures the most critical factors affecting its productivity. In a company where labor is the single most important factor in productivity, a base using labor only might be adequate, at least to start. In another company, where several inputs are equally important, a productivity base using only one factor might be inadequate. In one case, it was found that labor productivity could be increased by overworking machines and tooling. The employees were earning bonuses while the company was incurring excessive tooling costs. This company changed the productivity base to a broader one that included the cost of tooling.

A careful analysis by knowledgeable production, accounting, and engineering people will enable any company to determine the proper factors for the productivity base. Many of the productivity centers around the country are hard at work developing new and better ways to measure productivity. These organizations can be very helpful in suggesting what to include and how to develop a good base productivity measure.

DATA FOR THE PRODUCTIVITY MEASUREMENT

Once the proper factors for the productivity base have been identified, the next step is to measure base productivity and establish a starting point from which to determine gains or losses. There are three ways to measure the productivity base: history, standards, or plans.

Historical Records

After a product or service has been produced, there is a record of how much time, materials, energy, and other resources have been used to produce it. Historical records often provide the best data for measuring the productivity base. Gains are defined as improvements over the historical base. For instance, if it can be accurately determined from historical records that labor costs have been 30 percent of the selling price, this is a good base measurement of labor productivity. The same is true for materials, energy, and other inputs. Most Scanlon Plans use historical data for their base productivity measurement, and Rucker Plans use history exclusively. Where historical data are available, they are for many organizations not only the most reliable for the productivity base but also the easiest to explain to employees who are not experts in such matters. Psychologically it works like Olympic track records: Let's see if we can beat the old record. Beating records seems to have universal appeal. Perhaps there should be a Guinness Book of World Records for workers.

Historical records can be used only when the historical period is long enough to provide everyone with confidence in the measurement. Three to five years of experience are generally accepted as enough to provide a reliable base. The historical period can be shorter when operations are fairly simple and not likely to fluctuate. When using historical data, it is important to select time periods when operations are stable and near normal. To avoid an inaccurate productivity base, it may be necessary to exclude certain years in measuring the base. For instance, periods of exceptionally high or low sales volume may not be normal, and cost records for abnormal years may distort the base. In these situations, a company would use only the normal years from the recent past to determine the base productivity measurement.

New organizations do not have a history, and in others, major product or process changes render accumulated historical data obsolete. In these cases, standards are often the next best alternative.

Standards

Standards show the costs or quantity of each input needed to produce a unit or dollar of output, which is a productivity measurement. Engineered standards are productivity bases developed by engineering formulas, work measurement, or other mathematical techniques and refer to quantities and units. Standard costs come from formulas and show how much each input should cost to produce each dollar of output. Engineers determine how many widgets can be produced on a machine in an hour or a day using machine-loading formulas, work measurement, and other techniques. Cost accountants provide similar information but in the form of costs. Standards can be developed for any input factor. Properly set and maintained, standards provide good base productivity measures.

However, standards are not useful when they are out of date. They get out of date when changes occur in materials, methods, tools, or equipment, and they lose their reliability when they are not adjusted to reflect changes. Standards are not accurate where rates are negotiated or compromised due to employee grievances or management pressure. The organization must have confidence that a standard is reasonably accurate for it to be useful as a measure of productivity. An organization cannot have confidence in a standard that was developed mathematically and then negotiated to fit people's opinions or preferences.

Another drawback to the use of standards for the base productivity measure occurs when standards do not cover all jobs in the company. In companies that have standards, they are often available only for direct labor jobs. In a few cases, there are standards for indirect labor jobs. Standards seldom exist for overhead jobs.

Perhaps the biggest problem with standards is credibility. Standards are more refutable than history, and many people have seen them poorly administered. For any measurement to be useful, people have to believe that it is a fair way to measure and reward their performance. An organization that wants to use standards to determine the productivity base may have to clean up its standards before people will accept them as the measurement.

Despite some deficiencies, standards are being used successfully in many gainsharing programs. Improshare plans, for instance, use direct labor standards plus indirect labor to determine the base productivity factor (BPF). A few companies have neither history nor standards and must use the final alternative, which is the relationship between performance and plan.

Performance to Plan

In situations lacking reliable history or standards, financial plans can be used as a productivity base. Most organizations prepare an annual financial plan, including a budget, which contains the output/input information needed for a productivity base. The annual financial plan shows expected output (units or dollars) based on sales forecasts. It also shows how much labor, material, and other costs are to be used to produce the expected output. If these figures are a reliable estimate of expected productivity, they can be used as a base productivity measure for the gainsharing program.

Using plans for the productivity base also has its problems. In some companies, plans and budgets are not reliable. When plans are "guesstimates" and budgets are full of fudge factors, no one will accept the figures as a fair measure of productivity. However, in some organizations, this is the only alternative and should be used, provided the known risks are properly anticipated and managed: (1) Don't oversell the accuracy and reliability of plans, and (2) have some method to adjust the measurement retroactively if actual experience shows the original plan to be flawed.

COMPETITIVE LEVELS FOR THE BASE

The proper productivity base is that point where prices, wages, and profits are at reasonably competitive levels. With gainsharing, the company hopes to raise productivity to a level higher than the competition. Only then will there be an additional economic reward to be shared. So the starting point must be that level at which everything is equal to the competition.

Prices must be competitive. Competitive prices insure that the company can maintain its market share. A bonus paid from prices that are above the market will last only until the customers learn that they can save money by going to the competition. When prices are below market level, the company may not be generating enough money for bonuses. While there are, of course, many strategic issues that influence pricing decisions, a properly competitive price level should be used in the base productivity measurement.

Wages must be competitive. Wages and benefits are an individual reward, and most employees have a rather specific idea or expectation of what constitutes a fair or competitive wage for their job. A bonus that rewards extra effort can have impact only if it is in addition to a fair level of pay. When people regard a bonus as supplementing or making up for low wages and benefits, it simply does not work as a bonus. They are glad to see it when it comes, but it does not motivate greater productivity. Furthermore, employees are dissatisfied when there are no bonuses, because they feel it is their due, not something to be earned.

There is also a possibility that policies such as the above weaken management's credibility in the eyes of the employees. To employees it may appear that management is hedging its bet and may not really believe in the program. Although management says it will share increased productivity, to employees, the savings appears to be the money that was held back. Hence, the productivity base should include wages and benefits at a normal, competitive level.

Profits must also be competitive. The arguments here are the same as for wages. There is a competitive market for investments, and shareholders expect a competitive return. Most companies need to attract capital and require a competitive profit to provide an adequate return to investors. The base productivity measure must include a proper, competitive level of profit. The company's share of the productivity gain is the owners' profit bonus, just as the employees' share is a wage bonus.

To measure gains, the first step is to determine a satisfactory productivity base. The best productivity base is an output/input measurement using as many cost factors as possible. The base can be established using history, standards, plans, or some combination of the three and must include prices, wages, and profits at a normal, competitive level.

As with previous examples, the small, independent company has all of the options available to it. The division or plant in a large corporation may be limited in its choices because some data are not available. But any organization should be able to determine a productivity base from which gains and losses can be measured. To say otherwise is to admit that the company does not know what productivity is and therefore cannot manage it, which is intolerable.

EXAMPLES OF BASE PRODUCTIVITY MEASUREMENTS FOR GAINSHARING

The variety of base productivity measures that have been and can be used is virtually unlimited. In this section, we will examine eight common measurements based on the preceding criteria. Of the following examples, the first five measure labor cost only against various measures of output. Example 6 measures labor plus other costs against output and is preferred because of its breadth. Examples 7 and 8 are profit-sharing examples, and Example 8 is the only one of the eight that measures total productivity. Each example in this section stops at the point where the savings or gain is identified. How the gain is shared is a separate issue and will be covered in the next section of this chapter.

In Example 1, line 1 shows actual monthly sales. Most gainsharing programs measure productivity as the product is made rather than when it is sold. To do this, the sales figures must be adjusted.

Line 2 shows the inventory adjustment. Inventory increased by $12,000

Example 1. Gain based on ratio of labor costs to sales value of production.

1. Sales	$ 90,000
2. Inventory increase (or decrease)	12,000
3. Production	$102,000
4. Less returns and allowances	2,000
5. Adjusted production	$100,000
6. Labor ratio—productivity base	30%
7. Labor allowance	$ 30,000
8. Less actual labor	27,000
9. Gain	$ 3,000

and is added to sales to show how much was produced. If inventory decreased, it would mean that sales were greater than production, and the decrease in inventory would be subtracted from sales to reflect actual production.

Line 4 shows a deduction of $2,000 to cover defective goods returned from customers. Such returns are deducted from this month's production to recover bonuses that were paid in prior months. The system does not reward rejected parts, but some unacceptable parts will escape the best inspection process. The deduction corrects this error. Allowances or discounts given to customers to pay them for rework are treated the same way. In some organizations where quality is very critical to the success and reputation of the business, this deduction may be more than the actual cost of the bad parts. This is done to emphasize quality and to compensate the business for the loss of customer goodwill, which can hurt future business. The adjusted production figure, line 5, is the output for the productivity measure. Line 6, the productivity base, provides that 30 percent of production value is available to be spent on labor. Calculating 30 percent of the $100,000 adjusted production figure allows for labor costs of $30,000, line 7.

The actual cost of labor ($27,000) is shown on line 8. Line 9 shows a gain of $3,000 over the productivity base. This is the savings that will be shared between the company and the employees.

Example 2 shows how productivity is measured where there are two

Example 2. Gain based on ratio of labor costs to sales value of production, by product line.

	Product A	Product B
1. Sales	$50,000	$50,000
2. Inventory increase (or decrease)	5,000	5,000
3. Production	$55,000	$55,000
4. Less returns and allowances	2,500	2,500
5. Adjusted production	$52,500	$52,500
6. Labor ratio—productivity base	20%	32%
7. Labor allowance	$10,500	$16,800
8. Total labor allowed	$27,300	
9. Less actual labor	25,900	
10. Gain	$ 1,400	

Example 3. Gain based on ratio of labor costs to value added.

1. Sales	$100,000
2. Inventory increase (or decrease)	10,000
3. Production	$110,000
4. Less returns and allowances	5,000
5. Adjusted production	$105,000
6. Less purchased materials, supplies, services	50,000
7. Value added	$ 55,000
8. Labor ratio—productivity base	43%
9. Allowed labor	$ 23,650
10. Less actual labor	22,250
11. Gain	$ 1,400

products with much different labor ratios. Separate productivity bases are established and calculated for each product, as shown on lines 1 through 7. The separate product-line calculations are combined, line 8, and the productivity gain for the whole plant, store, or office is shown in line 10.

In Example 3, the output factor used in the productivity base is value added by production rather than the sales value. Lines 1 through 5 show an adjusted sales value of production, just as in the previous two examples. From the adjusted production amount, line 5, the cost of all purchased materials, supplies, and services, line 6, is deducted. The result, line 7, is the value that was added by the production process. The labor ratio of 43 percent is the base productivity measure. This ratio provides an allowance for labor costs of $23,650, line 9. Subtracting the actual labor costs, line 10, shows the productivity gain, line 11. This labor-to-value-added productivity measure is used by all Rucker Plans as described in Chapter 1.

In Example 4, the output factor is production, line 1, but in units rather than dollars. The productivity base is the allowance for labor to produce these units. The productivity base is $16,000 of direct labor ($16.00 per unit × 1,000 units), line 2, plus $8,000 of indirect labor ($8.00 per unit × 1,000 units), line 3, plus $7,500 of overhead labor ($7.50 per unit × 1,000 units), line 4. Actual labor, line 6, is subtracted from total allowed labor, line 5, to determine the gain, line 7.

This type of productivity measure might be used by a division of a larger company where the product is transferred to another division at cost and where sales value or value added is not known. Use of this

Example 4. Gain based on difference between allowed labor costs and actual labor costs.

1. Production	1,000 units	
2. Direct labor allowance	$16,000 ⎫	
3. Indirect labor allowance	8,000 ⎬ Productivity	
4. Overhead labor allowance	7,500 ⎭ base	
5. Total allowed labor	$31,500	
6. Less actual labor	28,500	
7. Gain	$ 3,000	

method varies. One company might show only one number, $31.50, for labor allowed per unit. Another might show even greater detail for each direct, indirect, and overhead department.

A variation of this plan, used when there are many different products, is to reduce each product to earned labor hours. There could be hundreds of products, as in a foundry. Each unit produced is recorded according to the number of labor hours allowed by standards to produce it. Standard hours would be the output, line 1, rather than units as indicated in the example. The rest of the example would be the same as shown.

Example 5 is essentially the same as the allowed labor cost formula shown in Example 4, except that all measurements are in hours rather than dollars. This method is the one used in Improshare plans as described in Chapter 1.

Example 5. Gain based on difference between allowed labor hours and actual labor hours.

1. Production	1,000 units
2. Direct labor allowed	1,600 hours
3. Indirect labor allowed	800
4. Overhead labor allowed	750
5. Total hours allowed	3,150 hours
6. Less actual hours	2,850
7. Gain in hours	300 hours
8. Gain in dollars (average rate $10/hour)	$3,000

Example 6. Gain based on ratio of a multicost productivity base to sales value of production.

1. Sales	$ 90,000	
2. Inventory increase (or decrease)	12,000	
3. Production	$102,000	
4. Less returns and allowances	2,000	
5. Adjusted production	$100,000	
6. Cost ratio—productivity base	76%	
7. Cost allowance	$ 76,000	
8. Less actual costs	72,000	
9. Gain	$ 4,000	

Output is production, line 1, in units produced. Input includes various labor categories such as direct, indirect, and overhead, lines 2, 3, 4, and 5. Production in units, tons, or any other measure yields the allowed hours. The actual hours, line 6, are subtracted from the allowed hours to determine the gain, line 7.

Bonuses in this type of plan are first shown as bonus hours, which are then paid at the employee's regular pay rate.

Example 6 is like Example 1 except that the productivity base includes labor, materials, and energy. As before, sales, line 1, are adjusted for inventory, line 2, and returns, line 4, to show output, line 5.

This method has most of the costs of labor, materials, and supplies included in the productivity base, line 6. In determining a multicost productivity base, a company will review all costs, such as the master list of inputs shown earlier in this chapter, and select those that are appropriate to the productivity base and gainsharing program. The selected costs are added together to provide a single productivity base. In a measurement period, monthly or otherwise, these base productivity costs, line 7, are compared to actual costs, line 8, to determine the productivity gain or loss, line 9. Of the partial measures, this comes closest to the ideal of a total productivity measure.

Example 7 shows a traditional profit-sharing calculation. Sales, line 1, minus costs, line 2, equals profit before taxes, line 3. This is an example of a plan in which the company has committed a fixed 25 percent of pretax profit to the employee profit-sharing plan. There are many other formulas for deciding the employee share in profit-sharing plans, some of which will be presented later in this chapter.

Example 7. Profit sharing, traditional method.

1. Sales	$100,000	
2. Less costs	84,000	
3. Profit before taxes	$ 16,000	
4. Profit share percentage	25% of pretax profit	
5. Profit share dollars	$4,000	

Profit may or may not measure productivity, but an increase in productivity will increase profit and result in a larger profit share. This type of plan, which is very common, does not really include a productivity base. There is no productivity standard against which to compare current performance. In plans of this type, the organization is committed to sharing 25 percent of profit regardless of productivity.

In some plans, there is a provision that sharing will not begin until a certain amount of profit has been earned, which does constitute a productivity base, similar to the following example.

In Example 8, the productivity base is a fixed-percentage return on investment. The gain is the amount of profit in excess of the ROI standard. The ROI standard was calculated as follows:

Capital invested in the business = $1,000,000

ROI standard percentage = 15% before taxes

$$\text{Monthly ROI requirement} = \frac{15\% \text{ of } \$1,000,000}{12} = \$12,500$$

This example of profit sharing is based on a productivity measure of profit to capital investment. Profit, which is the result of sales minus all costs, is the output. The capital investment in land, buildings, equipment, and working capital is the input.

Example 8. Profit sharing, based on return on investment (ROI).

1. Sales	$100,000
2. Less costs	84,000
3. Profit	$ 16,000
4. Less ROI standard	12,500
5. Gain	$ 3,500

Of all measures currently in use, the ROI profit sharing may be the ideal measure of productivity, because it includes all of the inputs required to determine true productivity. First, labor, materials, energy, purchased services, and other inputs (costs) are subtracted from output (sales) to determine profit. Then, capital investment is used directly in the productivity base. In this way, all inputs and outputs are included in the base.

Sharing the Gain

When a gain in productivity has been made, gainsharing provides that it be shared among the producers: owners and employees. The logic behind sharing the productivity gain between capital and labor is based on the reality that the interests of these two factors of production are inseparable and that a joint effort by the two is required to produce an output. The productivity base is set to insure that each receives fair and competitive base wages and profits. As productivity improves above the base, gainsharing provides an additional reward, a bonus for owners and employees.

Once it has been determined that a true increase in productivity has occurred, the issue becomes how to share the resulting gain. We can agree in principle that labor and management should share the gain, but this does not tell us what is a fair share for each. Should employees and owners receive equal amounts? Should owners receive twice as much as employees? Should there be a provision for reinvesting some or all of the company's share? If so, should this influence the sharing formula? Reinvestment benefits owners by increasing equity and security; it also benefits employees by creating growth, promotion opportunities, and security. Should the relative amounts of capital investment and labor be a factor in deciding an equitable gain? If so, in a company with a higher-than-average capital investment, the plan might award a larger share of the gain to the company than to the employees and vice versa.

What we need is a way to determine an equitable sharing ratio between owners and employees. What we have are the many questions listed above and only a few answers. Most of the available answers are from the experiences of many gainsharing companies—experiences that provide a good indication of what has worked in practice.

EXPERIENCE WITH SHARING RATIOS
Here is a summary of how the four major plans share gains between owners and employees.

Scanlon Plans

Most Scanlon Plans using a labor to sales productivity base share from 75 percent to 100 percent of the labor productivity gain with employees. The company share is the remaining 25 percent to 0 percent of the labor gain. To this smaller company share is added 100 percent of any productivity gains made in inputs other than labor. In general, it is correct to assume that as productivity of labor improves, the productivity of other inputs improves as well. Employees make less scrap, because the labor used to make scrap reduces labor productivity. As quality improves, so does the productivity of materials. It is very common to see a reduction in down time and, as a result, a reduction in repair costs. People take better care of equipment in order to keep it producing.

Scanlon Plan practice assumes that the larger employee share of the labor productivity gain (75 percent to 100 percent) becomes equitable with the company share, since the company receives the full benefit from the other productivity improvements. This assumption has generally been proved in practice, but there have been exceptions. In some machining operations, for instance, labor productivity can be increased (more widgets per labor hour) by operating machines and tools at excessive feeds and speeds. Running machines faster causes excessive wear and tear to tools and machines, which increases those costs. As labor costs per widget go down, tooling and other costs per widget may go up. Therefore, one critical issue to be dealt with in deciding an equitable sharing formula is to determine or estimate what additional productivity improvement can be anticipated that is not included in the productivity base.

Rucker Plans

Rucker Plans use a ratio of labor costs to value added for the productivity base. The Rucker standard establishes a fixed percentage of value added for labor costs. When productivity improvements increase value added, there is a gain to be shared. The Rucker standard defines what is available to pay labor, and money not used to pay wages and benefits is the bonus. This, in effect, gives employees 100 percent of the gain in labor productivity. The company's share is 100 percent of the productivity gain in the other inputs.

Improshare

Improshare plans measure labor productivity only, and gains are reported as hours saved. Savings in hours are shared 50/50. The employees' bonus is 50 percent of the hours saved. The company receives the remaining 50 percent of the hours saved plus other productivity gains that may occur along with increased labor productivity.

Profit Sharing
Profit-sharing plans include all costs, and there are several approaches
to sharing:

○ Fixed percentage of pretax profit.
○ Fixed percentage of pretax profit after a minimum profit threshold is
  reached.
○ Discretionary percentage of pretax profit decided by management
  when results are known.
○ Combination fixed percentage and discretionary award.

Deferred profit-sharing plans often start with a goal of providing a
bonus of 10 percent to 15 percent of employees' pay and work backward
to determine the necessary share. Deferred profit-sharing plans are limited
by law to a maximum of 15 percent of employee base pay. That is, taxes
may not be deferred on any amount in excess of 15 percent of pay. This,
in effect, places a ceiling on the employees' share in most deferred plans.
In such plans, all profits above the maximum employee allocation amount
are retained by the company. Cash profit-sharing plans are not subject to
the IRS regulations governing qualified deferred plans and do not place a
ceiling on employee earnings.

Multicost Gainsharing Plans
Multicost plans include labor plus materials, supplies, energy, and other
costs in the productivity base. Where the productivity base includes more
inputs, the share shifts to 50/50 or to 25 percent employee/75 percent
company, depending on the inputs in the base.

SHARING GUIDELINES
How to share productivity gains between owners and employees is perhaps the most difficult issue facing the organization in developing a gainsharing program. The company new to gainsharing will have no experience to guide it. Most managers know, or have heard, horror stories of
runaway incentives and windfall bonus programs. This lack of experience
and the knowledge of disasters causes managers to be extremely conservative in making a commitment to a sharing formula. Guidelines are
needed, and fortunately some have emerged from the experience summarized above.

Permanence
First of all, it is not necessary to establish a sharing formula for all
time, although many organizations try to do so. Management knows if it
tinkers with the formula every year, employees will be suspicious that it

is manipulating the plan to the benefit of the company. Permanence is nice, but it is not always possible. Changes in markets, technology, and economics are realities to be dealt with, not wished away. Ignoring reality to keep people from feeling bad is not a formula for success. A company considering gainsharing should put together the best plan it can devise and be ready to change it as soon as there is evidence that a change is needed. This advice pertains to every feature of the plan, including the sharing of the gain. It may be necessary to start with a conservative share for employees in order to win management support. Then, if experience shows a different sharing formula to be more equitable, a change should be made. It may also happen that a sharing formula that is equitable today becomes inequitable as circumstances change. In deciding the sharing ratio, it is important that the ratio's long-range implications be examined and factored into the decision.

Equity
The essense of a proper sharing formula is equity, meaning fairness or justice. It does not necessarily mean equality. Equity in sharing the productivity gain may mean equal shares to owners and employees in one situation and unequal shares in another. In a company with a very high capital investment and low labor content, it would seem equitable that a larger share of the gain be awarded to the company and a smaller share to the employees. The larger company share would make funds available from the gain to maintain and replace capital resources, which wear out in the process of production. The converse also seems proper. In a company with a very low capital investment and high labor content, perhaps a larger share of the gain should be awarded to employees.

Because there are no absolute rules to guide us in these decisions, they must be made according to the best judgments available at the time. Experience has shown that when this decision is dealt with in an open and responsible climate, employees will support the right decision. People have a good sense for what is fair and equitable. The spirit of partnership, which is the foundation for gainsharing, is the most reliable guide for making this decision.

A FORMULA FOR THE SHARING RATIO
From the accumulated experience, a pattern has emerged, which has been developed into a formula. In the following material, the development of the sharing-ratio formula will be presented. But, first, it is necessary to examine some additional examples to clarify the issues addressed by the formula.

Let us assume that, after a careful study, it has been decided that an equitable share of benefits requires that owners and employees each receive the same dollar amounts. The dollar amounts to be compared are the employees' share in dollars to the company's share in dollars after corporate taxes have been deducted. The employees' share is shown before corporate taxes because current tax laws permit the employee bonus to be shown as a before-tax expense. The company's share passes through a few more accounting procedures before there is a true benefit to the owners. The company's share of the gain is first shown as pretax income. Next corporate income taxes (usually 46 percent) are deducted, and the share becomes net profit. Finally, it becomes income to the owners in one of two ways: It is either paid out as dividends or reinvested in the company, which increases the value of the company and the owners' shares of stock. Dividend income is subject to the owners' personal income tax rate, similar to wages. Equity increases are subject to capital gains income tax procedures.

Thus, in Example 9, the $750 company share will be reduced to $405 by corporate income tax. In order for the owners to receive a share equal to that of the employees, there will have to be an additional $1,845 in the after-tax income, or $3,417 of pretax productivity gains from the nonlabor inputs. In this example, the other inputs from which the owners must derive their additional share are in excess of $50,000. A productivity gain of about 7 percent would be needed to produce an additional $3,417 in savings. That the productivity of other resources such as ma-

Example 9. Sharing the gain: traditional 75%/25% split. (Calculations continue from Example 1.)

Sales	$ 90,000
Inventory increase (or decrease)	12,000
Production	$102,000
Less returns and allowances	2,000
Adjusted production	$100,000
Labor ratio—productivity base	30%
Labor allowance	$30,000
Less actual labor	27,000
Gain	$ 3,000
Employee share—75%	$2,250
Company share—25%	$750

terials, supplies, energy, and so forth will improve by 7 percent seems reasonable. This sharing ratio offers a good opportunity for equity.

In Example 10, the owners' share is $920 less than the employees' share. For the owners to receive a share equal to that of the employees, an additional pretax productivity gain of $1,704 would be necessary to produce the $920 for the equal share. The original $4,000 savings is a 5.3 percent increase in productivity over the $76,000 productivity base. In this example, it does not seem likely that a $1,704 productivity gain would be possible from the inputs not covered in the productivity base. In a multicost formula, the inputs not covered are expenses such as depreciation, interest expense, insurance, and other corporate costs, which seldom produce significant productivity gains and certainly not the 20 percent or more that would be necessary to generate a savings of $1,704. If having equal dollar amounts for owners and employees is considered equitable, this sharing formula will not achieve it. A different share ratio is needed. We can try different combinations, such as 25 percent employees/75 percent company:

Gain	$4,000
Less employee share—25%	1,000
Company share—75%	$3,000
Less tax at 46%	1,380
Net company share	$1,620

Example 10. Effect of corporate tax on net share to owners of company. (Calculations continue from Example 6.)

Sales	$ 90,000
Inventory increase (or decrease)	12,000
Production	$102,000
Less returns and allowances	2,000
Adjusted production	$100,000
Cost ratio—productivity base	76%
Cost allowance	$76,000
Less actual costs	72,000
Gain	$ 4,000
Employee share—50%	$2,000
Company share—50%	$2,000
Less tax at 46%	920
Net share to owners	$1,080

In this case, the company share is 62 percent higher than the employee share, which does not provide equal dollar amounts. Something between Example 10 and the preceding example is needed; let's consider a 40 percent employee/60 percent company ratio:

Gain	$4,000
Less employee share—40%	1,600
Company share—60%	$2,400
Less tax at 46%	1,104
Net company share	$1,296

This sharing ratio also fails to provide the desired equity, but it is getting closer. Perhaps 35 percent/65 percent will do it.

Gain	$4,000
Less employee share—35%	1,400
Company share—65%	$2,600
Less tax at 46%	1,196
Net company share	$1,404

The shares are now very close.

These calculations show exactly what many organizations have done: search for the right combination by trial and error. However, there is a better way: A formula that can help determine the sharing ratio has been developed following the pattern expressed in the previous calculations.

When the measured productivity base included only a small percentage of the total productivity inputs, the employee share of the gain was fairly large. When the productivity base included more inputs, the employee share of the gain was proportionately smaller. Robert J. Keeler, of Honeywell, Inc., has developed the following formula to help determine an appropriate sharing ratio. The formula, which does with precision what the preceding examples were trying to do by trial and error, is:

$$\frac{\text{Employee share}}{\text{percentage}} = \frac{\text{ratio of total costs to sales} \times (1 - \text{tax rate})}{\text{ratio of productivity base to sales} \times [1 + (1 - \text{tax rate})]}$$

Employee share percentage is the percentage of measured gain that is awarded to the employees. The company share percentage is the difference between 100 percent and the employee share percentage.

Ratio of total costs to sales is all profit and loss statement costs that are subject to productivity improvement, whether they are in the productivity base or not. Included would be labor, materials, supplies, energy, overhead, and other expenses. Excluded would be profit and, depending on the nature of the business, such other expenses as depreciation, interest expense, property and local taxes, and expensed investment such as research and development.

Ratio of productivity base to sales is the ratio to sales of those costs that are included in the productivity base.

Tax rate is the average corporate income tax rate. For the examples that follow, we will use the simple incremental tax rate of 46 percent. This formula would have to be recalculated any time there was a significant change in the average corporate tax rate.

For Example 9, under the formula and the assumption that other inputs will become more productive to the same degree as labor, the dollar shares to the company and the employees will be equal. The calculation is shown in Example 9-A.

Example 9-A. Using the formula (with a labor productivity base) to make company and employee shares equal after corporate tax.

Ratio of total costs to sales   80% (assumed)
Productivity base rate   30% (labor only)
Tax rate   46%
Formula:

$$\text{Employee share} = \frac{.80 \times (1 - .46)}{.30 \times [1 + (1 - .46)]} = \frac{.432}{.462} = .935 = 93.5\%$$

Company share = 100% − 93.5% = 6.5%
Gain (see Example 9) = $3,000
Employee share = 93.5% of $3,000 = $2,805
Company share = (6.5% of $3,000) −(tax on resulting
                                      amount at 46%)
        = $195   − $90   = $105

The $3,000 gain in labor productivity is a 10% improvement. A similar gain is assumed in the factors not included in the base productivity measurement, with 100 percent of these additional gains going to the company to equalize the shares.

Total costs subject to productivity improvement	$80,000
Less costs included in base productivity measurement	30,000
Costs not in base	$50,000
10% productivity improvement	$5,000
Less tax at 46%	2,300
Additional savings to company	$2,700
Company gainshare	105
Total company share	$2,805

For Example 10, under the formula and the same assumption, the company and the employees each receive equal dollar shares, as shown in Example 10-A.

A Formula for Unequal Shares

As stated earlier, there may be cases where equity does not mean equal dollar shares. In such cases, the formula can be modified by the ratio of employee share to company share, represented by K in the examples that follow. In the first example, 10-B, the employee share is half of the company share. In the second, 10-C, the employee share is twice the

Example 10-A. Using the formula (with a multicost productivity base) to make company and employee shares equal after corporate tax.

Ratio of total costs to sales	80%
Productivity base rate	76% (multicost allowance)
Tax rate	46%

Formula:

$$\text{Employee share} = \frac{.80 \times (1 - .46)}{.76 \times [1 + (1 - .46)]} = \frac{.432}{1.17} = .369 = 36.9\%$$

Company share = $100\% - 36.9\% = 63.1\%$
Gain (see Example 10) = \$4,000
Employee share = 36.9% of \$4,000 = \$1,476
Company share = (63.1% of \$4,000) − (tax on resulting
amount at 46%)
= \quad \$2,524 \quad − \quad \$1,161 \quad = \$1,363

The \$4,000 gain in productivity is a 5.3% improvement. A similar gain is assumed in the factors not included in the base productivity measurement, with 100% of these additional gains going to the company to equalize the shares.

Total costs subject to productivity improvement	\$80,000
Less costs included in base productivity measurement	76,000
Costs not in base	\$ 4,000
5.3% productivity improvement	\$ 212
Less tax at 46%	98
Additional savings to company	\$ 114
Company gainshare	1,363
Total company share	\$1,477

(The \$1 difference between \$1,476 and \$1,477 is due to rounding.)

Example 10-B. Using the formula (with a multicost productivity base) to make employee share half as much as company share after corporate tax.

$K = .5$

Formula:

$$\text{Employee share} = \frac{.5 \times .80 \times (1 - .46)}{.76 \times [1 + .5 - (.5 \times .46)]} = \frac{.216}{.9652} = .224 = 22.4\%$$

Company share = $100\% - 22.4\% = 77.6\%$
Gain (see Example 10-A) = \$4,000
Employee share = 22.4% of \$4,000 = \$896
Company share = (77.6% of \$4,000) − (tax on resulting
                                                    amount at 46%)

| | | = | \$3,104 | − | \$1,428 | = \$1,676 |

Additional savings to company (see Example 10-A)   114
Total company share   \$1,790

The company share is twice that of the employees: $\$896 \times 2 = \$1,792$. (The \$2 difference between \$1,792 and \$1,790 is due to rounding.)

---

company share. Both of the following examples use the data from the previous multicost calculation, Example 10-A. The formula is:

$$\text{Employee share} = \frac{K \times \text{ratio of total costs to sales} \times (1 - \text{tax rate})}{\text{ratio of productivity base to sales} \times [1 + K - (K \times \text{tax rate})]}$$

Using the Sharing Formula

The preceding sharing formula should be used with some caution. A proper application of it requires two careful judgments. First, judgment is needed in deciding which costs to include in the total cost figure. The intention is to include all costs that can be impacted by the gainsharing program, whether they are in the productivity base or not. It is common to receive suggestions that improve the productivity of materials even in labor-only plans where the savings go entirely to the company. There are no guidelines about what to include or exclude. Each company must review a complete list of accounts and select those that are subject to productivity improvements through the gainsharing program.

Judgment is also required to determine the ratio of employees' share to owners' share. Fifty/fifty (equal shares) is an easy decision because it sounds fair, but it may not be the best ratio. If, for instance, the growth of the business is important for the company and the employees, growth

Example 10-C. Using the formula (with a multicost productivity base) to make employee share twice as much as company share after corporate tax.

$K = 2$

Formula:

$$\frac{\text{Employee}}{\text{share}} = \frac{2 \times .80 \times (1 - .46)}{.76 \times [1 + 2 - (2 \times .46)]} = \frac{.864}{1.5808} = .5466 = 54.66\%$$

Company share = 100% − 54.66% = 45.34%
Gain (see Example 10-A) = $4,000
Employee share = 54.66% of $4,000 = $2,186
Company share = (45.34% of $4,000) − (tax on resulting
amount at 46%)

=	$1,814 − $834	= $ 980
Additional savings to company (see Example 10-A)		114
Total company share		$1,094

The employees' share is twice that of the company: $1,094 × 2 = $2,188. (The $2 difference between $2,188 and $2,186 is due to rounding.)

is limited by the company's capital base. Reinvested profits are the least expensive, and therefore the best, source of capital funds for growth. Awarding a large share of productivity gains to the company for reinvestment is clearly a benefit to the shareholders, whose equity is increased. It also benefits the employees when the company reinvests profits, since future income, job security, and career opportunities are greater in a growing firm. What is given up today may well yield two or three times the benefit in years to come.

The entire process of deciding how to share productivity gains between the company and the employees is a judgment matter. The preceding formula will be helpful if used as a guide and not as a rule; the spirit of partnership serves as the rule.

Other Reward Issues

The major reward issues are the base productivity measurement and the reward ratio. Several other important issues are bonus payments and distribution, noncash bonuses, participating payroll, frequency of reward, reserves, bonus ceilings, changing the base, employment security, who participates, and bonus size.

BONUS PAYMENTS AND DISTRIBUTION

Bonus payments in Scanlon Plans and Rucker Plans are usually in cash and in a separate check. The separate check is good publicity for the program. In deferred profit-sharing plans, the employee receives a statement showing how much has been contributed to his or her account and the status of the total account. Improshare plans pay weekly bonuses combined with regular pay.

There are three ways to distribute the gainshare: (1) by percentage of pay, (2) by hours worked, and (3) by equal dollar shares. Percentage of pay means that each employee receives the same percentage applied to his or her total pay for the period. This method is by far the most common and is generally considered the most equitable. It provides greater rewards to those who worked more hours, on the premise that, while doing so, they produced more output and gain. It also gives greater rewards to those in higher pay grades, because holders of higher-skilled and higher-paid jobs contribute more to productivity improvement. The engineer who designs a complex machine makes a greater contribution to productivity improvement than the operator who suggests a new jig or fixture.

The second method divides the total bonus by total hours worked, which yields a bonus value per hour worked. Each employee then receives a bonus based on the number of hours worked in the period. This method does reward the greater contribution of those who work more hours but does not take into account different levels of contribution.

The third method is equal dollar shares. Every participant in the program receives an equal share of the bonus. This method rewards cooperation but does not reflect different contributions.

The accompanying table shows how the different methods compare for a group of five employees for an average month. Regardless of which method a company uses, complaints will arise, and someone will suggest that another method be used. The most common complaints are with the first option, percentage of pay, because over 90 percent of current gainsharing programs use this method.

Experience shows that there are two situations that aggravate any dissatisfaction with the method that involves paying all employees the same percentage of pay. The first is related to performance. Complaints, when they occur, come mainly from production workers. When they see staff people earning higher salaries and receiving a larger bonus, production workers will complain if they feel that the higher-paid people are not performing—that is, not providing a valuable contribution to the gain. If workers' suggestions are poorly handled or delayed by the accounting department, or if engineers do not respond to requests for service, there

Job	Hours	Pay	Bonus	Percentage of Pay
By Percentage of Pay: 10% Bonus				
Engineer	173	$2,176	$217.60	10.0
Supervisor	173	$2,076	$207.60	10.0
Mechanic	183	$1,880	$188.00	10.0
Operator	178	$1,073	$107.30	10.0
Secretary	173	$1,038	$103.80	10.0
Totals	880	$8,243	$824.30	
By Hours Worked: $0.9367 per Hour Worked				
Engineer	173	$2,176	$162.05	7.4
Supervisor	173	$2,076	$162.05	7.8
Mechanic	183	$1,880	$171.42	9.1
Operator	178	$1,073	$166.73	15.5
Secretary	173	$1,038	$162.05	15.6
Totals	880	$8,243	$824.30	
In Equal Shares				
Engineer	173	$2,176	$164.86	7.6
Supervisor	173	$2,076	$164.86	7.9
Mechanic	183	$1,880	$164.86	8.8
Operator	178	$1,073	$164.86	15.4
Secretary	173	$1,038	$164.86	15.9
Totals	880	$8,243	$824.30	

is validity to their complaints of inequity. However, the problem in this situation is not in the way the bonus is distributed. It is a problem of performance, which will not be corrected by a different distribution method.

The second situation is where the company's job evaluation system does not establish internal equity throughout the organization. If an employee feels that his or her base pay is unfair in relation to that of others, bonuses distributed as a percentage of pay compound the problem. A different distribution method will not solve this problem, either. A company should select the distribution method that is best for its circumstances and resolve any legitimate complaints by correcting their basic cause.

NONCASH BONUSES

Almost all gainsharing programs use cash bonuses as the reward, but there is a lot of room for experimentation on this point. Noncash bonuses, such as premiums, gifts, trips, stock, and so forth, all have potential as a way to pay a bonus. An electronics company in New England used trips to Rome, London, and Disneyland as one-time performance bonuses with excellent results. Many companies use premiums in various performance contests, such as sales and cost-reduction campaigns. There is no gainsharing experience to draw from, but gainsharing programs could easily employ methods other than the cash bonus. In addition to the general interest other approaches might generate, there are some tax advantages to methods that use premium and gift items. There are companies that will manage such programs for a fee and eliminate the administrative headache.

PARTICIPATION IN THE BONUS

There are two aspects to this issue: what pay to include as participating payroll for bonus calculation, and whom to include in the program for the sake of teamwork. Participating payroll is the pay for people who will receive a gainsharing bonus. In some programs, not everyone participates in the bonus, and some pay is excluded from bonus awards. For instance, new employees often do not participate for their first 30 to 90 days. The rationale is that while they are learning their jobs, their work is more of a cost than a contribution to the bonus. Pay for nonparticipating employees must be subtracted from total payroll before calculating individual bonuses. Year-end bonuses paid from the reserve exclude the payroll of employees who have left the company and include the pay of new employees only from the time of their bonus eligibility. Total payroll minus the pay of ineligible employees is one calculation for participating payroll.

A second participating-payroll calculation concerns fringe benefits and nonworked pay benefits. Where there are thrift plans or matching-stock plans, it must be decided whether company contributions will be included or excluded from participating payroll. A decision must also be made about holiday, vacation, and paid sick leave pay. Generally, fringe benefits are not included in participating payroll, even though they may be labor costs in the productivity base.

A common rule for determining this second participating-payroll issue is to use only pay for actual time worked. Many companies follow this rule. However, vacation pay is a common exception. The argument in support of this exception is that to exclude vacation pay from participating payroll penalizes senior employees who are eligible for more vacation. The opposing argument is that the bonus is earned, and therefore paid, for work done and that vacation pay is a reward in its own right and completely separate from productivity. The issue of participating payroll must be deliberated and resolved by each organization according to its needs and preferences.

As for the teamwork issue, there is no standard as to who participates in the bonus portion of the gainsharing program. Improving productivity requires the participation and cooperation of everyone in the organization, but many different options have developed as to who participates in the bonus. Because a major goal in gainsharing is to achieve total, organizationwide cooperation, it is strongly recommended that everyone in the company participate in the program.

In practice, many successful gainsharing programs exist without everyone participating. The most common exclusions are executives and commissioned salespeople (because they are often on different bonus systems, as will be explained later). Some plans exclude all salaried employees. Exclusions of some employees occur in every possible combination. Among the major programs, the following employees are typically included:

- Improshare—hourly employees only.
- Rucker Plans—hourly employees, and sometimes supervisors and professional, technical, and administrative employees.
- Scanlon Plans—all employees, sometimes excluding executives.
- Profit sharing—all employees; sometimes executives have separate programs.

Plans that include only hourly employees tend to be focused on factory and office workers, more in the tradition of incentive plans. Such plans sometimes pay nonparticipating salaried employees a matching bonus from the company share of the gain. Plans that include all employees focus on the total organization as the source of productivity improvement, which is more in line with the ideal in gainsharing. Experience indicates that the most difficult groups to include are senior managers and commissioned salespeople. However, excluding executives and salespeople from the gainsharing bonus risks the feeling by other employees that the executives and salespeople are not part of the team. While there should be no conflict between the goals of the executive bonus plan, sales commissions, and the gainsharing program, there is a risk that situations will arise where people feel a sense of conflict due to the separate bonus programs. These risks are avoided when everyone is in the same program.

Senior managers are often included in a separate incentive bonus based on annual profits. More than 80 percent of the industrial firms and 40 percent of financial firms in the United States have such incentive compensation plans for senior management. In these companies, it is felt that it would be unfair for the senior managers to participate in both bonuses. The choices are to drop the separate management bonus or exclude senior management from the gainsharing bonus. Neither of these alternatives is ideal. Management bonuses are so common today that companies must have them for a competitive executive compensation plan. Also, the use of bonuses that fluctuate with profits holds the executive payroll down in bad years and pays out in good years, which is more cost-effective than a higher fixed level of executive pay.

In companies where both programs are in operation and executives participate in both, only their base pay is included in participating payroll and eligible for a gainsharing bonus. This benefits the rest of the employees by omitting a portion of executive pay from participating payroll and increasing all other shares. This issue tends to be rather complex and requires a careful weighing of the alternatives and an equally careful explanation to everyone of the final decision. Company D experienced some serious problems in this area simply because it did not tell employees of the existence of the executive bonus. Eventually the bonus was discovered in such a way that employees felt that it had been deliberately kept secret from them. No one can measure the harm such events do to an organization. This company dropped the executive bonus, which was the only feasible option at the time.

Commissioned salespeople are more often than not excluded from the gainsharing program. The reason given is that they have a different incentive and it is difficult to determine how much of their pay to include as participating payroll. This is unfortunate, since the sales force is so vital to the success of the gainsharing program. Not only can salespeople contribute cost-reduction ideas from customer feedback but they have the major impact on the output half of the productivity base. It is recommended that salespeople be included fully in the gainsharing program and that a method be developed to accommodate their different compensation in the gainsharing bonus. The participating-payroll issue can be dealt with by:

○ Including all of the commissions as participating payroll.
○ Including a substantial base pay as participating payroll and excluding commissions over the base.
○ Eliminating commissions and paying the sales force a salary that is included in participating payroll.

FREQUENCY OF REWARDS

Most Scanlon Plans and Rucker Plans pay the bonus monthly, but quarterly bonuses are not uncommon; semiannual or annual bonuses are, however, rare. Improshare plans pay the bonus weekly, which is the most frequent of any gainsharing program. Profit-sharing plans usually pay or declare the bonus once a year when the books have been closed and audited. There is some movement among profit-sharing companies to pay bonuses more frequently. Quarterly and semiannual payouts, and even monthly bonuses, are beginning to be used. In deciding on an appropriate frequency of bonus payments, the following points should be considered.

Reward theory says that the closer a reward is to the behavior that produced it, the better. As employees work more productively, the reward has its greatest impact when it is received soon after the productive work. This theory would indicate that weekly is the best and once per year is the worst of the options. Most will agree that once per year or even semiannually is too infrequent for the bonus to have real impact on current work. Company P, a once-per-year profit-sharing firm, reported that employees showed little or no interest in the annual profit share during the first three quarters of the year, but that interest and effort picked up in the fourth quarter as the bonus day approached. Of all the options, monthly bonuses are the most common, including companies that use 13 four-week accounting periods per year.

Scott Myers, in his book *Every Employee a Manager* (see Bibliography), makes the point that the bonus is one aspect of the information feedback process to employees. He argues that frequent feedback is better and recommends monthly bonuses for the profit-sharing plans.

Accounting system capability may influence the frequency decision. The basic widget-making manufacturing company can produce complete accounting figures weekly and monthly. Other organizations may only be able to close the books on a quarterly basis and therefore cannot produce reliable bonus information more frequently. Companies manufacturing large capital equipment that is in process for several months, or construction companies, may have to choose quarterly bonus payments as the only practical answer.

A point to consider in deciding on bonus frequency is the size of the bonus. The following examples are of a company paying a 10 percent bonus to a worker whose hourly wage is $8.50.

$$\begin{array}{lll}
\text{Weekly} & 40 \times \$8.50 \times 10\% = & \$34.00 \text{ bonus} \\
\text{Monthly} & 173 \times \$8.50 \times 10\% = & \$147.05 \text{ bonus} \\
\text{Quarterly} & 520 \times \$8.50 \times 10\% = & \$442.00 \text{ bonus}
\end{array}$$

The weekly $34.00 may be too small to have real impact. The monthly bonus of $147.05 is big enough to have significant impact. The quarterly payout of $442.00 is a large bonus and one that will have a very big impact. Between the monthly and quarterly bonuses, both of which are big enough to have impact, it can be argued that the monthly bonus will have a big impact more often: 12 times per year versus 4 times per year. Are 12 big impacts better than 4 very big impacts? We don't really know which is better. Each organization will find its own answer to the question. Clearly the most common bonus frequency among practicing gainsharing companies is monthly. This frequency has many advantages and few drawbacks and can be recommended as a standard.

An alternative to all of the preceding options is a variable-frequency bonus that would pay out whenever the gain was sufficient to produce a certain-size bonus, for example, 10 percent. Present practice is a fixed-time variable amount. A fixed-amount variable-time bonus is an interesting option to consider. It would probably require some changes in accounting systems, but such changes should not be beyond the reach of modern computers. A daily or weekly accounting would be required, and many firms have produced daily efficiency reports for years. The potential psychological impact of the fixed-amount variable-time bonus prompts some interesting speculation. This payout method would carry the message that the gainsharing program pays off when productivity improves, and not until it improves. This would link the bonus more directly to productivity rather than to the calendar.

RESERVES, AVERAGING, AND CONTINUOUS ACCRUAL

Productivity fluctuates from month to month in all companies, fluctuating in some more than in others. It is typical for productivity to rise above the base for one or several months and sink below the base in following months. If a bonus is paid in one month when productivity is above the base, losses must be recovered when productivity drops below the base in subsequent months. There are three ways to deal with fluctuating productivity.

Reserves. This technique involves withholding an amount from each bonus and creating a reserve account. Rucker Plans refer to this as the balancing account. The amount is accrued from month to month (or other period) as bonuses are earned. In a month where productivity is negative, when actual costs exceed the costs allowed by the productivity base, an amount equal to the excess is taken from the reserve to compensate the company. The size of the reserve, from 10 percent to 30 percent, depends on the size of the anticipated fluctuation. The reserve is accrued for the full year and resolved with year-end audited results. If there are funds in the reserve account at year's end, they are paid out as an additional bonus to eligible employees and the company. The year-end bonus is paid in the same way as are other bonuses: as a percentage of actual pay, by hours worked, or in equal shares. Employees who leave during the year forfeit their portion of the year-end bonus, which is divided among the remaining employees. If the reserve account shows a loss at year's end, it is absorbed by the company, and the reserve begins accruing from zero each year.

Averaging. Improshare plans use averaging to cover fluctuations from week to week. The length of the averaging period depends on the size of the anticipated fluctuation, with most Improshare plans using four to six weeks. A four-week average will be used to demonstrate this method. At the initiation of the plan, no bonuses are paid until the end of the fourth week, at which time a bonus equal to the average gain over the four weeks is paid. This provides a constant reserve equal to three weeks' average gain. Short-term fluctuations reduce but do not eliminate the bonus. If productivity dips to negative for only one week, the bonus is decreased but not eliminated. Continued negative weeks will eliminate bonuses and put the plan in a deficit, which is dealt with by continuous accrual.

Continuous accrual. This method eliminates the need for a reserve or balancing account. Productivity gains and losses are accrued continuously, and bonuses are paid when the account shows a positive balance. Losses, when they occur, must be made up before any further bonuses are paid. This process continues from week to week, month to month, and year to year. There is no year-end reserve payout or losses absorbed by the company. Any adjustments required by audits are made on a current basis.

Deciding which of these methods to use in dealing with inevitable fluctuations requires a careful analysis of past performance. Where fluctuations are not severe, any of the three methods should work quite well. When anticipated fluctuations may be great, consideration must be given to protecting the company's interest and maintaining the employees' motivation. Paying out bonuses during the first half of the year, only to suffer greater losses during the second half, increases the company's cost, which is unfair to the company and unwise for everyone else. Employee motivation tends to sag during no-bonus periods and may disappear completely if large deficits accrue that seem insurmountable. One company using this method absorbed a large deficit that had accrued during a long recession in the automobile industry. This was done to encourage the employees who had worked hard to increase productivity during very difficult times and to provide an incentive for greater effort as the company returned to a healthy state.

The prospect of major fluctuations presents a difficult problem in gain-sharing. Such a problem is best dealt with openly by all who will be affected by the decision. Unpleasant surprises and false expectations are to be avoided. Gainsharing experience has shown that people are able to deal with difficult organizational problems intelligently when the problems are well communicated.

BONUS CEILINGS

Inevitably the question of bonus maximums comes up while a company is first exploring gainsharing. Deferred profit-sharing plans, by law, limit to 15 percent of an employee's pay the amount for which tax can be deferred. Improshare plans have a 30 percent maximum on employee bonuses. Gains that result in an employee share greater than 30 percent are banked and used when future bonuses drop below the 30 percent level. When bonuses exceed this maximum regularly, there is the "buy-back" provision in Improshare that pays employees a substantial one-time bonus in exchange for an adjustment to the base productivity factor.

There are no provisions for a maximum bonus in other plans, and they are generally not recommended. A maximum puts a ceiling on productivity improvement and employee earnings, which benefits no one. However, managers often fear runaway bonuses, which they have experienced or heard about in other incentive plans. From a manager's point of view, ceilings are seen as a way to protect the company from excessive costs. Yet, as long as the productivity base and the sharing formula have been well devised, there should be no runaway bonuses. When employees are earning big bonuses, the company should also be receiving a large amount as its share of the productivity gain. And if productivity is improving, everybody will be winning. If, however, bonuses do become excessive and the company is not receiving an equitable benefit, the basic plan must be changed. While a maximum might be a comforting safeguard, it produces negative employee attitudes. Good formulas for the productivity base and the sharing ratio are recommended over a bonus maximum.

CHANGING THE SHARED REWARD

Should the shared reward ever be changed and, if so, when and how? The answer is yes, whenever it must be changed. How to change it depends on how the reward was originally established and what has happened that requires a change to either the productivity base or the reward ratio or both.

The Base

A problem with changing the productivity base only arises in plans using either history or standards. When the reward is based on plans, it seems well understood that plans change each year, which automatically produces a new, annual productivity base.

But where the productivity base is established with historical data or standards, a problem does occur. The process of analyzing three or four years of actual data or of using sophisticated engineering or cost accounting standards tends to give the productivity base an aura of permanence. The careful weighing of cost records and data, which in some cases is a rather elaborate process, gives the impression that the resulting productivity base will be correct for all time. A moment's reflection, however, is enough to dispel this myth. With the possible exception of nails, there is hardly an industrial or consumer product that has not changed in the past 20 years. And there are fewer still for which the manufacturing process has not undergone extensive change. Changes in output, materials, technology, production processes—all impact productivity. Some of these changes render the productivity base obsolete, which means it is time for a change.

The productivity base should be reviewed every year but changed only when necessary. Setting the productivity base, communicating it, and obtaining everyone's acceptance are difficult tasks. Once this is accomplished, there is a desire to leave well enough alone. But gainsharing is not intended to be a "well enough" program. It is designed to be a program of excellence, and a commitment to excellence is a commitment to growth and change. Changes must be made as new information becomes available, as each year's experience with the gainsharing program accumulates, as new products replace old ones, as new methods and processes are developed, and as markets and the economy change.

The annual review must consider everything that was considered in the original design. If nothing has happened to change the productivity base, the program continues as is for another year. If something has happened that invalidates some aspect of the productivity base, changes must be made. The productivity base may have to be changed when:

○ Major capital investments significantly alter other inputs.
○ New products are introduced with significantly different labor and/or material content.
○ Old products are dropped.
○ A major change occurs in marketing or pricing, causing the input/output ratio to become obsolete.
○ Additional information shows an error in the original base.

The productivity base should not be changed when:

- ○ Productivity improves as a result of employee suggestions or better work habits.
- ○ Wages or other input costs change.
- ○ Normal selling price changes occur. These changes should be anticipated in the input/output factors in the original productivity base.

Capital Investment

The introduction of new machines or other capital equipment is the most common reason for changing the productivity base. The decision to purchase expensive capital equipment is always based on the return to be realized. The expected return can be greater output (new sales) or reduction of inputs, especially labor. When an investment is made in a new, more productive machine, the resulting productivity gain is mainly due to the machine and the capital used to purchase it, not to labor. Most of the return must therefore go to the owners, who made the investment. Because investment in new equipment has such a predictable impact on the productivity base, the original design of most plans includes provisions for dealing with changes resulting from new capital investment. Several techniques have evolved. For example:

Full adjustment. All factors in the base are adjusted to the extent that they are changed by a new machine or other capital investment. Some companies using this approach do not change the productivity base for 6 to 12 months following the installation of the new equipment. During this start-up period, the base stays the same, and all gains in productivity remain in the savings pool for sharing. This allows the employees an opportunity to earn additional bonuses during start-up, which is an incentive to install the machine and get it to full production as quickly as possible. The employees receive extra savings, and the owners have greater assurances that new investments will be quickly and successfully installed.

Partial adjustment. Elements of the productivity base that are changed by the new investment are partially adjusted. If, for instance, a new machine saved 100 hours of labor, the productivity base might be adjusted by 80 hours rather than the full 100. This is another method of sharing productivity gains between owners and employees that recognizes that employee effort and cooperation are needed to make capital equipment productive.

Payback and share. This method provides that the productivity gains resulting from the investment will first be used to pay back the cost of the new equipment and then shared. This means that 100 percent of the new productivity benefit is credited to the company until the investment has been recovered, after which the new productivity gain is shared as are all other gains.

No adjustment. Another approach anticipates new investment in the original sharing formula and needs no further adjustment to accommodate capital investments. Some companies are able to plan accurately for future growth and know in advance how much capital investment will be required to achieve planned growth targets. In these situations, the original sharing of productivity gains between the company and its employees can be set to provide funds for the necessary capital investment. Where this is done, no future adjustments are needed when new equipment is introduced. If, for instance, analysis showed that a 50/50 split of the gain would be an equitable sharing formula, a decision could be made to award a 40 percent share to employees and a 60 percent share to the company to provide funds for new capital investment. With this approach, the company would make a commitment that the extra funds will be applied to new investment and that the gains from new equipment will not cause the productivity base or the sharing formula to be adjusted.

It is reasonable to predict that many companies could maintain this commitment over an extended period of time. Such an approach would probably accommodate 75 percent to 90 percent of the capital investment most companies must make in order to remain competitive. On the other hand, there would still have to be a provision for exceptions. An unanticipated, massive, or radical change in markets, materials, or processes could force a company into a huge capital investment that could not be covered by the no-adjustment sharing formula. Changes from machining metal parts to plastic injected parts, or from vacuum tubes to transistors and integrated circuits, are examples of radical changes that will obsolete the best gainsharing formulas.

These are some approaches to handling capital investments that have grown out of past gainsharing experience. Others may be developed that will work as well or better, but some method must be anticipated and made a part of the original plan. We cannot avoid the process by which technology displaces manual or even knowledge work. In 100 years, 90 percent of the farm labor force was displaced by technology. The same changes are inevitable in the manufacturing and service sectors of the economy. Every business must make provisions to accommodate these unavoidable changes. Gainsharing, because it seeks the best interests of all parties, will help to provide more positive and creative responses to such changes.

Wage Increases

A very common question is "How do annual wage increases affect the gain and the bonus?" In all plans based on costs, pay increases are automatically included in most base productivity measures and are recovered by improved productivity; otherwise the bonus automatically decreases.

In Example 11, nothing changes except for a 10 percent wage increase from year 1 to year 2. (For the sake of example, other factors are assumed to be equal.) The gains, line 9, made in year 1 are almost completely offset by the wage increase, line 8, in year 2. Both the gain and the bonus are reduced. Additional productivity improvements must be made in year 2 to increase the gain and the bonus. It is this feature of gainsharing that produces noninflationary wage increases. This automatic feature does not occur in plans that are based on hours, such as Improshare, as shown in Example 12.

Example 11. Effect of wage changes on productivity gain in a cost-based plan.

	Year 1	Year 2
1. Sales	$ 90,000.00	$ 90,000.00
2. Inventory increase (or decrease)	12,000.00	12,000.00
3. Production	$102,000.00	$102,000.00
4. Less returns and allowances	2,000.00	2,000.00
5. Adjusted production	$100,000.00	$100,000.00
6. Labor ratio	30%	30%
7. Labor allowance	$30,000.00	$30,000.00
8. Less actual labor	27,000.00	29,700.00
9. Gain	$ 3,000.00	$ 300.00
10. Less reserve—10%	300.00	30.00
11. Sharing pool	$ 2,700.00	$ 270.00
12. Company share—25%	$675.00	$67.50
13. Employee share—75%	$2,025.00	$202.50
14. Total payroll	$27,000.00	$29,700.00
15. Less ineligible payroll	500.00	500.00
16. Participating payroll	$26,500.00	$29,200.00
17. Gainsharing bonus	7.6%	.7%

Example 12. Effect of wage changes on productivity gain in an hours-based plan.

	Year 1	Year 2
Production	1,000 units	1,000 units
Direct labor allowed	1,600 hours	1,600 hours
Indirect labor allowed	800	800
Overhead labor allowed	750	750
Total hours allowed	3,150 hours	3,150 hours
Less actual hours	2,850	2,850
Gain in hours	300 hours	300 hours
Employee share—50%	150 hours	150 hours
Average wage	$8.00	$8.80 (10% increase)
Total bonus	$1,200	$1,320

There are two provisions in Improshare plans that offset the bonus growth as wage rates increase. First, the sharing formula does not pay as much of the gain as other plans do. Labor-cost-based plans typically pay 75 percent of the gain in labor productivity as the employee share, whereas Improshare plans pay 50 percent. Second, Improshare plans contain a buy-back provision that provides a large one-time payment to employees and retains all future benefits for the company. These additional company benefits offset the bonus growth due to annual wage increases.

The Sharing Ratio

The sharing formula may have to be changed when:

○ Experience shows a more equitable formula for sharing the productivity gain.
○ Business plans change, requiring a change in sharing to achieve new business objectives.
○ Economic or other external conditions are such that a larger share should go to either the employees or the company.

The guiding principle for sharing is equity. A change must be made when it is necessary to establish or restore equity. The process used for changing should be the same as that used in preparing the original design. Data should be analyzed carefully and judgment used to establish the revised sharing ratio.

Acceptance

The key point in changing either the productivity base or the sharing ratio is that the change must be accepted by the organization, just as were the originals. It is of utmost importance in a gainsharing program that the productivity base be accepted as a realistic measure of productivity and that the sharing ratio be accepted as fair. First, no one is motivated by an unrealistic performance measure. There is ample evidence to support the position that goals, to motivate, should be challenging. There is just as much evidence that people simply reject goals that are unrealistic. Second, employees cannot be expected to warm up to a sharing program when they feel that the sharing is unfair. When the productivity measure and sharing ratio are presented to the organization, everyone will form an opinion as to the realism and fairness of the bonus provisions. Individual opinions will be influenced by:

○ The facts—How real? How fair?
○ How well the facts are understood.
○ The opinions of other employees.
○ Past experience of realism and fairness.
○ The process used to develop the productivity base and sharing formula.

In order to obtain a high degree of acceptance:

○ Be realistic and fair.
○ Keep it simple to avoid misunderstanding, and provide thorough explanations of all aspects of both formulas.
○ Win the support of influential employees early.
○ Anticipate and deal openly with any problems of mistrust growing out of past experiences.

All things considered, the easiest way to insure acceptance of the reward plan is to involve people in its development. When the plan is developed behind closed doors by a few, it must be sold to the many. When the plan is developed by the many, there are fewer left to be sold on its merits. (Chapter 9 will present ways to involve more people in processes such as this.)

EMPLOYMENT SECURITY

There is a growing conviction among motivation watchers that job security may be a more important motivational factor than any bonus. It was employment security that brought the automobile industry and the UAW back to the bargaining table in early 1982. Clearly, in planning the gainsharing program, employment security should be given high priority.

Many people believe that increasing productivity results in workers' losing their jobs. This is reasonable because improving productivity does result in the elimination of work. However, eliminating work does not necessarily mean that people become unemployed. In the past 100 years, we have eliminated 90 percent of farm work, and we now have more people employed than ever before. The workers displaced from the farm are doing different jobs to be sure, but they are working.

In the individual firm, work can be eliminated without eliminating workers. This is true in all but the most extreme cases. In a company with 100 people and a turnover rate of 10 percent, ten jobs can be eliminated each year without any layoffs. Seldom does a company eliminate work at a rate greater than 10 percent per year. More often, as productivity improves, the organization increases its market share and sales, with the result that employment actually grows as improved productivity eliminates some work.

In recession periods where unemployment is high, turnover rates drop dramatically. Sales drop as well, making it virtually impossible to absorb increasing productivity. Nevertheless, it is both necessary and desirable to improve productivity in good times and bad. A company that is not improving productivity cannot provide security for either workers or owners. This lesson has been brought home dramatically by events in the United States auto industry in the late 1970s and early 1980s. One million people lost their jobs, and many companies faced bankruptcy, including the giant Chrysler. For marginally productive companies, economic recessions can be fatal. The more productive organizations suffer as well, but they can survive.

Policies that provide realistic employment security must be established for the gainsharing program to be successful. For the company to realize major gains in productivity, employees must be free from concerns about employment security. The plan must make it possible for an employee to make the ultimate suggestion: the elimination of his or her own job. This requires firm guarantees against loss of employment. Jobs are continually being obsoleted by new products and technology and cannot be unconditionally guaranteed. However, a reasonable policy of guaranteed employment is not only possible but highly practical and mutually beneficial to employees and owners. A reasonable policy is one that guarantees employees that they will not be laid off due to productivity improvements growing out of the gainsharing program. Employment guarantees are generally not possible when major process or product changes are made that eliminate more work than attrition or increased sales can absorb. Nor are guarantees possible during extended recessions, when the organization cannot sell its products or services.

It is interesting to note that while employment guarantees are a big stumbling block when a company is first exploring gainsharing, the opposite is true of companies that have had a successful gainsharing program for several years. As time goes by and experience accumulates, the company begins to realize that a stable, experienced workforce is one of the keys to major productivity improvements. It becomes obvious that employment security benefits both employees and owners. Once a workforce reaches a high level of performance, companies are very reluctant to disturb such a valuable resource. Layoffs, especially where bumping according to seniority is practiced, disrupt every work group in the company. This may have a greater negative impact on productivity than the savings from the workforce reduction.

Experienced gainsharing companies use the layoff as a last resort and only in the worst of circumstances. These companies are developing new and creative approaches to reducing labor costs during business downturns. Vacations, leaves, and voluntary layoffs are encouraged to effect a reduction. Shorter work weeks and wage reductions are used to cut costs. Workers are assigned to training, maintenance, and other special projects that have a long-term positive impact on productivity. Where used, these approaches have been worked out by joint labor/management processes to insure that company and employee interests are properly considered.

Each company must decide this issue on the basis of its own circumstances, just as with every other aspect of the gainsharing program, but it is an issue that must be addressed. An enthusiastic employee response to the gainsharing program is not possible if people feel that the program places them in jeopardy of losing their jobs.

WHAT SIZE BONUS?

A frequently asked question is "How big must the bonus be to be truly motivating to employees?" One answer frequently given is "Ten percent is usually big enough to elicit a favorable reaction." We could leave the question there, but we might miss an important gainsharing point. Though people delight in receiving substantial bonus checks and will put forth effort to insure a big payout, a gainsharing program built on just a bonus is not a strong program. The principal motivator in the gainsharing program must be participation. Meaningful participation is the human use of human beings. The inhuman use of human beings results in demotivation or antiorganizational motivation.

If the gainsharing program results in better management practices, effective employee participation, and improved job security, the size of the bonus is not as important as many believe. More is always better in bonuses, but good gainsharing programs have remained healthy during low-bonus or even extended no-bonus periods. In plans where the bonus has been allowed to occupy a position of too great importance, low- or no-bonus periods are times of crisis. In such plans, when bonuses are down, more energy tends to go to blaming other people or departments for the low bonuses than to finding and correcting problems.

In a mature gainsharing organization, the primary function of the bonus is to identify how well the organization has performed. The major source of satisfaction is the performance. The bonus is only a sign, not the goal. It is recommended that any company designing a gainsharing program put its effort into the program's important features and let the bonus serve its proper role as a measure of improvement, not as the goal of the program. When management practices and employee participation are given the proper attention, productivity and bonuses will increase.

Part II
HOW TO PLAN AND INSTALL A GAINSHARING PROGRAM

As in any important endeavor, systematic and thorough planning is the master key to success. There is no better adage to apply to gainsharing planning than

PLAN THE WORK   *and*   WORK THE PLAN

Because most organizations will consider gainsharing as a way to solve a current or anticipated productivity problem, a basic four-step problem-solving, planning sequence is recommended. The time, cost, and intensity of each step in the sequence will depend on:

The severity of the productivity problem.
The readiness of the organization to change.
The complexity of the plan to be installed.
The size and nature of the organization.

The severity of the productivity problem adds urgency that, without thorough planning, can result in a "haste makes waste" solution. Serious problems deserve serious planning.

Gainsharing usually represents a major organization change requiring an adjustment of long-standing habits and thought patterns. Though difficult, such major changes are possible with careful, thoughtful planning. Plans that involve complex productivity measurements and participation systems require more attention to detail than simpler plans. The planning task is easier where parts of the plan, such as the participation system, are already in place. In larger, more complex organizations, communications about the program will be more difficult. Divisions and plants within larger companies have more steps in their decision and communications processes. Developing and installing a gainsharing program is not a simple task, but a successful outcome can be virtually assured with careful and thorough planning.

Four-Step Planning Procedure

Although every organization must adapt each step to fit its own situation, a successful gainsharing installation will generally follow these four planning steps:

Step 1—Feasibility studies
 One or more studies to learn about gainsharing and to determine if it is an appropriate strategy for the organization.

Step 2—Program design
 The detailed planning and design of five components of the gainsharing program that fit the unique business and human characteristics of the organization.

Step 3—Program start-up
 Presentation of the gainsharing program to the organization for approval and start-up.

Step 4—Program development
 Adherence to a plan of ongoing analysis and evaluation to refine the program as experience accumulates and circumstances change.

The following chapters will describe in detail how each of these steps can be used to plan a successful program.

Although it is difficult to predict the time and cost involved in planning a gainsharing program, the basis for estimating each will be presented in

Figure 13. Sequence and timing of steps in planning a gainsharing program.

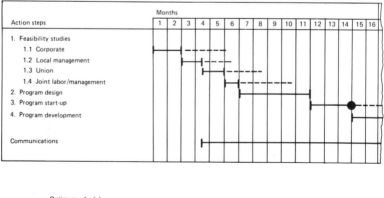

 Optimum schedule
Alternative schedule
Installation

the following chapters. Figure 13 provides an overview of the sequencing and time required to complete each step of the process. The times represented by the solid lines are for an ideal situation; the broken lines show an alternative schedule. In actual cases, the time needed to complete Steps 1 and 2 has been two or three times greater than shown in the figure. Also, as will be discussed in Chapter 8, communication may begin earlier than shown in the figure, depending on the wishes of management.

Chapter 8

Step 1 – Feasibility Studies

Gainsharing is still a relatively new idea, and few organizations possess the knowledge and expertise necessary to plan, design, and install a successful program. Therefore, a careful and thorough planning process is highly recommended.

Planning must begin with the very basic step of determining feasibility. First, the organization must learn about gainsharing in some detail. Second, it must decide if a gainsharing program is appropriate to its current or anticipated productivity problems. Only when gainsharing is understood and a decision made that gainsharing is appropriate can detailed design and planning commence.

There is a possibility in Step 1 for as many as four separate feasibility studies. In a large multidivision or multiplant organization, it may be necessary for each of the following groups to conduct its own feasibility study: (1) corporate management, (2) local management, (3) union, and (4) management and employees jointly. Figure 14 is a flowchart depicting the use of all four feasibility studies.

A smaller, single-plant company would not need study (1) and a company without a union would not need study (3). Each of the four studies has its own unique features and purposes, which will be presented in the following sections.

Corporate Management Feasibility Study

Large multidivision or multiplant companies have a need to maintain consistent strategies, policies, and programs from one division to the next. Gainsharing can be a fairly radical departure from past practice and requires a study of certain corporatewide issues. A program in one division may affect another division. Gainsharing may require a change in some

Figure 14. Flowchart of the relationship among the four feasibility studies.

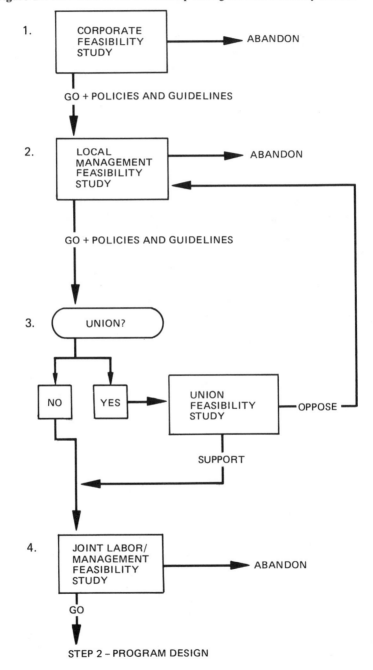

144

corporate policies to insure its success. For best results, gainsharing must be decentralized; each division, plant, or similar operating unit should have its own plan. The purpose of this corporate study is to decide issues of feasibility and consistency. Some corporations establish firm policies and guidelines for gainsharing in their operating units; others give their units complete freedom to plan local programs. As more and more large corporations use gainsharing, the complete spectrum of approaches—from highly controlled and centralized plans to full freedom for local units—will undoubtedly be seen.

A clear corporate position regarding gainsharing is highly recommended, and the corporate feasibility study is conducted mainly for that purpose. As noted, the actual gainsharing programs need to be designed by local units to meet local needs and circumstances. However, to facilitate design work at the local level, a corporate policy statement is very helpful. Without some guidance, local people may spend a good deal of time in unnecessary work and worrying. In the company that gives full freedom, the corporate policy statement can be as simple as "There is no corporate policy on gainsharing; units may do as they wish." In a corporation that prefers to control such programs for the sake of consistency, a lengthy statement of do's and don'ts and other guidelines may be issued. Neither approach is preferred in gainsharing, but whatever the policy is, it must be clearly communicated. Only since the mid-1970s have major corporations shown any real interest in gainsharing, and only a handful have issued policy statements. Appendix B shows two examples of types of gainsharing policy statements that might be issued by corporate management to guide its local units.

WHO CONDUCTS THE STUDY?

The corporate management feasibility study can be conducted by a staff group or a task force. A multidiscipline task force will insure that the perspectives and interests of operating managers as well as key staff departments such as finance and human resources are thoroughly considered. The final result should be a clear statement from the highest level of management for the guidance of the entire organization. One major corporation appointed a task force composed of the presidents and general managers of ten divisions and the heads of corporate finance, engineering, research and development, and human resources. This task force produced a comprehensive set of recommendations that were then adopted by the executive management committee as corporate policy. In this corporation, local units can now move as they wish, knowing at all times what they must do to obtain corporate approval for their plans. In other corporations, units have tried for as long as three years to obtain corporate approval for a gainsharing program. Because so much time and energy can be wasted, a clear yes or no is much preferred to an ambiguous position or a postponed decision.

THE ISSUES TO BE EXAMINED

The issues constituting the agenda for the corporate feasibility study generally include:

- Is the basic concept of gainsharing consistent with the values, policies, strategies, and goals of the corporation?
- Do we have productivity or quality-of-work-life problems for which gainsharing is an appropriate response?
- How will gainsharing fit with other management, employee, and/or labor relations programs and strategies?
- Are accounting and other information systems able to support gainsharing?
- What are the potential benefits of gainsharing to the corporation, to local units, and to employees?
- What are the proper gainsharing units for us?
- What changes in organization structure might be needed to establish proper gainsharing units?
- What changes in our compensation programs might be needed to implement gainsharing?
- What changes in other corporate policies might be needed to take full advantage of gainsharing?
- What risks can be anticipated if some units use gainsharing and others do not? Are those risks acceptable and manageable? Will the risks be offset by potential benefits?
- How much uniformity between units will be necessary to utilize gainsharing effectively in our company?
- What policies, rules, and/or guidelines should the corporation issue to insure the successful use of gainsharing and minimize adverse impacts?
- Do we need a corporate staff to coordinate and administer gainsharing?
- How should gainsharing be introduced in our corporation?

THE STUDY

Whether performed by staff or by task force, this study usually proceeds through a sequence of data collection, analysis, evaluation, deliberation, and conclusions. During the data-gathering step, the members of the task force learn about gainsharing theory and practice by reading, attending seminars, holding conferences with consultants, and visiting other gainsharing companies. Once the members are adequately informed about gainsharing, a list of issues specific to the corporation is drawn up. Organization data are collected, and each issue is deliberated until an appropriate conclusion is reached. The study concludes with formal recommendations prepared and presented to top management for adoption. The presentation to top management may result in the adoption of an official corporate position, or it could produce additional issues to be studied and decided. Once all issues have been decided, the resulting corporate position or policy should be communicated to operating units for their guidance and action.

Corporate feasibility studies have been completed in two months. Others have gone on for two years. The time required to complete the study will depend, for the most part, on the issues involved. A few simple issues can be decided quickly. A longer list of more complex issues will require more thorough study, more careful deliberation, and more coordination to determine an appropriate policy. A central staff group can generally complete this study in less time than a task force composed of subsidiary unit representatives, who are more difficult to assemble for meetings. The budget for this study will include the time of the managers who work on it and additional costs for seminars, travel for visits to gainsharing companies, and consultation.

RESULTS OF THE STUDY

The task force will conclude that gainsharing is or is not feasible for the corporation. When the conclusion is in favor of gainsharing, some corporate studies will issue the simple recommendation to endorse gainsharing and allow total autonomy to divisions and plants. Others may recommend any or all of the following elements:

- ○ A strong exhortation or a mild recommendation to use gainsharing.
- ○ Firm corporate policies.
- ○ Guidelines that are recommended but not binding..
- ○ Addition of corporate gainsharing staff for consultation, coordination, or control.
- ○ Introduction of gainsharing with pilot programs prior to general use.
- ○ Study of additional issues prior to general use.

When the results of the study indicate that gainsharing is not feasible, the study report should include the basis for the conclusions.

Further Use of the Study Task Force

Once a gainsharing position or policy has been decided, the work of the study team is complete, and the team may be dissolved. On the other hand, the study team has grown to be a resource on the subject of gainsharing and can therefore be of further service to the corporation. The team, or certain members of it, could fulfill any of the following roles:

○ Internal gainsharing consultants.
○ A panel to review and/or approve local unit plans.
○ A committee to audit the overall corporate experience with gainsharing and recommend further refinements in policy as experience accumulates.

Local Management Feasibility Study

If a gainsharing program is to be installed, it will be done at the plant or other operational unit level by local management and employees, whether they are part of a large corporation or an independent company. Before any serious planning occurs, local management will want to conduct its own feasibility study. It is not practical to suggest a joint employee/management study as the first step in the process. Experience has shown that management simply is not comfortable conducting a joint feasibility study until it determines that a gainsharing program is safe and advantageous to the organization. Managers say they see no point in raising, and risking having to disappoint, employee expectations. Managers are also concerned that once some momentum develops, it may be difficult to stop the process should their feasibility study show that the organization is not ready for gainsharing. Managers feel that both of these risks can be avoided entirely by conducting a low-key, management-only study until they are satisfied that a gainsharing program would be feasible and beneficial to the company. Management should not be criticized for quietly studying gainsharing in depth but rather should be encouraged to do so. Management is responsible for everything that happens in an organization, and gainsharing will have a major impact on what happens.

The only danger in the management-only study is that the inquiry may go further than necessary. A study can delve into too much detail and preempt a necessary joint employee/management feasibility study. How far is "too far" will differ somewhat from organization to organization. The rule is for this study to go no further than is required to satisfy management's legitimate concerns. The local management feasibility study should generally proceed along the following lines.

WHO CONDUCTS THE STUDY?

This study is usually conducted by the top management team or committee. However, it may be assigned to a staff such as human resources, finance, or industrial engineering or to a task force with members from operations and the key staff departments. A task force representing several major departments is recommended, since it provides greater perspective to the study. If a task force or staff is assigned to conduct the study, it will return to top management with recommendations. The final decision to proceed or stop must be made or approved by the chief executive officer (CEO), the general manager, and/or the top management team.

The study and assignment should be initiated by the CEO or general manager, who should outline the scope, mission, purpose, and other details of the study. The assignment, written or oral, from top management should include the following points:

- The clearest possible definition of the organization's current or anticipated productivity and quality-of-work-life problems.
- Reasons for exploring gainsharing as a possible strategy for dealing with productivity and quality-of-work-life problems.
- Personnel assigned to the task force and reasons for each assignment.
- What specifically the task force is expected to accomplish.
- When the study should be completed.
- A budget.
- Any restrictions or limitations on the work of the task force, such as involvement of others and communications about the progress of the study.

THE ISSUES TO BE EXAMINED

The questions on the agenda for this study may include some or all of the following:

- What is gainsharing, and what has been the experience of organizations similar to ours?
- Is gainsharing consistent with our organization's values, policies, goals, and strategic plans?
- Do we have sufficient corporate support and direction to proceed? (For units of larger corporations.)
- Will gainsharing address the current or anticipated productivity and quality-of-work-life issues of our organization?
- What will it cost to develop and implement a gainsharing program, including management time, consultation, training, education, communications, and additional staff?
- Will the potential benefits from gainsharing be sufficient to offset the costs and effort to develop and implement a plan?

THE STUDY

As with the corporate study or any staff study, this local management study follows the process of data collection, analysis, evaluation, deliberation, and conclusions. The important point to remember is that this is only *one* feasibility study and, more important, this is *not* the design study. The final feasibility study should be accomplished by a task force with representatives from other employee groups, which will be discussed as study No. 4. There are no limitations about the depth to which this study should go. However, it should go no deeper than is necessary to determine that there is or is not sufficient potential in the idea to warrant further study.

To accomplish its study, the task force may need to examine some of the following types of information about gainsharing and its own organization:

- ○ Theory and practice of gainsharing in the literature and the experience of practicing companies.
- ○ The nature of the organization's productivity and quality-of-work-life problems and opportunities, to determine if gainsharing is appropriate.
- ○ The history and present status of the organization's climate, to determine if gainsharing is possible and to what extent employee participation can or should be increased.
- ○ The current status of compensation programs, labor/management relationships, and other human-resource policies that might influence the success of a gainsharing program.

This study can be completed in one to three months and will require a budget for seminars, travel, visits to gainsharing companies, and consultation.

RESULTS OF THE STUDY

This study should result in one of three possible recommendations:

1. Gainsharing is not feasible for the organization, and other methods should be considered to deal with productivity and quality-of-work-life problems. This recommendation will also explain why gainsharing is not feasible and why other approaches may be more appropriate.
2. Gainsharing is feasible but not now. This recommendation will also explain when or under what conditions the organization should reconsider gainsharing.
3. Gainsharing is feasible from management's standpoint and should

be pursued. This recommendation will include suggestions on how to proceed, such as:

○ An invitation to the union to conduct its own feasibility study and join in a joint study.
○ The appointment or election of a joint employee/management or union/management task force to conduct a thorough and final feasibility study, including the timing and budget for the study.
○ Any policies or guidelines that management feels must be adhered to as the study proceeds.
○ Communications to the organization.

These recommendations conclude the specific assignments of the task force, and the group may be dismissed. As a practical matter, members of this group are often assigned roles in additional feasibility studies and in the design, implementation, and ongoing administration of the gainsharing program. The members of this task group are a valuable resource and should be used in any appropriate continuing role.

Union Feasibility Study

Where there is a labor union and management has decided to pursue a gainsharing program, there is a need for the union to conduct its own feasibility study. This study may be performed by the local, regional, or international union, depending on the union's internal structure. It may also be conducted jointly by two or more unions that have contracts with the company.

The experience has been that unions do not conduct as thorough a feasibility study as previously described for local management. Local unions tend to examine fragments of information and take a position for, cautiously for, or against management's proposal. The prospect of developing a successful joint labor/management program would be greatly enhanced if the union were to conduct its own feasibility study similar to the management study previously described. The union would explore similar data and work through a similar agenda but with a different perspective. The union would focus its attention on how gainsharing would benefit the employees as individuals and the union as an organization. This additional perspective should enhance the joint study that must eventually occur.

The following is an outline of the principal elements to be included in a union feasibility study.

WHO CONDUCTS THE STUDY?

The feasibility study could be assigned to an existing board or committee or to a specially constituted task force. Local union officers could be joined by others from regional or international offices as needed, or as required by the union constitution or general practice. Many unions have expert resource personnel, among them research directors and their staffs and incentive specialists, who can assist in a study of this type. Consultants could also be useful to the study team.

THE ISSUES TO BE EXAMINED

From the union's standpoint, some of the primary questions to be addressed in a gainsharing feasibility study would include:

- ○ What is gainsharing, and what experience have other unions had with gainsharing programs?
- ○ Is gainsharing consistent with the union's values, policies, goals, and strategic plans?
- ○ What are the benefits to the union and its members from a gainsharing program?
- ○ What risks are there to the union or its members in a gainsharing program?
- ○ What will be the impact of gainsharing upon labor/management relations, in general, and the collective bargaining agreement, in particular? Are these impacts acceptable or unacceptable?
- ○ What is the union's position concerning any specific features of management's present proposal?
- ○ How does the union wish to be involved in the planning, implementation, and development of the gainsharing program?

The systematic analysis of an agenda such as this would enable the union to approach any joint planning effort as an informed party able to contribute to the joint effort. The lack of such a study places the union in the position of always having to react to management initiatives, often without adequate information or a well-developed position. Joint labor/management projects, which have not been spectacular to date, will continue to limp as long as management continues to initiate and the union only reacts. The way out of the reactive mode is for unions to do their homework. When a union is present, the most successful gainsharing programs are those in which the union is a knowledgeable and strong partner.

THE STUDY

The union feasibility study should proceed along the same lines as the previously described studies: data collection, analysis, evaluation, deliberation, and conclusions. This study can be completed in one to three months. A low-budget study can be done in the local office by mail and phone. If funds are available, they can be used for seminars, visits, and consultants.

RESULTS OF THE STUDY

The results of the union feasibility study are a decision to support, remain neutral toward, or oppose the management proposal, depending on whether gainsharing is seen as beneficial for, having no effect on, or harmful to the union and its members. This decision, when made, is usually communicated to the membership.

Joint Study by Local Management and Employees

This joint employee/management feasibility study is the most important of the four studies. If the three previous studies have recommended gainsharing, corporate management, local management, and the union will have stated that gainsharing is feasible for the organization. However, these groups have only a partial influence on the program's success. The total organization will ultimately determine if gainsharing will succeed. Thus, the total organization must pass the final judgment on its feasibility.

The purpose of the joint employee/management study is to determine finally whether or not to proceed with a gainsharing program. Some organizations will skip this phase of Step 1 and go right to Step 2, program design. They do this with the assumption that feasibility has already been sufficiently determined and it is O.K. to move on. This approach may or may not lead to trouble later on.

The organization may indeed accept this determination of feasibility and be willing to plunge into Step 2. On the other hand, this decision denies the bulk of the people in the organization an opportunity to consider the issue of feasibility and influence the course of the program. A few may resent this slight and resist the program as a way to get even. We can only guess about the potential harm this might do. The major known harm in omitting this study is that of a lost opportunity, because the study allows the entire organization to have ownership of the program from the very beginning. To create this ownership early is a definite advantage. Therefore, as an opportunity, this study should not be passed over.

WHO CONDUCTS THE STUDY?

To conduct a joint employee/management study, representatives from both management and nonmanagement employees are needed, as well as union officers or members where there is a union.

A typical task force for the Acme Widget Company or the Spokane Division of United Gismo, Inc. would include:

○ Three or four senior or middle management representatives from operations, finance, human resources, and engineering.
○ A union official in unionized companies.
○ A nonmanagement professional employee from engineering, accounting, sales, or some other department.
○ A first-line supervisor from operations.
○ A clerical or administrative employee (white collar).
○ Three or four operations and support employees (blue collar—union members in union companies).

Appointments to this task force are critical. In addition to having broad representation, the task force must be composed of people who are experienced, well known throughout the organization, and respected. If the right people conduct the study, their conclusions will have credibility with the organization and smooth the way for all subsequent steps in the planning process. If the task force members lack credibility, the results of their study may be rejected by the organization or at least burdened with a skepticism that will be difficult to overcome.

Management task-force members are usually appointed by top management to represent operations and the key staff departments. Managers who participated in prior feasibility studies are often appointed, since they are already knowledgeable and are therefore good resources. Such managers need to be careful not to dominate new members.

Where there is a union, the union generally appoints the hourly representatives. The top local union official is usually an ex officio member of this task force. For the other positions, unions generally appoint stewards, committee chairpeople, or other union officials. The company should not attempt to influence the union's appointments. No matter how well meant, the attempt will cause the union to be suspicious of management's intentions. On the other hand, it is entirely proper for management to make it clear to the union that the project is very important, that the task force must have a high level of credibility to be successful, and that strong, capable, respected people are needed to give the task force that credibility.

If the union conducted its own feasibility study, as recommended above, it would be desirable for it to appoint the experienced personnel from the previous study to this task force. The union may also ask to have an international representative participate in the study. This is especially true in unions that have staff experts for such matters. Such requests are usually approved to insure the union's cooperation in the joint effort.

In organizations without a union, the selection of hourly representatives is an entirely different matter. Nonmanagement employees, particularly hourly employees, are not accustomed to participating in joint studies of such importance. The task force must be small to be able to work efficiently, which means that four to six people will have to represent a large number of hourly employees. A careful selection process is needed to insure that the majority of the workforce feel properly represented as the study proceeds.

There are two acceptable approaches to the selection and assignment of hourly and other nonmanagement employees to the task force: appointment by management or election by their peers. Management appointment carries the risk that management will choose "safe" people who may lack credibility with the rest of the organization. However, like all risks, this one is manageable, and when appointments are the best alternative, they can be successful as long as management exercises discretion and sensitivity.

A much-preferred approach is to have the hourly and other nonmanagement members of the task force elected by their peers. An election insures that the task-force members are representatives in fact, not just in title. This participative process is also in keeping with the spirit of gainsharing—an example of things to come.

If the organization eventually adopts a gainsharing program, there will be other occasions to elect employee representatives, such as elections to other task forces and suggestion committees. This first assignment is therefore a good time to establish an effective elective process. The following process is recommended for use both in the initial election and in all subsequent ones.

Employee Elections
Determine constituencies. There should be four to six nonmanagement representatives on the task force, each elected at large or elected to represent specific employee groups. Specific representation is preferred to give balance to the task force. At Acme Widget, this would result in one

employee representing the office force; one or two from assembly; and one or two representing manufacturing support departments such as maintenance, tool room, quality control, and warehouse. The number of representatives should be based on the size of the group and be as proportional as possible. In at-large elections, smaller departments are often outvoted by large groups, such as manufacturing and assembly, and are not represented.

This process need not be limited to hourly or nonexempt employees. An organization with a number of professional nonmanagement personnel, such as engineers or scientists, may also use the elective process to select a task-force member to represent professional employees.

Nominations. Nominations can be solicited informally by allowing anyone to submit any employee's name in nomination. Prior to soliciting nominations, an educational program should be conducted to explain what the job of the task force is and what will be expected of the employee representatives. This is best done in group meetings, but a letter may be sufficient. The objective is to nominate those who can do the job best. The best representatives will be those who, by education or experience, will be able to understand and participate meaningfully in the work of the task force. Ideally, the representatives will be people who are well known and able to communicate easily with their constituents as the study progresses.

Elections. Ballots should be prepared and a date and time set for the election that is convenient for all employees. This will be the first opportunity for participation by the organization, and every effort should be made to have a large voter turnout. Additional short educational meetings may be conducted before the voting begins to emphasize the importance of the program and the election of competent representatives. Because management will be conducting the elections and educational program, there is a risk that its efforts may be seen as an attempt to unduly influence the election outcome. Regardless of the possibility of criticism from cynics, management should provide leadership at this point and exert proper influence on the outcome. The outcome it should try to influence is to have the best possible representatives of the employees elected.

50 per cent + 1 majority. To insure that the candidates elected have the backing of a substantial number of employees, it is suggested that a rule be established that the successful candidate must receive votes equal to 50 per cent + 1 of the *eligible* voters. This may result in runoff elections, but it prevents a person's being chosen as a representative by a very small minority of the people. Effective employee representation in participative programs is too important not to take steps to insure that most employees vote and that there is a clearly preferred candidate.

If the organization has difficulty getting people to vote, there is a need for more education. If management believes that gainsharing is important, it is its job to convince everyone that it is important. There is no point in even starting this feasibility study if no one really cares. The same is true for other elections. At Company W, the employees did not take these representative roles seriously and made poor choices of representatives. It became a practice to "stick" new employees with representative positions, which resulted in a very weak representative corps and a mediocre gainsharing program. This practice continued for several years, apparently without management's realizing it. A simple structure, such as the one outlined above, is enough to insure satisfactory results. Attention to details at the outset will pay substantial dividends in the long run.

THE ISSUES TO BE EXAMINED
The issues for the joint employee/management study are similar to those examined in the earlier feasibility studies. The differences are that the issues are deliberated jointly and in greater detail than previously. For instance, if the previous studies determined that there were some employee/management conflicts that might inhibit the planning for a gainsharing program, this study might explore the conflicts and their causes to determine just how they might influence such planning. The agenda for the study might include:

- What is gainsharing, and what has been the experience of other companies?
- Is gainsharing consistent with the values, goals, and policies of the organization?
- What are the benefits and risks of a gainsharing program?
- Should we proceed? If so, how?
- What features and options are desirable or undesirable for our situation?
- What safeguards, limitations, or restrictions must be followed in the design of the gainsharing program?
- How will gainsharing be introduced to the organization?
- When should a program be started?
- What resources will be needed to design and install the program, such as personnel and budgets?
- How will employees and/or the union be involved in designing the program?
- What must be done or changed prior to the design and installation of a program? (Compensation, union/management relations, or other.)

THE STUDY

The joint employee/management feasibility study proceeds along the same lines as those previously described: data collection, analysis, evaluation, deliberation, and conclusions.

One approach to this study is for the task force to meet, share the data already available, conclude that gainsharing is feasible, and recommend that the organization go directly to Step 2, program design. On the other hand, the task force may decide to study feasibility in more depth than previous studies. If it does, it will want to approach the task systematically and thoroughly. This may call for a comprehensive organizational audit of marketing, financial, operational, and climate data. A diagnostic study will have to be conducted sometime in either Step 1 or Step 2. In-depth information about the organization will be needed before a proper program can be designed. The task force may decide that some or all of the information is needed to properly complete the feasibility study agenda. The options to consider are:

1. A full organization audit now. The information is collected, analyzed, and used to determine feasibility questions and is then turned over to the design team for its use.
2. A partial audit now, looking in-depth at selected information and leaving the rest to be completed by the design team in Step 2.
3. No study now, since sufficient information is available to determine feasibility; leave entire audit to be completed by the design team.

A detailed description of the organization audit will be found in Chapter 9. The feasibility task force should review the audit information and decide if any or all of the audit should be completed to properly deal with its agenda.

This feasibility study can be completed in one to three months. A few meetings to share data and decide to move on to Step 2 can be done with little cost and not much time. A study involving extensive data collection, visits, seminars, and consultation will require a substantial budget.

RESULTS OF THE STUDY

The conclusion reached by this joint task force will be either to abandon planning for a gainsharing program, to postpone planning for a gainsharing program, or to proceed with planning for a gainsharing program. A decision to proceed should include recommendations about the program and the remaining planning steps. For example:

○ Suggestions about the three major plan elements: management practices, employee participation, and shared reward.

- General or specific gainsharing policies and guidelines.
- A target installation date.
- How to establish the design team.
- Budget and other administrative details for the design process.
- Communications.

Communications

Communications is a very important ingredient of each of the four steps in the planning process. However, this step has one special communications problem that requires careful treatment. Step 1 begins with the decision not to tell people that any or all of the first three feasibility studies are under way. The reason for withholding information at first is to avoid raising expectations until organization leaders, both management and union, are satisfied that a gainsharing program would be appropriate and beneficial. The probability that the studies will remain a secret is very low. The information will get out to people in the organization. No harm comes from leaks at this point because the low-profile study and the leak both send a message to people that it is too early to get hopes up.

If, as a result of the first three feasibility studies, it is decided to conduct a joint employee/management study, the communications problem occurs in full force. For feasibility study No. 4, a task force is appointed or elected to conduct the study on behalf of the entire organization. Whether task-force members are elected or appointed, other employees must know that a study is under way and that everyone is represented in the process. Although few will take advantage of it, the opportunity to influence the process through their representatives should be available to all employees.

Doesn't this then raise expectations and create the very problem the organization has tried to avoid? It could happen. However, the chances are low. First of all, if the study has progressed through three feasibility studies, or even only one, the odds are quite high that the joint study will also recommend proceeding. Second, if the task force maintains contact with the organization, shares information, and listens to suggestions, everyone should come to the same conclusion at about the same time. And if the study arrives at a decision to abandon the gainsharing effort, there should be a consensus, and therefore no serious expectations will be disappointed. Disappointed expectations occur only when someone promises to do something and doesn't. So if there are no promises, and if people decide themselves not to have a program, no disappointment should occur.

Communications should include general or department meetings to present information, answer questions, and provide a forum for suggestions. Letters and other written communications are also useful. This is a good time to start a special gainsharing bulletin board for posting meeting minutes and making various announcements.

During these early stages, individual task-force members go through periods of uncertainty as they learn about gainsharing and the many options that must be decided. Nonmanagement members, in particular, not having participated with management in a project as important as this before, tend to be unsure about what to communicate to whom. These problems can easily be managed in the task force, first, by giving priority to the need of the organization to be informed. Second, each task-force meeting should include time at the end of the meeting to decide what to communicate and how best to do it.

When the joint feasibility task force has completed its study, and the organization has accepted its recommendations, the process moves to Step 2, program design.

Chapter 9

Step 2 – Program Design

Designing the program is the second step in the planning sequence and the most important event in the life of the gainsharing program. Although gainsharing is still a relatively new idea, it is a strategy that will work in organizations—provided that it is designed to work, which means that the program must be carefully planned to fit the individual organization's characteristics. It must be designed to fit the nature of the business; the skill and experience of management and the workforce; the size and structure of the organization; and the needs of owners, employees, and customers. No two organizations are identical or have identical needs, and therefore no two gainsharing programs will be identical.

This does not mean that every minor detail will be unique in every program. Experience already exists from past gainsharing programs, from other organization and management development programs, from past incentive programs and efforts in the field of employee participation. Wheels that already exist need not be reinvented. They can be used but must be adapted to fit each organization. Although invention is not necessary for every detail, adaptation certainly is, and this is the challenge for the design team.

The complete design, to be planned in this second step, has five principal parts:

1. The base productivity measurement.
2. The formula for sharing the gain between employees and the company.
3. The employee-participation system.
4. A detailed plan for installing the gainsharing program.
5. A development plan for evaluating and upgrading the gainsharing program.

The details pertaining to each part of the design are presented in other chapters of this book and in other references listed in the Bibliography. This chapter deals with the planning process itself, rather than the content of the design. The following pages suggest ways to approach the design task for best results, including procedural steps, a design checklist, and some exercises to facilitate discussion and planning in the design team.

The Design Process

The program is best designed by a representative team appointed and/or elected to the task. This design team must organize itself, become knowledgeable about gainsharing, collect and analyze data about the organization, and design the five components of the gainsharing program. And while they do all this, team members must stay in close contact with the employees they represent so that their finished product belongs to the entire organization. Let's examine all these components of the design process a bit more closely.

THE DESIGN TEAM—SELECTION AND ASSIGNMENT

When a gainsharing plan is designed by management alone, the final design must be "sold" to the organization. When the whole organization, through representatives, designs the program, there is no one left to be "sold." If a representative group was assigned to conduct the joint management/employee feasibility study, it may be used to design the program, or a new group may be assigned.

Some points to consider in setting up the proper design team for this assignment are:

○ The team must be large enough to represent the total organization.

○ The group must be small enough to be able to work efficiently.

○ Some or all of the following groups should be represented on the design team:

Top management	Other key staff departments, depending on
Operations management	the nature of the organization
Finance staff	Professional and technical employees
Human-resource staff	Office, administrative, and
First-line supervision	clerical employees
Labor union officials	Production or operations employees

○ The design team should have access to and should use expert resources from within the organization to help with the design. For instance, accounting and engineering departments are expert in productivity measurements and should be called on to help design the productivity base; human-resource departments are expert in employee-involvement techniques and should be used to help design that part of the program.

The human-resource department may include a training unit, which should be called upon to help plan and conduct training and educational programs. Outside consultants can also be used to supply expertise for general planning or detailed design of specific aspects of the program.

○ Subcommittees can be used to involve many people actively in the design task without any one work group becoming excessively large. A design team of about 8 people could coordinate the overall project, with as many as 30 or more people involved in specific design assignments for the productivity base, the sharing formula, the participation system, and the installation and development plans.

○ Design-team members must maintain good communications throughout this design process with those they represent. If the members closet themselves while they design the plan, obtaining organizational support for the plan will be unnecessarily complicated. First, the organization will be asked to approve the whole master plan at one time. A gainsharing program can be fairly complicated, and is easier to grasp if presented a piece or two at a time. Second, the design team will understandably look at many options in its deliberations. It will help people to understand and accept the final design if they know that the task force has thoroughly explored other options. Third, one of the purposes of the representative team is to allow everyone in the organization to participate, even indirectly, in the design process. Open communication between the team and the rest of the organization is essential to this purpose.

○ If the joint task force assigned in Step 1 is used as the design team, it can begin the design work as soon as approvals are given to its feasibility-study recommendations. If a new group will be formed, a selection process similar to that described in Chapter 8 should be followed. It is common that some or all of the people who served on the feasibility task force will serve on this design team. However, design work is different from a feasibility study, and it is just as common to have new members added for this step.

ORIENTATION

If all or some of the members of the design team are new, they will need a period of orientation in which to study all of the gainsharing and organization information generated by the feasibility studies. In addition, they need to know that:

○ There is a basic commitment by key leaders, both management and labor, that gainsharing can be beneficial to the organization and to the employees.

○ There is agreement among all key decision makers regarding broad guidelines and program objectives. In other words, those who must approve the design have defined the basic conditions that will be necessary to obtain their approval.

This orientation can usually be completed in one to two weeks and involves readings and one to three days of briefings and meetings.

WORK PLAN

Once the task and all of its dimensions are clearly understood, the design team develops a work plan, which includes elements such as a schedule of activities, meeting times and place, use of internal and external personnel as resources, communications to and from the organization, the decision-making process (vote or consensus), and other rules of order.

GAINSHARING INFORMATION

Depending on how much information about gainsharing was obtained during Step 1, the design team may want more details about successful gainsharing programs. This is accomplished through readings, seminars, visits to gainsharing companies, and consultants. In Step 1, the need was to learn about the concept of gainsharing and what it would do to help the organization. In Step 2, the need is to learn more about how to do it. If the "how-to" information is missing, the design team will have to obtain it.

ORGANIZATION INFORMATION

The studies in Step 1 involved collecting and analyzing some information about the organization to determine if gainsharing was feasible. The design team must have even more information about the organization to select the proper optional features for the gainsharing program. If a thorough diagnosis of financial, marketing, operational, and climate data was conducted to determine feasibility, the same information can be used for design. If the diagnosis was omitted, or is lacking in any way, it must be completed to insure that the program will be designed to fit the unique characteristics, needs, and opportunities of the organization. A thorough diagnosis will result in several sets of data to be used in design and implementation:

- Some of the data will be used to select and design the most applicable gainsharing features for the organization.
- Some of the data will point to the need for action or changes prior to installing a program.
- Some of the data will point to areas where productivity improvements can be made or should be explored. This information will be

communicated to the organization as the plan is installed and operated, to stimulate problem solving, suggestions, and action.

If the organization's major productivity problem is one of quality rather than efficiency, the gainsharing program should be designed to emphasize quality improvement. If the organization has had no experience with employee participation and a history of authoritarian management practices, it may be folly to design a third-degree work-team participation system. An assessment of management practices will provide data to determine management-training needs and to design an appropriate employee-participation system.

There are many techniques available in the area of organization analysis. Some may already be in use by the organization, and information from them need be made available only to the design team. Organizations without internal diagnostic expertise can obtain help from consultants who specialize in organization analysis and from the firm's auditors. The organization diagnosis will cover some or all of the following areas.

Financial

Are there financial problems that can be solved by increased productivity? Are there financial problems that must be solved before gainsharing can be considered?

Generally, the need is to look beyond traditional balance sheet and profit and loss statements to determine the causes for productivity or the lack of it. Whereas traditional accounting looks at wage rates and total wage costs, this analysis will examine trends in unit labor cost. This study should also look at financial information compared to industry trends. Trend analysis examines future impacts of current and past financial decisions. Specifically, it examines:

Profit	Historical trends and industry comparisons of return on investment and percentage to sales.
Volume	Real growth rates (adjusted for inflation). Sales per employee and sales to labor-cost trends.
Investment	Industry comparisons of total and per-employee investment and trends.
Systems	Are current accounting systems able to provide timely and necessary information? The gainsharing program thrives on such information.

In Appendix D of their book *The Scanlon Way to Improved Productivity,* Moore and Ross present several excellent checklists to use in this financial analysis.

Marketing

Does the organization need to increase its market share for adequate employee and owner security? Are improvements needed in quality, cost, and/or delivery to win greater customer satisfaction? Can market share be increased as productivity increases?

This information will first be used in design and then shared within the organization so that more people know what the potential or limitations are for increasing the output part of the productivity calculation. This analysis will indicate the strength or weakness of the company's present market position and the extent to which improved productivity is necessary to strengthen or secure its position. This diagnosis explores:

Market share	Current status, trends, and opportunity to increase share.
Competition	Which firms, their strengths, weaknesses, and prospects for the future based on trends.
Products	Status of current products and prospects for new ones.
Price	Trends and controlling factors.

Operations

Are operations causing problems in quality, cost, and/or delivery toward which the program should be aimed?

This analysis examines the health of operations and provides information of great value to the design team. It shows how much room there is to improve productivity and some of the specific areas where it can be improved. This analysis also shows how extensive the employee-participation system should be and provides data for a cost/benefit analysis of alternative participation systems. A third-degree system with weekly work-team meetings is costly to set up and maintain. The analysis of the type and extent of operations problems will indicate how much program costs can be justified by the potential gain in productivity. This diagnosis should explore:

Manufacturing	Age, condition, and adequacy of facilities and equipment.
	Efficiency.
	Maintenance costs and down time.
	Quality assurance costs and results.
	Scrap and rework costs.
Standards	Accuracy and employee acceptance.
Staff and technical support	Adequacy, costs, competence.
Systems and procedures	Adequacy, costs, reliability.
Safety	Status and trends.

| Labor/management relations | History, trends, current and past use of incentives. |
| Compensation and benefits | Costs, competitiveness, and employee satisfaction. |

Management Style and Climate

Does the management style argue for or against certain approaches to employee participation? Are there issues of employee dissatisfaction, communications, trust, labor/management, or other conflicts that must be addressed in the gainsharing program or solved before the program can commence?

Climate and management style are less tangible elements of an organization than the accounting systems or operations, but they are powerful determinants of an organization's ability to meet its objectives. The task force should conduct a climate analysis as part of the organization study prior to installing a plan, because:

- It will provide a benchmark from which to measure change. A successful gainsharing program will improve the organizational climate.
- It can be extremely useful in pinpointing problem areas that must be addressed prior to or as part of the gainsharing program.
- It begins or advances the process of two-way communications with employees.

There are many different approaches to assessment of organizational climate and management style, but they are usually combinations of employee surveys and interviews. Surveys vary in depth, detail, and usefulness in pinpointing problem areas. One of the best climate surveys available for this analysis is the Survey of Organizations described in Chapter 5. Another survey, developed by Moore and Ross specifically for Scanlon Plan installations, can be found in their book. (See Bibliography.) Among the exercises at the end of this chapter there is a brief example of a climate survey, which may serve to acquaint the design team with the concept. (For a more comprehensive description of the use of surveys and other data in organization assessment, see Nadler in Bibliography.)

Generally speaking, more is better in this diagnosis of an organization, since all the data developed represent useful management information, which, if not needed to design the plan, can be put to other uses, such as employee communications and management planning. There is a definite need for a single comprehensive diagnostic package that would include organizational, financial, marketing, and operational data. An ideal package would correlate and facilitate the analysis of data that are now being examined separately with no attempt at correlation. Such an all-inclusive diagnosis would be very useful, not only for gainsharing design, but also for strategic management planning. Although the ideal package does not yet exist, an effort is under way at the Oregon Productivity Institute in Corvallis, Oregon, to develop a more comprehensive diagnostic instrument. Its development is being made quite feasible by advances in the areas of data collection, quantitative methods, and the ability of computers to process many complex variables.

Diagnosing the organization can be a major undertaking. When the diagnosis is completed, it should be summarized in a way that relates the information to the task of designing the gainsharing program. In Figure 15, for example, such a diagnosis is summarized in the form of a force-field diagram. All the known positive forces pushing for improvements are identified, as well as the negative forces pushing to prevent them. (The strength of each force is shown by the length of the arrows.) The design team then uses this information to develop a program that will strengthen the positive forces and weaken the negative ones.

DESIGN

Armed with the necessary information about gainsharing and the organization, the team begins to design the five parts of the gainsharing program:

1. Productivity base (see Chapter 7 for details).
2. Sharing ratio (see Chapter 7 for details).
3. Employee-participation system (see Chapter 6 for details).
4. Installation plan (see Chapter 10 for details).
5. Development plan (see Chapter 11 for details).

The team may do all the design work for each of the five parts, or it may delegate the work. There are two reasons why the design team might delegate rather than personally perform these tasks. First, it may prefer to involve more people from the organization in the work of designing the parts of the gainsharing program. Designing a program leads to a high degree of ownership in the final product; people will support what they have helped create. It will be better for the gainsharing program if 30 people are its designers rather than only 8. Second, especially in small organizations, the resource people needed to produce a good design may not be available internally. The team may need to use outside consultants to help design parts of the program. When this is done, it is very important that people from the organization work closely with any outside consultants. The internal people will learn from the consultants and insure that the organization controls the work being done for it.

Figure 15. Force-field diagram summarizing the diagnosis of an organization.

Positive Forces	Negative Forces
Firm's need to compete and survive	Lack of good productivity measures
Opportunity to increase market and market share	Firm's lack of awareness of productivity need or problem
Pressure from management to perform	Resistance to change: management and workers
	Worker resentment of management policies and practices
	Supervisors too busy fire fighting to plan, schedule, supervise
Worker desire to do good work	Group pressure to restrict output
Worker desire to achieve	Worker fear of speedup
Worker desire for rewards: pay, benefits, security, promotion	Worker fear of working self out of job
Worker fear of loss of job	Inequitable or noncompetitive base pay and benefits
Worker experience and knowledge of operations	Outdated or ineffective incentives
	No system to use worker creativity and experience for problem solving
Mutual desire for teamwork, cooperation	Lack of teamwork, cooperation between individuals and departments
Mutual desire for labor/management harmony	Restrictive labor/management climate or contract
Tools, equipment, facilities, and systems to aid productivity	Inadequate worker and management training
	Lack of feedback and information to workers
	Excessive down time, scrap
	Lack of incentive to use and care for tools, systems, etc.

If the design work is delegated, internally or externally, it is important that the design team place itself in a steering-committee or executive-committee posture relative to the people actually doing the design. Tasks can be assigned to internal staffs or consultants, or people can be attached to the design team like subcommittees. For instance, the task of designing the productivity base can be delegated to an internal staff department such as cost accounting or industrial engineering. Or it could be assigned to the company's CPA firm or gainsharing consultants. The final option might be to form a subcommittee of the design team made up of a design-team member, a cost accountant, and an industrial engineer. Whichever method is used, the work should come back to the design team as a recommendation. The full design team should review the recommendation and decide whether or not to accept it.

PRESENTATION

The design team performs its task on behalf of the organization. Its mission is not the long-range success of the gainsharing program but the short-range acceptance of the program by the organization. Once the organization accepts the design, the responsibility for making it work belongs to the entire organization. This goal—that the organization accept the program and make it work—should guide the design team in all of its deliberations, communications, and work.

The final five-part design, when complete, is presented in full for the organization's approval and implementation. In some situations, it will first be necessary to obtain formal approval from management and union leaders where there is a union. Because of the sharing nature of the program—splitting the gain between the employees and the company—someone must formally accept the plan on behalf of the company. Union leadership approval is needed to insure the union's support.

The next step is formal approval by the organization, which will be described in Chapter 10. The design team's work is complete once the design has been accepted by the organization. At this point, the design team may be disbanded. However, the team's members, individually or collectively, are now a valuable resource and are often used to help install and develop the program in various official or unofficial assignments.

Summary

A well-designed gainsharing program has both immediate and long-range benefits. The immediate benefit is acceptance by the organization and the initiation of gainsharing. Over the long range, a well-thought-out design is easier to evaluate and improve than one that was hastily thrown together. Troubles are bound to occur in any program, but when they do, they can be more accurately diagnosed and resolved if the design work is well documented. If people know why each program element exists and what effect it is supposed to produce, they can revise those elements more effectively. (Methods for keeping gainsharing programs up to date are discussed in Chapter 11.)

Organizations are often tempted to shortcut the design process or to use a gainsharing program already developed by someone else. Such halfhearted measures, however, are unnecessarily risky. A careful, thorough design, suited to the specific organization, is highly recommended.

Checklist and Exercises

Following are a design checklist and three discussion exercises for use by the design team. The primary purpose of the exercises is to facilitate communications within the team. The ideal design team is made up of members from all parts of the organization, who will have different perceptions of issues critical to a successful design. These different perceptions will be a curse or a blessing, depending on how they are used. Used incorrectly, they will lead to interminable bickering in the design team. The team can be like the three blind men, out for a walk, who bumped into an elephant. Each described what he thought the obstacle to be. The first, feeling the leg, announced that a tree blocked their way. "No," said the second, feeling the elephant's body, "It's a large rock." "Wrong," cried the third in alarm, "It's a snake." He was feeling the trunk. These three could continue to argue, or they could pool their information and correctly conclude that they had encountered an elephant. Likewise, the members of the design team can argue, or they can pool their different perceptions and correctly define the organization. These exercises are designed to help the individual members describe their "piece of the elephant" and share the information with each other.

DESIGN CHECKLIST

The design checklist can be used to help the team plan its tasks and assess its progress.

GAINSHARING DESIGN CHECKLIST

Objectives
○ What do we want the program to do for the organization? For the employees?
○ What short-term results do we expect? What long-term results?
○ Is there consensus on the objectives and expected results?

Information
○ Do we need more information about gainsharing? What? How will we get it?
○ Do we need more organization information? What? How will we get it?

Communications
○ What information will be given to people about productivity? How will the information be communicated?
○ How will we determine what other information people need or want?
○ How will we get the information to them?
○ Do we need a bulletin board or newsletter?

Suggestions
- How will suggestions be handled?
- To whom are they made?
- How are they to be approved?
- How do we keep track of ideas and suggestions to be sure they don't get lost or delayed?
- How fast will they be processed?
- How will we communicate acceptance or rejection to the suggester?
- Shall we use suggestion boxes, representative committees, or work teams?

Productivity Measurement
- What will be measured? What output? What inputs?
- What base will be used to determine gains?
- Who will develop the measurement?
- Who will approve the measurement?
- Can the measurement or base be changed? How?

Sharing
- How will gains be shared? Employee? Company?
- How will employee share be distributed?
- If percentage of pay, what pay—base, overtime, vacation?
- Will a deficit reserve or a balancing account be used?
- How often will payments be made?
- Can this be changed? How?

Installation
- What approvals do we need to begin installation?
- How will this be done?
- How, what, and when will employees be told about the plan?
- Will the program be installed on a trial basis? For how long?
- How will renewal or continuation be decided?
- What special training is needed prior to installation? For whom?
- Can we/should we install the program in full at one time or in steps—a piece at a time?

Maintaining the Program
- Will a steering committee be set up to guide the program?
- What, if any, will be the ongoing role of the design team?
- What will be measured to determine progress: productivity, ROI, climate, number of suggestions, speed of processing suggestions, absenteeism, turnover, grievances?
- How often will we measure the program's progress? After six months? One year? Two years?
- How will changes be handled?

READINESS EXERCISE

The readiness exercise is also a checklist. Ideally, an organization must be able to answer "yes" to all 20 questions before it is ready to install a gainsharing program. With some questions, a "no" answer may not block installation if the design includes a process to deal with any negative areas. All of the questions on the exercise can be scored "yes," "no," or "?". Design-team members should complete the questionnaire individually and then compare their perceptions and discuss differences until they reach a consensus. This exercise may be used several times in the planning process as a way to check progress.

GAINSHARING—ARE WE READY?

	Yes	No	?	Notes
Goals, Policy, Practice				
Gainsharing is consistent with the values and policies of the organization and top management.				
Gainsharing will contribute to the achievement of the organization's goals.				
Gainsharing will contribute to the achievement of the individual goals of employees.				
Gainsharing is consistent with organizational practices such as compensation, decision making, communications, and so forth.				
Skills Managers and supervisors have the communications and problem-solving skills required to operate a gainsharing program.				
Employees have the problem-solving skills to contribute useful ideas and suggestions.				
The organization has the training capability to develop the necessary management and employee skills.				
The necessary internal and external consultants are available to support and administer a gainsharing program.				

	Yes	No	?	Notes
Motivation Managers are motivated to improve productivity.				
Managers are motivated to improve the quality of work life.				
Employees are motivated to improve productivity.				
Employees are motivated to improve the quality of work life.				
Systems Necessary accounting systems are in place to measure and evaluate productivity gain.				
Diagnostic and auditing systems are available to identify productivity problems.				
Diagnostic and auditing systems are available to identify quality-of-work-life problems.				
Information systems are available for feedback and problem solving.				
A communications structure is in place to process employee ideas and suggestions.				
Planning Other alternatives for improving productivity and quality of work life have been properly explored.				
The pros and cons of gainsharing have been thoroughly examined.				
The process for exploring, planning, and communicating the gainsharing program has been thorough and properly executed.				

PRODUCTIVITY ANALYSIS

The productivity analysis exercise is designed to help the task force clarify its understanding of the organization's productivity problems. The way to use the exercise is to have each team member (and other resource people) complete the questionnaire individually. Questions 1, 4, and 5 are to be scored. Individual scores can be shared (posted on a flip chart) and discussed to develop a team consensus. The other questions produce information that can be compiled and refined to produce a team consensus.

GAINSHARING PRODUCTIVITY ANALYSIS

1. Overall, how do you rate the current level of productivity in the organization?

Very poor	So-so	Very good
1 2	3	4 5

2. Which are the most productive units in the organization? Why?

1. _____

_____

2. _____

_____

3. _____

_____

4. _____

_____

3. Which are the least productive units in the organization? Why?

1. _____

_____

2. _____

_____

3. _____

_____

4. _____

_____

4. Who is concerned about productivity? Rate each of the following classes of employees according to the extent to which they are aware of and consciously working to improve productivity.

	Not aware or don't care		Somewhat aware		Very aware or active
Top management	1	2	3	4	5
Middle management	1	2	3	4	5
First-line supervisors	1	2	3	4	5
Professional/technical	1	2	3	4	5
Administrative	1	2	3	4	5
Production/operations	1	2	3	4	5

What percentage of the total workforce rates 4 or 5? ____
What percentage of the total workforce rates 1 or 2? ____

5. To what extent do the bulk of the employees in the organization see top managers demonstrating an active concern for productivity improvement? How often is productivity discussed in staff meetings, and so forth?

Seldom Occasionally Regularly
1   2   3   4   5

Are productivity problems and opportunities for improvement identified?

Seldom   Sometimes Regularly
1   2   3   4   5

Are productivity improvements specifically requested of people?

Seldom   Indirectly Definitely
1   2   3   4   5

Are productivity improvements recognized and rewarded?

Seldom   Sometimes Regularly
1   2   3   4   5

6. How do you think the organization defines productivity?

7. How does the organization measure productivity? (List different methods for different operations, if appropriate.)

_____

_____

_____

_____

_____

_____

8. What are the three major opportunities for improving productivity in the organization?

     1. _____

     2. _____

     3. _____

9. What are the principal forces pushing for or against improved productivity in the organization?

For	Against
1.	1.
2.	2.
3.	3.
4.	4.
5.	5.

10. What action steps can or should the organization now take to increase productivity?

     1. _____

     _____

     2. _____

     _____

     3. _____

     _____

     4. _____

     _____

     5. _____

     _____

CLIMATE ANALYSIS

The climate analysis questionnaire is an abbreviated version used primarily as a training exercise to acquaint people with the nature of a climate survey. It can be used for that purpose by the design team. It can also be used as a preliminary exercise to determine whether a more extensive climate survey might be needed. As a preliminary exercise, individual team members are asked to predict how the whole organization might score each question. These predictions are shared, and as team members explore the differences in one another's scores, they develop greater insights about the organization, which are invaluable when they start to design specific features of their plan.

GAINSHARING CLIMATE ANALYSIS

Rate each of the following climate questions according to this key:

1	To a very little extent	4	To a great extent
2	To a little extent	5	To a very great extent
3	To some extent		

Organization   *Ratings*

1. To what extent do employees know and understand the organization's goals and mission?   1 2 3 4 5
2. To what extent do employees support the organization's goals and mission?   1 2 3 4 5
3. To what extent are the organization's values, principles, and policies well defined?   1 2 3 4 5
4. To what extent do employees support the organization's values, principles, and policies?   1 2 3 4 5
5. To what extent are top managers and executives well known throughout the organization?   1 2 3 4 5
6. To what extent do employees know how the organization is performing (productivity, quality, profit, and so forth)?   1 2 3 4 5

Jobs

7. To what extent do employees know and understand the what and why of their jobs?   1 2 3 4 5
8. To what extent do employees know how to do their jobs well (training)?   1 2 3 4 5
9. To what extent are employees motivated to achieve on their jobs?   1 2 3 4 5
10. To what extent do employees know how well they are performing (productivity, quality)?   1 2 3 4 5

Problem Solving

11. To what extent do employees receive feedback to solve   1 2 3 4 5
    problems of cost, quality, scheduling?
12. To what extent do employees know how to get help   1 2 3 4 5
    when they need it?
13. To what extent do employees get help when they need   1 2 3 4 5
    it?
14. To what extent are employees' ideas for solving job-   1 2 3 4 5
    related problems solicited and used?
15. To what extent are supervisors good problem-solving   1 2 3 4 5
    facilitators?

Rewards

16. To what extent are employees rewarded for good   1 2 3 4 5
    individual performance?
17. To what extent are employees rewarded for good group   1 2 3 4 5
    performance?
18. To what extent are compensation plans (wages and   1 2 3 4 5
    benefits) tied to performance?
19. To what extent are there psychological rewards for   1 2 3 4 5
    good performance (recognition, promotion, and so
    forth)?
20. To what extent are poor performers dealt with   1 2 3 4 5
    appropriately (training, placement)?

Chapter 10

Step 3 — Program Start-up

In this, the third step in the planning process, the gainsharing program is installed and begins to function. The installation plan is like a script from a play that describes the details of who does what and when. In this step, the script should be followed precisely as it was prepared by the design team. This chapter will present the steps and issues of installation and start-up.

A critical issue in this step is the transfer of responsibility. Up to this point, the responsibility was assigned to one or more task forces to conduct the feasibility studies and complete the detailed design. Now the responsibility returns to the whole organization. The task force cannot install and maintain a gainsharing program. Such an important project can be carried out only by the entire organization working in unison. Therefore, the installation of the plan becomes the responsibility of management, the formal leaders of the organization. This transition of active leadership from the task force to management takes place when management and the organization accept and approve the program as recommended by the task force.

Leadership Support

Experience has shown that no gainsharing program will go far without strong and active support from organization leaders: management and labor, where there is a union. A first step in start-up is to obtain formal approval from top management and from union officials. While top management may have given approval to proceed with a program in Step 1 and reaffirmed approval throughout Step 2, there should be a formal approval and acceptance of the gainsharing program's final design, including the installation and development plans.

The nature of this approval is also very important. The approval of management and union leaders must be of the active-support variety; passive support is not sufficient. People at all levels in the organization must know that their leaders not only want the program to be successful but will work to insure that success. The response from the leaders must be: "This is great, let's do it!" not, "We don't see anything wrong with it, so give it a try." When the gainsharing program develops momentum, ideas for change will come up to top management, bonus checks will be going out, and problems requiring top management approval will emerge. If, when these things happen, top management is surprised or hesitant, the whole program could stumble and fall.

An enthusiastic approval by the leadership based on a thorough understanding of the plan is the first step in a successful implementation. It is better to delay the installation than to proceed in the face of any doubts or reservations by the leadership.

In seeking top management and union approval, the design team must be sensitive to the leaders' concern: that it is impossible to predict everything that may happen once the plan is installed and begins to function. Top management is responsible for organization results, and union officials are responsible for protecting the interests of their members. Each will review the plan for assurances that their interests are protected. There will be a tendency for them to be conservative and protective until experience shows that the program is safe. This is a principal reason for the development plan, which spells out when and how the program will be changed to correct any problems that arise.

The design task force must anticipate these concerns and present a proposal that will be acceptable. If it encounters problems in this approval process, it may have to go back to the drawing board and make some changes to obtain the proper top leadership approval.

Memorandum of Agreement

A second phase of leadership approval in organizations where the employees are represented by a labor union is executing a memorandum of agreement between the organization and the union. The memorandum of agreement is separate from the collective-bargaining agreement but is signed by the same parties. It is fairly common practice to use this device for matters that require management and union agreement but that the parties wish to exclude from the formal labor contract. The gainsharing program must be kept separate from the collective-bargaining agreement, and the memorandum of agreement is a proper vehicle to satisfy the needs of both parties. Gainsharing may add to employees' income but does not guarantee to do so. Wage rates are a proper subject for negotiation, but pay for productivity gains above a predetermined base is not. Productivity is a market and economic necessity and is therefore not a proper subject for negotiations.

The meeting of managers and workers to solve production problems is a different matter than their meeting to resolve grievances, and the two issues must be kept separate and distinct. The gainsharing program must not interfere with or preempt any part of the collective-bargaining agreement and vice versa. The memorandum of agreement is the way to keep the proper relationship and distance between the contract and the gainsharing program.

In Appendix C, there are two examples of the language for a memorandum of agreement. The first was prepared by Roy Ockert, research director for the International Woodworkers of America. It refers to Rucker Plans but could be used for any gainsharing program. The second is the current agreement at American Valve & Hydrant Manufacturing Company of Beaumont, Texas, and pertains to its Scanlon Plan. It, too, can be used for any gainsharing program. Other examples can be found in *The Scanlon Plan* by Lesieur and in *The Scanlon Way to Improved Productivity* by Moore and Ross. From these examples, an organization should be able to construct an appropriate memorandum for its program.

Communications and Education

Once the program has been accepted by the organization's leaders, it must be communicated to and accepted by the rest of the organization. The organization must understand what the program is, how it works, and why it is being proposed before it can decide to support the program. Figure 16 is a matrix that visually represents different combinations of understanding and support. Understanding is represented by the horizontal continuum from full understanding to no understanding. Support is represented by the vertical continuum from strong support to strong opposition. Combining the two yields four quadrants that show typical support/understanding positions.

When the installation process begins, the organization might be distributed on the matrix as follows:

Quadrant 1: Support with understanding	15%
Quadrant 2: Support without understanding	65%
Quadrant 3: Opposition with understanding	5%
Quadrant 4: Opposition without understanding	15%

The communications and education program should move the bulk of the organization to either quadrant 1 or 3. If enough move to quadrant 1, the

Figure 16. Understanding and support matrix.

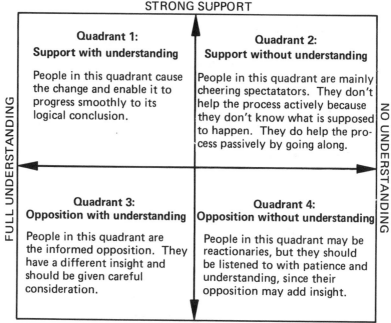

installation will progress smoothly. If too many move to quadrant 3, the design team may have to go back and do some more work on its design. The following are some suggestions about how to proceed with this communications task.

WHAT TO COMMUNICATE

Why the organization is being asked to approve and support a gainsharing program:

- To solve certain productivity or other problems.
- To strengthen the organization.
- Because the concept is consistent with the organization's values and policies.
- Because the gainsharing program will benefit the organization and the employees.

Management commitment to:

- Solicit and use employee ideas and suggestions.
- Provide information to the organization about productivity, quality, and other organization goals and problems.

- ○ Organize and sustain a system to facilitate problem solving throughout the organization.
- ○ Train supervisors to lead and facilitate problem solving in their departments and work groups.

Employee participation:
- ○ The structure, such as forms, committees, and representatives.
- ○ How suggestions are submitted and processed.
- ○ What training and other help will be provided to facilitate employee problem solving.

Reward:
- ○ The base productivity measurement and how it was determined.
- ○ How gains will be shared.
- ○ That the gainshare is a bonus reward over and above competitive wages and benefits.
- ○ How employment security will be provided for as productivity improves.

Other program features:
- ○ How the program was developed.
- ○ How it will be monitored and evaluated.
- ○ How it will be refined and changed.
- ○ When, where, and how information about the program will be provided.
- ○ Where to go for more information about the program.

HOW TO COMMUNICATE

Communicating the program to the organization to obtain understanding and support is critical to its success. The degree of difficulty presented by this task is generally underestimated. Surveys have shown that workers in the United States view productivity-improvement efforts as benefiting management, the organization, and the owners at the expense of workers. People tend to regard productivity-improvement programs as speedups that cause workers to work harder with little or no added benefit. There is also a general feeling among people in the United States that workers are laid off due to productivity-improvement programs. If even as few as 30 percent of the employees in an organization hold these negative attitudes about productivity-improvement efforts, the new gainsharing program will be in trouble before it starts.

Those who plan the gainsharing communications and education programs must be sensitive to, anticipate, and deal with these negative attitudes. Employees must be shown that the gainsharing program is different from other similar-sounding programs they may have experienced or heard about. They must also be given the opportunity to express their reservations freely in an atmosphere of patience and understanding. They must be allowed to ask their questions and not receive glib platitudes in response.

The following are the most commonly used methods for communicating the program to the employees:

○ Booklets distributed to all employees describing in varying degrees of detail the program's purpose, benefits, and principal features.
○ Formal presentations with slides or flip charts to explain the program's purpose, benefits, and principal features.
○ Small-group meetings conducted by department supervisors assisted by task-force members, consultants, or other resource persons.
○ Bulletin boards reserved for gainsharing information, such as plan details, announcements, bonus information, meeting minutes, and suggestions.
○ Employee newspapers specifically designed for gainsharing or with a special section for gainsharing news and information.

A plan for the initial explanation of the program during the installation process might proceed as follows:

Day 1—Booklets are distributed to all employees.
Day 2—Formal presentations are made to one or more large groups.
Day 3—Supervisors, assisted by resource person(s), conduct small-group discussions with department personnel.

An installation activity that generates good publicity, stimulates interest, and provides a bit of fun for everyone is a contest to name the gainsharing program. Companies often give their programs names that reflect one or more of the programs' features. Some examples of gainsharing program names are:

○ WIN/WIN (*W*orking *I*n uniso*N*, *W*e're *I*nvolved *N*ow)
○ PAL Plan (*P*eriod *A*llowance for *L*abor Plan)
○ Facts of Life Plan
○ Security Plan (*S*ecurity, *E*quity, *C*ooperation, *U*nity, *R*eward, *I*nvolvement, *T*rust, *Y*our Plan)
○ 50/50 Plan
○ Gainsharing '82

Training

The communications described previously are designed to explain to people what the program is all about. Beyond a knowledge of the program, people may need skills to operate the plan. The design team will have prepared an overall training recommendation. During installation, an organization need only be concerned with training that must occur before starting the plan. There will also be a need for training that extends beyond start-up, which will be part of the development plan.

Depending on the program's details, some personnel may require special training to enable them to perform duties or responsibilities specific to the program. The following is a list of the kinds of training that might be necessary for installation or during the early stages of the program.

All employees. The role of all employees in the program is to solve problems and make suggestions. Prior to start-up, it may be important to hold training sessions for all employees in rudimentary problem solving and how to complete the suggestion form. After start-up, additional problem-solving training will be very useful.

Management. Managers may require orientation to the theory and practice of participative management. The extent and nature of this training will depend on the degree of participative management required by the program and the style of management currently practiced in the company. The gainsharing program design will specify what is required, and the climate analysis from Steps 1 or 2 will identify current practice. The difference between the two defines the extent of the training program. There are literally hundreds of approaches to this training—too many to list here. Larger companies should be able to obtain the necessary training programs from their in-house management-training staff. Smaller companies should seek help from consultants, their trade associations, or local business schools.

Prior to installation, all managers should receive a thorough orientation to participative management and what will be expected of them under the gainsharing program. More in-depth training in participative management can be incorporated into the development plan. Extensive management training, if required before start-up, will delay the installation, however.

Supervisors. Any type of second- or third-degree participation system will require supervisors to conduct problem-solving meetings. To do this, supervisors may need training in meeting leadership and in group problem-solving techniques. There are several good programs available to deal with this training need. For meeting leadership, the Interaction Method, developed by Michael Doyle and David Straus and described in their book, is a good one. For problem-solving training, programs such as Work Simplification, Kepner-Tregoe, and Quality Circles are excellent.

Some current approaches to employee problem-solving groups recommend the use of meeting facilitators with a stronger role than that of the supervisor. The use of skilled facilitators can be very helpful to the group and to the supervisor, but the facilitator should not preempt the supervisor's leadership role. The proper execution of supervisory and managerial roles is very important to the success of any organization. Gainsharing works best when appropriate leadership roles are enhanced, not. diminished.

Supervisors must receive extensive education about the gainsharing program prior to installation, but skill training in group problem solving does not have to be completed before the official start-up date. Such training can be phased in over several years, becoming progressively more sophisticated and technical.

Coordinator. If the company decides to appoint a coordinator or administrator for the gainsharing program, he or she may need some specialized training to perform the duties of the new position. There are no formal training programs to teach someone how to administer or coordinate a gainsharing program. The best method to prepare someone for this role would be for the newly appointed coordinator to visit experienced coordinators in other gainsharing companies and learn about the role from the actual experience of others.

If a coordinator is to be used, the design team should prepare a thorough position description (see Chapter 11). Describing the specific duties of the coordinator will provide an easy method for determining what training an individual will need to properly perform the job.

Other training. In most new gainsharing programs, the preceding categories are sufficient for the start-up phase. Other training needs may surface as experience accumulates. The process for determining what training may be needed is straightforward. The plan prepared by the design team will directly or indirectly describe tasks and duties (including who must perform them) as well as responsibilities that must be accomplished for the program to operate successfully. A simple analysis should indicate whether the designated people have the knowledge and skill required for satisfactory performance. Those who lack such knowledge and/or skill need training.

Information Systems

When the program is installed, the organization's information systems must be able to generate productivity gain or loss information for each bonus period (weekly, monthly, quarterly, or other). Sometimes this requires changes in some accounting systems and procedures, which must be completed prior to installation. The program will also require information about productivity, performance, and problems for the suggestion and problem-solving process. Any deficiencies in current systems should be corrected during this start-up phase. Refinement and improvements can be made as experience with the gainsharing program shows the need.

Organization Structure

Some organizations may find it necessary and desirable to make certain major or minor organization-structure changes to take full advantage of gainsharing. There are three general situations where this is most likely to occur, and there are others specific to individual organizations.

In large multidivisional organizations, the natural gainsharing unit is a complete operational unit, such as a profit or cost center. Designating divisions or plants as gainsharing units leads immediately to questions of what to do with the corporate, group, or division staffs that support several operating units. Staff personnel contribute to productivity improvement by virtue of their support services and should therefore share in productivity gains. It is usually difficult to measure how much of each staff's contribution applies to a given unit. One approach is to determine some form of proportional sharing. Where it can be determined that 30 percent of a staff person's time is in support of Plant X, that person could receive a gainshare from Plant X's program based on 30 percent of his or her pay. Thirty percent of the person's pay should also be included in Plant X's productivity base. Where all of the plants in a corporation have gainsharing programs, staff personnel are often paid a bonus equal to the average of all the plants. Such bonuses are usually paid from the company share and are provided for in the sharing ratio.

Deciding this issue may lead to organization-structure changes. Sometimes the contribution analysis shows that some staff people, or groups of people, support Plant X 100 percent of their time. When that is the case, it may be better, from a gainsharing standpoint, to transfer such people to the divisions or plants for which they work. The transfer to the division or plant may also be better from an organization standpoint. Organization theorists generally agree that keeping the bureaucracy lean and resources in local control is best.

Another situation that occurs in large organizations has to do with identifying proper operating units for gainsharing. The analysis leading up to these decisions may show that two units should be combined or that a single unit should be split into two separate units. Changes such as this should be made before installing the gainsharing program(s).

At the plant level or in the small company, it is fairly common that minor changes in the organization are needed to facilitate employee participation. This is especially true of a third-degree participation system as was described in Chapter 6.

Participation System

Setting up the gainsharing participation system involves several administrative tasks. The tasks will be defined in the plan outlined by the design team and include the following:

- Designing and printing suggestion forms.
- Organizing suggestion committees or work teams.
- Electing or appointing committee representatives and coordinators, or making other special assignments. Elections, if used, should follow the process described in Chapter 8.

Timing

A key decision for the design team is when to install the gainsharing program. The design team should pick a date that is both appropriate and reasonable. An appropriate date is one that:

- Avoids conflict with union collective-bargaining agreements; a plan should not be installed within six months before or after contract negotiations.
- Synchronizes the plan with the fiscal year, since it ties the gainsharing program in more closely with business goals and business planning.
- Catches the upside of the business cycle; it is best to start the program at a time when volume is expected to increase.
- Provides adequate time for design and installation activities.

Companies usually try to hit the start of the year in order to have a full 12-month year for the first trial. This is ideal, but generally no serious harm is done when the first trial period is 8 or 9 months rather than 12. Less than 6 months is probably not sufficient as a trial period, and it may be better to wait for the beginning of the following year.

Programs that use a reserve account with the bonus are sometimes timed so that the end-of-the-year bonus (if there is one) is paid just before Christmas or just before the vacation season.

The design team must weigh all relevant factors in selecting a starting date and the plan year. It is strongly recommended that the plan year coincide with the fiscal year to reinforce the mutuality of the business plan and the gainsharing program and to avoid any conflict between the two.

Start-up Date and Installation Schedule

The design team will have selected a target start-up date. The entire start-up sequence is scheduled so that all necessary preinstallation activities will be completed before the program's planned start. People will become anxious to get on with the program, but haste can make just as much waste in gainsharing programs as in anything else. As the start-up phase progresses, problems will occur, which may or may not cause delays. Each problem must be examined to determine if the official start-up date should be postponed. Some problems definitely call for postponement, such as the failure to obtain full leadership support or not having the productivity base measurement. Other problems may not require postponement. For instance, some of the management and supervisory training can be completed after start-up, even though it was planned to take place before.

The decision to postpone start-up is seldom as traumatic as it might first appear. A great deal of work has usually been done to get ready for a gainsharing program. Designers and leaders normally feel that a postponement will lead to disappointment and frustration. The circumstances surrounding a decision to postpone determine whether the reaction will be positive or negative. If the situation is something that could have and should have been avoided, there will probably be a negative reaction to a postponement decision. If the situation is something that could not have been anticipated, a postponement will be seen as reasonable. Regardless of reason or reaction, the gainsharing program should not be started until all necessary installation steps have been properly completed. The design team should anticipate the possibility of delays and have a contingency plan ready to deal with the situation.

There are a number of ways to handle a start-up postponement. One is to begin from one to six months late and let the first trial period be whatever time remains of the originally planned first year. Another is to start part of the program and phase in the postponed features as soon as possible. The bonus can be started before the participation system has been fully developed. Likewise, the participation system can be started before the bonus plan has been developed and/or approved. Both of these scenarios are less than ideal, but neither is fatal. While postponements should not be viewed as fatal mistakes, neither should they be treated casually. When interest and enthusiasm are high, a postponement might be seen as a lack of interest or commitment on the part of those responsible for the delay. A failure to deal with the issues causing postponement will make matters worse, so any such situation needs to be resolved expeditiously.

Vote

Usually the last step in the installation plan is the formal acceptance of the gainsharing program for a first trial period.

The entire organization votes on the program as designed and proposed. A successful start-up requires a strong expression of commitment by the organization to the gainsharing program. The vote is a test of that commitment and acceptance. To insure a strong commitment, a favorable vote of from 80 percent to 90 percent of the *eligible* employees is often set as a minimum requirement for implementation. This may sound difficult but is regularly achieved in gainsharing start-ups. When the design team and management agree to this very high level of acceptance, it forces them to plan and communicate the program in order to achieve an 80 percent to 90 percent favorable response. Both the planning and communicating job are therefore done better and more thoroughly.

If the required minimum acceptance is not achieved, there can be only two causes. Either the design of the program is not acceptable, or the program has not been sufficiently communicated. Either problem must be corrected before the program can be successfully installed. If the design is not acceptable, the design team should be asked to change it to make it acceptable. When this is done, the revised plan (or at least the changes) must go through the same process of education and communication and approvals as did the original plan.

If the organization fails to obtain the minimum vote because not enough people understood the proposed program, then more or better education and communication are needed. The program should be communicated and explained until the necessary acceptance is achieved.

This vote should be taken by secret ballot. A common practice, however, is to conduct the vote by department to determine the degree of support in different major areas of the organization. An unusual occurrence, but one that could be very critical, is when the overall organization accepts the program but one group rejects it. For example, an organization might vote by as high as 90 percent to accept a program, but one small department might reject it entirely or by a significant majority. Technically, the vote has passed, and the small group of dissenters could be ignored. Practically, it is not a good idea to ignore such opposition. To force the program on even one department or one group is inviting trouble. This kind of trouble can be rather severe if it comes from a key department, such as maintenance or engineering, or if it involves, for example, all first-line supervisors. The cause of the opposition should be carefully examined. This situation also indicates either a design or a communications problem. If, by correcting either problem, the dissenting group accepts the program without causing the rest of the organization to withdraw approval, the installation will be more successful, and the program will be off to a stronger start.

Such problems are usually resolved to everyone's satisfaction. When they are not dealt with during installation, the organization and the program suffer until the source of the problem is fully resolved. A situation like this occurred in a company with several unions. The plan, as proposed, was accepted by everyone except one union, which did not approve the bonus. After much discussion, it was decided to proceed with all of the program features except the bonus. Removing a major element such as the bonus is tantamount to having no gainsharing program, but apparently that was the best this organization could do.

When the necessary minimum vote is reached, the program is started for its first-year trial. A common procedure, following the trial year period, is to have a second vote to install the plan permanently. In the next chapter, on development, the idea of voting on the plan every year will be presented.

After Start-up

As has been suggested throughout this chapter, there may be some installation work that continues beyond the official start-up date. Any important installation work that was not completed prior to the start-up date should be wrapped up as quickly as possible. Installation, Step 3, flows directly into development, Step 4, which will be discussed in detail in the next chapter.

Chapter 11

Step 4 – Program Development

Every organization starting gainsharing designs the best program possible for its time and particular circumstances. But time and circumstances change, and experience brings new insights. No matter how well designed a program is when started, it can be made twice as good by the end of the third year and twice as good again by the end of the tenth year. Such fourfold improvement, of course, is not achieved automatically, but it can be achieved by hard work, creativity, and a systematic development plan. Keeping an organization lean, mean, and in a state of high performance is like the queen's croquet game in *Alice in Wonderland:* "You must run to just keep up and run faster to get ahead."

To get ahead in gainsharing, there must be change. As situations and circumstances change, the program must adapt to keep current. As experience accumulates, bugs will be discovered, and new opportunities will arise. The purpose of the development plan is to insure that the right changes are made at the right time.

History shows that few gainsharing companies have had a well-organized development plan. Experience also shows that sooner or later every program develops problems. One difference between successful and unsuccessful programs is in the way companies deal with problems when they occur. Although many gainsharing programs have been abandoned because they coped poorly with problems, companies that react properly and quickly have developed very healthy programs. The best example of good development is described by John Donnelly in the article "Participative Management at Work" (see Bibliography). Donnelly Mirrors, Inc. has developed the best example of a successful gainsharing program available today. The article identifies at least 13 specific changes made to its Scanlon Plan over the plan's 25-year life. Since the article was written, the company has made an additional major change in its reward system. It has invented what may well be the first gainsharing program to use profit as a true productivity measure and basis for the reward. Donnelly developed the ROI method shown in Example 8, Chapter 7.

Too many of the early gainsharing programs began with the naive idea that their original design would be good for all time and that external changes would not happen. Reality has never been kind to people or organizations with their heads in the sand. Gainsharing programs that have failed to adapt have tended to wilt. While survival of the fittest has been the order up to now, careful monitoring and systematic development must be the order of the future. The development plan can be simple or sophisticated, depending on the needs, style, and preference of the organization. The important thing is that there be a plan to insure development rather than leaving this critical aspect to chance. This chapter will outline the dimensions of the development plan, Step 4 in the overall planning process. The plan is prepared by the design team in Step 2 and is then carried out by the organization over time.

Commitment to Change

The development plan begins with the awareness that change will be needed and will be beneficial to the overall program. Throughout the organization, there should be a solid understanding that what is important about gainsharing are the principles and not the techniques or structures. The gainsharing principles of participation, organizational excellence, and equity through shared rewards are permanent, but how participation, excellence, and equity are achieved will change. That a method works well today is no guarantee that it will work at all tomorrow.

Management practices have a long way to go before anyone will agree that we have reached an ideal system. New and better techniques of employee participation are evolving constantly, and we can be absolutely certain that better management practices and employee-involvement methods will continue to be discovered. The commitment to gainsharing is therefore a commitment to change. This commitment is so important and the dangers of failure to change so great that it is recommended that the development plan include an annual program renewal. Each year the organization should evaluate its experience with gainsharing and formally approve the program for the following year. This method provides an opportunity to examine the program and correct minor problems before they become serious. It insures that the program will be conscientiously and continuously fine-tuned to changing markets, products, and internal conditions. But, most important, it avoids creating the impression that the plan is unchangeable.

If a program is started with the notion that it will never change, change inevitably causes suspicion and mistrust when the organization is forced to deal with it. With the expectation firmly established from the start that change will occur (as often as annually), changes are much easier to accept and implement. For instance, many gainsharing companies report that it is difficult to change the productivity measure and bonus base once they have been established. Contrary to this popular notion, Atwood Vacuum Machine Company in Rockford, Illinois, has changed its productivity base every year for 30 years with no adverse reactions. It was part of the original plan; it is expected each year and causes no problems when it occurs.

Having a vote each year to formally adopt the program for the next year is a simple and expedient measure to insure that the plan will be examined and modified when and as necessary. The annual vote also makes it easier to deal with problems in a timely fashion when they occur. When individuals or groups sense a problem, they know that at the most they will only have to wait a few months until there is a formal opportunity to raise their issue and have it reviewed by the entire organization. People can relax and wait until the proper time to bring their issues up for consideration. Without such an opportunity, people often feel compelled to mount an aggressive campaign to have their issue heard and acted upon. With a status quo, change always creates two factions: those who want to maintain the status quo and those who want to change it. Without a status quo, this conflict does not develop.

Change is an essential feature of a successful gainsharing program. The annual review and vote is a way to incorporate this feature into the program.

Performance

The gainsharing program, when successful, will affect the organization's performance in many ways. The development plan should identify the more important expected results and monitor performance to see that they occur. The following are some examples of the type of performance goals that might be monitored in the development plan:

Productivity improvement.
More output or volume.
Improved quality of products or services.
Less scrap and/or rework.
Greater share of present markets.

Entrance to new markets.
New product introductions.
More on-time deliveries.
Greater profit.

To be useful, each of the performance goals to be measured should include specific standards or targets, such as:

Productivity	Improve productivity by 10% over preceding year.
Volume	Increase volume by 20% over preceding year.
Quality	Reduce field returns by 25%.
	Reduce final inspection rejects by 25%.
Scrap	Reduce scrap by 20%.
	Reduce scrap to 10% of output.
	Reduce rework by 15%.
Market share	Increase market share from 32% to 38%.
New markets	Enter northeastern supermarkets within the next two years.
New products	Introduce two new models next year.
Deliveries	Achieve 98% on-time delivery.

These performance targets will be recorded in strategic plans but should also be included as an expectation for the gainsharing program. As a feature of the gainsharing program, this information is communicated to everyone as part of the organization's overall productivity-improvement strategy.

Time periods must also be included in performance plans, such as six months, one year, two years. The development plan, then, provides a system for measuring actual performance at appropriate times. When the performance is measured and the organization determines whether it has succeeded or failed, these questions can be asked: To what extent has the gainsharing program contributed or failed to contribute to the achievement of these performance goals? What should/can/must we change now to reach our goals?

Quality of Work Life

In addition to enhancing business results, the gainsharing program should contribute to an improvement in the quality of work life. As with performance results, the development plan must include ways to measure or evaluate the quality of work life. Specific criteria such as these might be used: scores on attitude or climate surveys, rate of turnover, rate of absenteeism, accident frequency and severity, and number and type of grievances.

These measures should also be quantified with specific scores, rates of improvement, rates of reduction, or achievement of a specific level of performance. The development plan should provide that measurements be taken at appropriate times to see how the gainsharing program has contributed to improvement in the quality of work life.

The Gainsharing Program

Specific measures should also be established to determine how well the gainsharing program is working, such as:

Frequency of suggestions (per employee or work group).
Quality of suggestions (cost savings, quality improvement, or other).
Average time to process suggestions.
Size and frequency of bonuses.
Number, frequency, and cost of meetings.
Attendance at meetings.

These should also be specific as to achievement and time, such as 1.5 suggestions per employee per year and three weeks average time to process suggestions with a maximum of six weeks.

The design team should recommend, as part of its original proposal, specific targets and measurements in all three of the above categories. The measurements can be derived from the organization data collected in either Step 1 or Step 2. Base measurements or indices should be set and targets selected. The targets should be challenging but attainable and related to real organization needs. They should also allow the organization ample time to adjust to the new program; the gainsharing program will start slowly but will develop momentum. A target of one good productivity-improvement suggestion per employee per year is a reasonable second- or third-year goal but may not be reasonable for the first six months of a new program. A first-degree participation system will typically produce a high volume of minor suggestions. A third-degree system will produce fewer but better suggestions. On the basis of its situation and type of plan, each organization should set realistic expectations for itself.

The design team should ask what levels of accomplishment are reasonable to expect in the first six months, first year, second year, and so forth. These reasonable goals are set and then used to measure progress. To build interest and enthusiasm for the program, achievement or over-achievement of goals should be reported to the organization as accomplishments. Failure to achieve a reasonable goal should result in action to strengthen the gainsharing program.

Assignment of Responsibility for Monitoring

The development plan, like the rest of the gainsharing program, belongs to and is the responsibility of the entire organization. However, the task of monitoring the plan can and perhaps should be given to someone or to a group to be sure that measurements are taken and analyzed and that actions to improve the program are initiated. Some or all members of the original design team could be formed into a review committee. As designers, they know how the program was intended to work; they looked at many alternatives in selecting the various features of the program. If something is not working as planned, the designers have the background and expertise to suggest program modifications. The design team also prepared the development plan and knows how to use the plan to modify and/or improve the gainsharing program. It is highly recommended that the design team be used in some capacity for program development, at least during the first few years of a new gainsharing program. Where a coordinator is used, some of this development work will be delegated to that position.

Coordinator

Some organizations appoint a full-time or part-time gainsharing program coordinator or administrator. For others, such a position will be unnecessary. Generally, this decision will be influenced by the size of the organization and the complexity of the program. Larger organizations with more complex programs will be more likely to use a coordinator, whereas smaller organizations with simple programs will most likely assign coordinating tasks to one or more employees as additional responsibilities. In the absence of a full-time coordinator, controllers and personnel managers are often given special assignments. Regardless of who is assigned, there will be some administrative and coordination activities that must be performed.

The coordination tasks that have to be covered one way or another include the following, which can be incorporated into one job description for the coordinator or included in the job descriptions of several people:

○ *Communications.* Collecting and posting meeting minutes; maintaining gainsharing bulletin boards; expediting the flow of information important to the gainsharing program up, down, and sideways; publicizing successes, problems, and other information important to the program.

- ○ *Training.* Educating all employees in the purpose and process of the gainsharing program; educating and orienting new employees; training managers and supervisors in meeting leadership, group process, and problem-solving methods; training groups in effective problem-solving methods; orienting and training newly elected/selected committee representatives; maintaining materials and equipment resources for training.
- ○ *Auditing.* Auditing activities required by the development plan to monitor the progress of gainsharing, such as operations audits and organization surveys.
- ○ *Suggestion processing.* Recording, transmitting, expediting, and following up suggestions.
- ○ *Research and innovation.* Studying new developments in the field of gainsharing and introducing innovation as needed or possible, especially in such matters as measurement and participation.
- ○ *Scheduling.* Arranging elections, meetings, and special events related to the gainsharing program.

This coordinator position should not duplicate other resources already available in the organization. For instance, if the organization has a training department, it would perform the actual training mentioned above. In these situations, the administrator would coordinate training activities between the training department, the needs of the gainsharing program, and the organization.

If a full- or part-time coordinator is used to perform these and other activities in support of the gainsharing program, it is important that this position not diminish in any way the responsibility of general managers, department managers, or supervisors to provide active leadership for the gainsharing program throughout the organization and in their respective areas. Titling a coordinator position as "manager," such as "gainsharing manager," should probably be avoided, to prevent the incumbent from assuming inappropriate power and influence over the program and/or to keep others from expecting too much from the position.

Development Checklist

In addition to the preceding suggestions for the development of the gainsharing program, the following checklist may suggest additional points to monitor to determine how well the program is operating:

- ○ Employees know and understand the details of the program.
- ○ Employees are showing more interest in the company; understand the nature of the business; and are suggesting ways to improve operations, reduce waste, and upgrade the quality of product or service.
- ○ Managers and supervisors are more receptive to the ideas and suggestions of other employees, and there is a high level of meaningful participation.
- ○ Employees are being involved in important decisions and contributing to better decisions.
- ○ Individuals, shifts, and departments are cooperating with each other in solving problems and improving the way work gets done.
- ○ Communications are improving. People are receiving the information they need to do their jobs and sharing information with others. There is frequent contact among employees at all levels.
- ○ Staff departments are performing their support and facilitating roles better. Line departments are more receptive to help from technical and functional experts.
- ○ Grievances, formal and informal, are less frequent. Problems that once turned into grievances are being solved in a more rational, understanding manner before they become formal grievances.
- ○ There is a new spirit throughout the organization, more trust, more helping, greater satisfaction, more fun, and a new feeling of mutual respect between labor and management.
- ○ Employees understand better how their work contributes to total organization success.
- ○ Bonuses are being earned and are appreciated, but the bonus has not become the central theme of the program. The central theme is organization excellence.
- ○ Change is becoming a way of life in the organization. Everyone is eager for changes that will improve the organization.
- ○ New employees are carefully selected and welcomed by their work groups as a source of new ideas.
- ○ The quality of management, supervision, and leadership is improving. The openness, mutual respect, and greater trust have strengthened the manager's status in the organization. Managers and supervisors are delegating better and doing more managerial and supervisory work.
- ○ Customer satisfaction is growing as a result of better value, quality, and delivery.
- ○ There are positive signs of greater employee satisfaction, such as less absenteeism, lower turnover, fewer accidents, and more applicants for jobs with the company.

Summary

Successful gainsharing programs cannot be purchased, nor do they happen by chance. They occur only as a result of careful planning, hard work, sincere effort, and creativity. The necessary work can be made easier and the results more certain with a well-thought-out development plan.

Part III

SOME OTHER CONSIDERATIONS

Previous sections of the book have described gainsharing and how to do it. This section will examine some additional issues that have not been dealt with so far.

The first is about the unions and gainsharing: Does a gainsharing program work with or without a union? What do the unions say about gainsharing?

The second has to do with adapting gainsharing to the service sector: Is the industrial experience applicable to other organizations and, if so, how?

The third is: Why gainsharing? Does it really address today's problems?

Each of these issues will be dealt with in its own chapter.

Chapter 12

Unions and Gainsharing

Can gainsharing work with a union? Can gainsharing work without a union? These questions are asked regularly by people with gainsharing experience. Those in companies without a union ask the first question. They believe that unions will oppose or hinder gainsharing. People from unionized companies ask the second question, because they see the union as important to the success of their program.

When people from nonunion companies are told that gainsharing works very well with a union, they are surprised. When people from unionized companies are told that gainsharing works very well without a union, they too are surprised. If these confusing reactions come from people with gainsharing experience, imagine the confusion among those without any gainsharing experience.

A classic instance of curiosity about union participation in gainsharing concerns the United Steelworkers of America and the Scanlon Plan. The Scanlon Plan was invented by the president of a Steelworkers local, Joseph Scanlon. The first plan was so successful that in the late 1930s the Steelworkers promoted Scanlon to the position of research director in its Pittsburgh headquarters, where his job was to promote his gainsharing program to other companies with Steelworkers contracts. Today, however, few Steelworkers officials know about the Scanlon Plan, and none are experts.

What Is the Union Position on Gainsharing?

One correct answer to the question of a union position on gainsharing is that there is none. While correct, that answer is not complete. Recent interest in and experience with gainsharing is causing some ripples in union circles, and a variety of reactions are beginning to emerge, which may result in some form of official position. The AFL-CIO began in 1981 to develop a position paper or manual about joint labor/management com-

205

mittees and worker-involvement programs such as quality-of-work-life programs and Quality Circles. When available, this manual may provide a clear and official union position about gainsharing and similar matters. However, even with an official AFL-CIO position, individual unions will still establish their own official positions.

Individual unions have not taken a firm stand for or against gainsharing. However, some have developed guidelines to help their affiliated locals when they are asked to consider or adopt a gainsharing program. This chapter presents the pros and cons of gainsharing from labor's point of view in an effort to clear up some of the current confusion. It also presents an approach to joint labor/management gainsharing planning.

An Overview of the Union Perspective

Labor unions, just like many managements, have very little experience with gainsharing and, for that reason, have not developed a firm position, pro or con. Labor unions, like management, are busy with many other affairs of the organization and have not given the subject the priority or the time necessary to develop expertise in gainsharing.

As a first reaction, union officials see gainsharing as something midway between profit sharing, which many do not trust, and individual incentives, which most do not like. This naturally leads to an initial position of caution. This cautious first reaction is intensified by bad experiences and moderated by good ones. The good experiences include:

- An increase in worker earnings over the negotiated base.
- Worker involvement in the day-to-day operation of the company.
- Better management—"It keeps management on their toes," as Don Rand of the UAW put it.

The bad experiences include:

- Gainsharing plans being proposed as a substitute for equitable wages and benefits.
- Plans being used to prevent organization in some cases and to weaken the union in others.
- Plans resulting in excessive peer pressure unfavorable to union members.
- Interest in plans waning after an initial few months of high interest.
- Plans promising great things that do not materialize.
- Incentives based on factors over which employees have little or no control.

○ A feeling that management failed to provide complete and accurate financial reports to employees about plan results.
○ Unemployment of union members.

In the minds of most union officials there are, as the above lists would suggest, more reasons to be cautious and skeptical than to be open and supportive.

The reaction to gainsharing is influenced to a great extent by past experience with other types of incentive plans, which generally has been unfavorable. Thus, most unions are hesitant and negative when it comes to any so-called productivity-improvement effort. The collective experience of the unions has convinced them that productivity improvement is synonymous with speedups, layoffs, and unequal distribution of benefits. This general opinion is not limited to labor officials but rather is held generally by a large percentage of the total workforce of the United States. A 1980 United States Chamber of Commerce poll asked who benefits from productivity improvements. The response, which represents the opinion of workers throughout the United States, is summarized below:

If all the organizations and companies in the country improved their performance and productivity, who do you think would benefit the *most*—workers, management, stockholders, or consumers?

Workers	9%
Management	15
Stockholders	17
Consumers	39
All of the above; everybody benefits equally (volunteered)	18

Who would benefit the *least*—workers, management, stockholders, or consumers?

Workers	44%
Management	12
Stockholders	15
Consumers	13
All of the above; nobody benefits (volunteered)*	9

*Reprinted with the permission of the Chamber of Commerce of the United States of America, from *Workers' Attitudes Toward Productivity: A New Survey* (1980). Percentages do not add up to 100% because of rounding of numbers and exclusion of nonresponses.

An Official Position?

The closest to an official labor position comes from the United Auto Workers. In 1958, the executive board of the UAW issued guidelines for collective bargaining that included a proposal providing for a share of year-end profits over and above requirements for shareholders and executive bonus. This proposal called for a sharing of the excess profits as follows:

50 percent to the corporation
25 percent to workers
25 percent rebate to customers

Again, in 1979, the national UAW collective-bargaining convention adopted a resolution in favor of gainsharing. The text of that resolution follows:

PROFIT OR EQUITY SHARING

Workers, like executives, are entitled to the basic equity represented by their wages and fringe benefits. But their total share in the success of the company requires supplementation of basic compensation through profit sharing, similar to that which is provided to executives and stockholders.

For many years, the executives of corporations have enjoyed the enormous benefits of a profit sharing program, commonly known as an executive bonus plan. In 1978, for example, General Motors executives received bonuses totaling one hundred sixty eight million dollars on top of their incredibly high salaries; stockholders shared in the wealth by receiving dividends which are related to profits, as are changes in the stock value.

Workers' efforts are essential to produce the wealth which permits the stockholders to receive dividends and executives to receive their high salaries and profit sharing bonuses; workers should receive their full share of the profit as well. Profit sharing would have the added advantage of being non-inflationary because its payout occurs only after the prices on the product have been established, the sales volume is known, and the profit figures are in. Extra dividends for stockholders are declared after profit is known. The extra equity owing to the workers should also be established after the profit figures are known.

Profit sharing must properly be understood not as a substitute for other demands but rather as a rational means by which workers, stockholders, executives, and consumers can share equitably in the increased productivity and profitability of the company after they are known.

The following paper provides a clear position on gainsharing from the International Association of Machinists and Aerospace Workers (also known as IAMAW or IAM).* This is not an official position paper, since it has not been adopted by a board or convention.

PROFIT SHARING AND GROUP INCENTIVE PLANS

For years, American industry has attempted to tie workers' earnings to levels of output or productivity, rather than reimbursing an employee for specific skills, job functions, etc. Historically, this has been done through a variety of individual type incentive systems. Companies have assumed that the incentive principle operates best by giving each individual an opportunity to perform and paying him for extra performance. Individual incentives have major application where workers exercise control over their output. As mechanization increases, however, there is reduced need for the traditional individual incentive systems.

Whether because of technological change or the general opposition of American labor to pitting one worker against another, individual incentive plans have been on the decline. This is evident in the fact that in 1967, 26 percent of IAM members were covered by some type of incentive system. In the first quarter of 1979, this percentage had dropped to 20. As a consequence of this decline, more and more American companies are attempting to introduce plant-wide or group incentive programs.

There are basically two (2) different approaches to plant-wide incentive (production bonus) plans. Profit sharing is one type of collective or plant-wide incentive payment system. The other general type is based upon some measure of production, cost, or sales, rather than profits. Of this second type, the most commonly used systems are the Scanlon Plan and the Rucker (Share the Production) Plan. Under both, workers receive a bonus for savings in labor costs.

These types of plans are not new and some have been around since World War II. They are, however, undergoing a revival for two reasons. First, the nation is being bombarded by the press concerning the relatively low productivity growth of the 1970's. We are supposedly facing a "productivity crisis." Secondly, under the so-called "voluntary" Carter wage and price guidelines, offsetting increases in productivity is one way an employer can exceed the seven (7) percent pay standard and remain within the guidelines. Thus, industry is looking at both old and new ways of increasing productivity and group incentives are at the top of their list.

The purpose of this article is to review the IAM's position on profit-sharing and discuss the two most common types of group incentive systems.

Profit-Sharing
The IAM has, through the years, maintained a suspicious regard of profit-sharing plans. This opposition is based upon several points which include difficulties experienced on the part of the employees having their hopes built up that they would receive a bonus at the end of a prescribed period, only to have their hopes end when no bonus payments are made. Also, profit-sharing plans were frequently introduced by employers as a means of circumventing a wage increase

*Paper prepared by Reginald Newell, research director of the IAM. Reprinted by permission from the *IAM Research Report,* Volume III, No. 2, Spring 1979.

that would be received by employees at each pay period, with the vague and uncertain prospects that a bonus would be paid six months or a year later.

If it is used in connection with pensions, profit-sharing plans are the least desirable of any form of retirement programs. This position is due largely to the fact that the employees of a company have no guarantee whatsoever that during a particular year the company will earn sufficient profits to add any credits to the individual employee's retirement fund. In other words, the money used to provide retirement benefits depends upon the company's ability to earn a profit. Since there are so many factors involved in the company's ability to operate profitably during a particular year, over which the employees have no control whatsoever, we consider it unfair to the employees to operate under such a plan. If business conditions are such that for a period of several consecutive years or several years within a different period of time the company does not make a profit, the employees would receive no credit toward their retirement fund.

It is true that some sincere employers have used a profit-sharing plan to the benefit of the employees; however, such cases are, unfortunately, the exception and not the rule. That is the reason why the IAM has opposed profit-sharing systems over the years. There have been instances in the past when profit-sharing plans, which were made to appear very attractive, were put into effect during a period of prosperous business, but when the period of prosperity ended, the employer insisted that the plan must work both ways since their business fell off and gross earnings were reduced. The experience of the IAM on the subject has also been the experience of other unions.

Naturally, there are occasions when, despite the IAM's position on profit-sharing plans, our negotiators have no choice but to accept them. When this happens, it is our duty to make sure that we negotiate the best possible such plan.

Types of Plans

Profit-sharing plans may take the form of (1) current distribution plan, (2) deferred payment plan, or (3) a combination of [the] two. Most current distribution plans provide for annual payment in cash. The amount distributed under current distribution plans is deductible for income tax purposes by the employer, and is taxable income as far as the employee is concerned.

Under deferred payment programs, a portion of the profits is placed in a trust fund and invested in stocks or bonds. Individual payments eventually are made from the fund in the case of death, disability, retirement, or separation for some other reason; or, in some cases, an employee may direct that part of each year's contribution be used to purchase life insurance or an additional pension. Some deferred plans permit borrowing or withdrawal for medical expenses, financial hardships, education of children, or any "worthy cause." In an increasing number of cases, distributions are permitted as a supplement to unemployment benefits.

When faced by a company proposal regarding a profit-sharing plan, the first thing to be examined is the wage structure. If it is up to standard, then a profit-sharing plan becomes slightly less objectionable. In too many cases, however, a profit-sharing plan is introduced as a means of covering up the very low wage structure. If this is the case, one should steer away from any profit-sharing plan.

Another question that should be answered is whether the company can be relied upon to furnish accurate financial statements. If it does, and meets all the other criteria, then one should not turn down a profit-sharing plan out of hand. If the employees can make real gains, the profit-sharing plan should, at least, be explored.

Scanlon Plan

Like profit-sharing schemes, the Scanlon Plan is affected by the economic success of the company. Because company sales will have a great effect upon bonuses, it may be expected that the plan will look very appealing during periods of heightened economic activity but may lose its appeal during periods of economic contraction. This is especially true in industries in which demand fluctuates greatly. Bonus payments may disappear entirely during periods of slack demand when labor costs tend to be higher, in relation to the value of output, than they would otherwise be. The Scanlon Plan is of necessity streamlined to the individual needs of the company where the plan is in effect. However, basically the plan is a group incentive rather than an individual incentive.

At first glance, the method of determining savings appears complicated and may have many varieties. Basically, the ratio between total payroll and sales value of production (net sales plus inventory) during some historical period is adapted as a norm or standard of labor cost. This ratio or percentage is then applied to the sales value or production for the month in question. The difference between the resulting figure and the actual payroll constitutes the savings in labor cost for the month. Thus, if the historical norm is 35 percent, in any month in which products worth $100 have been produced at a payroll cost of $30, the savings amount to $5 ($35 minus $30). Part of the savings, generally 25 percent, is put aside as a reserve to cover those instances where actual labor costs may be greater than the norm in any particular month. The rest is split, 25 percent going to the company and 75 percent being paid out immediately to participating employees. At the end of the year, if the reserve is greater than all of the deficits incurred during the year, the remainder is shared by the company and employees in the same proportion as the monthly payments.

The total savings to be distributed to employees may be calculated as a percentage of payroll and the percentage thus obtained applied to each employee's earnings to determine his share. Thus, if the share of savings going to all employees is 5 percent of the total payroll for the month, each employee will get 5 percent of his earnings for the month. However, under some plans, where the norm is also defined in terms of the ratio of labor costs to sales value, the total amount going to labor is divided by the number of hours worked and a uniform increase in wage rates is paid to each employee for each hour worked.

Role of Committees

Theoretically, the rise in productivity, leading to lower labor costs, is a result of higher morale, a greater sense of participation, and better motivation rather than a speedup in the usual sense. Allegedly, the rise in efficiency is brought about chiefly by suggestions as to how time and effort can be saved. These suggestions are processed by joint Production Committees for each department and an overall Screening Committee. The committees, whose function it is to encourage, develop, and implement suggestions, are of central importance in the Scanlon Plan.

The above may sound complicated, but in reality is quite simple, provided that the management and labor have a complete trust in one another. (This is very important because if there isn't complete trust, the plan cannot be effective.)

With regard to the IAM's view of the Scanlon Plan, the following observations are offered:

1. In spite of its somewhat unique nature the Scanlon Plan is purely and simply a work measurement and wage incentive plan. Disputes will arise during the life of the agreement and during negotiations, where the Plan is in effect, just as is true with any other work measurement and wage incentive plan.

2. Under an individual incentive plan each operator works at his or her own pace depending on personal preferences. Workers tend not to be too concerned when fellow workers "goof off." This is not the case under a group incentive plan such as the Scanlon Plan. A good deal of "self-policing" takes place. Indeed, one of the primary objections to any group incentive plan is its inherently divisive effect upon the work force. We believe that it is unhealthy for workers to be placed in a position of policing fellow workers.

3. The Production Committee and the Screening Committee, while they are not in theory a substitute for the grievance committee and the bargaining committee, may in fact assume a more important role in the eyes of the membership. It is easy to speculate about the impact of such an eventuality upon the local union.

4. Legitimate grievances may go unprocessed and unsolved because workers will hesitate to disrupt the production process. That is, grievances take the aggrieved and the steward away from their respective workplaces thereby adding to labor cost without increasing production.

5. During contract negotiations, in addition to all the other issues which must be resolved, there must be recalculation of the productivity ratio. If the recalculated ratio does not accurately and fully reflect the impact of improved wages and fringe benefits, the members of the bargaining unit will end up paying for their own bonus.

6. There is an assumption under any system, be it individual or group, that incentive earnings are as much a part of gross earnings as base pay. Therefore, it is common practice to use average incentive earnings as the basis for computing vacation pay. Under the Scanlon Plan bonus earnings do not apply to vacation pay. This means that workers incur an earnings penalty when they take their vacation. It also means that the more senior the worker the greater the penalty. The union, in essence, negotiates against itself. In the process of trying to obtain longer vacations for its members it, in effect, negotiates reduced gross earnings.

7. It is generally accepted that the more direct and immediate the relationship between a worker's effort and ingenuity and the resultant incentive payment or bonus the more effective the system. The relationship between a worker's productivity and the bonus, under the Scanlon Plan, is very remote. Not only that, but many factors beyond the worker's control, including production processes, demand, management efficiency, and quality of materials, help determine the extent of savings. Total sales, for instance, may be affected by seasonal demand

for the product or by the marketing skills of the firm. Since most low to middle income families budget their income to the hilt it is difficult to make adjustment for unexpected declines in income. Yet that is precisely what can happen under the Scanlon Plan.

8. One way to increase the bonus is to reduce the size of the labor force while maintaining output and sales at previous levels and while leaving the productivity ratio unchanged. From the company's point of view this would obviously be desirable. In the short run it may be desirable for the worker. But the concept of a fair day's work which emerges under such circumstances may be untenable in the long run. Remember, under the Scanlon Plan *all* jobs are on incentive. There are no indirect labor jobs which older workers can turn to, as would be the case under individual incentive standards, when incentive jobs are too strenuous.

9. Finally, for the Scanlon Plan to be of any benefit to the employee, the broadest base of employee participation must be sought. All work units must be represented by the production committees so that problems, which could divide workers, may be thoroughly discussed. It goes without saying, that workers' representatives should be appointed or elected through the union. These representatives should have access to company records that are used to establish or adjust bonus ratios.

Rucker Share-of-Production Plan
The Rucker plan is similar to the Scanlon plan in philosophy but is based upon much more sophisticated analysis. A historical relationship is established between total earnings (including indirect compensation) of hourly rated employees and production value created by the company. If major changes in products or production process occur, the plan is re-engineered. Because of the careful analysis that goes into the original ratio, adjustments occur less often than in a Scanlon plan.

An economic engineering audit of several years of past operation is conducted, including a detailed study of approximately two years, broken down by monthly operating results. Production value added by the company is sales value of output less cost of raw materials purchased and related costs such as supplies and power. A standard productivity ratio is calculated which expresses the amount of production value required for each $1.00 in wages paid including benefits. The productivity ratio also determines production shares, that is, the share of production attributable to labor and the share due the company. The analysis is conducted for each plant.

Assume that the company put $.55 worth of materials, supplies, and power into production to obtain a product worth $1.00. Value added or production value is thus $.45 for each $1.00 of sales value. Assume also that analysis shows that 40 percent of production value is attributable to labor. The productivity ratio becomes 2.5, and for a payroll (plus benefits) of $100,000 standard production value is $250,000. If actual production value for the month is $300,000, a gain of $50,000 is available for bonus and is distributed 40 percent to labor and 60 percent to the company. Labor's bonus share for the month is $20,000. Actually, 25 percent of the gain in any month is placed in a reserve account to offset months with poor results. The reserve account is distributed at the end of the year. The $20,000 bonus fund is distributed pro rata to individuals on the basis of their regular pay (including overtime and shift differential) for the month.

The plan is most often applied to production workers, but it may be developed to cover all the employees in the company. Analysis determines standard shares of production value for each group or team. A common arrangement is to determine the shares of the employee team (all hourly rated employees) and the company. The Rucker plan provides an integrated incentive to reduce costs of producing the same production value or produce a greater production value for the same costs. All savings go to the groups covered on the basis of their share of production value.

Employee committees are used to obtain and appraise suggestions for improvements in production costs. Typical "share of production" committees consist of worker representatives from each major department plus a lesser number of shop supervisors. Usually there are two chairmen, a top executive, and the union president. Committee members may serve terms of one year, or shorter periods may be specified to bring in new ideas.

Apparently these committees achieve results quite similar to those found under Scanlon plans. One study reports that committee members in successful Rucker plans are just as aggressive and critical of poor management as in Scanlon plan companies. It appears that the results and problems in Rucker plans are very similar to those existing in Scanlon plans. One difference may be that Rucker plans have been successfully added to existing individual incentive plans.

In summary, the IAM is very skeptical about any type of profit-sharing and/or group incentive plan. IAM negotiators are urged to avoid any system of indirect wage payment which is dependent upon factors over which the employee has little or no control. Instead, bargaining should center on obtaining single rates of pay for all job classifications. These rates should reflect skill level, labor market conditions, comparable rates of pay in the industry, the rising cost of living, improved productivity, and the need to increase a worker's real purchasing power.

Another example of the position of organized labor toward gainsharing is the following list of guidelines developed by Donald E. Rand, now retired administrative assistant to the secretary-treasurer of the UAW. These guidelines were issued to assist UAW locals in discussing Scanlon Plans with the Dana Corporation.

It is our intent to work with the company on a continuing basis in fashioning and developing our experiences in the so-called quality-of-work-life programs in which both the union and the company are cooperating. Insofar as the Scanlon Plan is concerned we have established a number of guidelines:

    1. Under no circumstances may a Scanlon-type incentive plan be substituted for a collective bargaining agreement with an equitable wage structure.

2. A bonus received from a Scanlon-type plan should not be considered as regular wages. In the collective bargaining agreement a fair and equitable wage rate should be established for all classifications without consideration to additional earnings obtained through a bonus system.
3. When management approaches a bargaining unit with a proposition for establishing an incentive plan, the local union officials should immediately contact their international representative and the UAW department involved.
4. If an incentive plan is established in a facility, it should be understood that such a plan affects wages and fringe benefits and is properly the subject matter for collective bargaining.
5. A bonus plan should be established on the basis that it will provide an opportunity for employees to achieve additional earnings over and above the negotiated wage rate established for a classification.
6. In plants where there is an incentive program and the parties agree to implement a Scanlon-type bonus system, it will be necessary for the company and the union to establish rates of pay for incentive classification based upon the average incentive earnings by classification or department. These new rates should fully protect the earnings of incentive workers. Bonuses earned under the Scanlon Plan will be based upon these new rates.
7. The agreement should provide that a third-party consultant be used in the development and installation of a new Scanlon Plan and that such third-party consultant be retained in order to insure that the original concept of the plan is being followed.
8. It must be clearly understood that such a plan does not conflict with, supersede, or in any way interfere with the collective bargaining agreement.
9. Union matters should not be discussed during the so-called screening and production committee meetings scheduled for the purpose of Scanlon Plan discussions.
10. The plan should include a provision whereby the union may, upon request, obtain the services of an outside certified public accountant to audit the company's records to determine if the financial data being provided is correct.

Unfortunately, in many instances, companies place great emphasis on the need to increase productivity, improve plant performance and efficiency, and so forth. We do not believe that it is necessary to judge these programs based upon an increased work pace. We agree with Mr. Ren McPherson, Chairman of the Board of the Dana Corporation, that "we can work smarter instead of harder."

Programs which we have advocated should result in a reduction of absenteeism, lower labor turnover, improved product quality, fewer grievances, and less discipline; but, above all, such programs must assure that workers are treated fairly and honestly.

Roy Ockert, research director for the International Woodworkers of America, had firsthand experience with the Rucker Plan while he was with the Rubber Workers Union. On the basis of this experience, he prepared three papers in 1972 pertaining to gainsharing. The first, an introduction to gainsharing, is presented below. The second is a sample memorandum of agreement, which appears in Appendix C. The third is a sample of a memorandum regarding the conducting of a joint feasibility study and is also reprinted in Appendix C.

PRODUCTIVITY SHARING PLANS

Workers in virtually every industry have been aware for years of the onrush of technology. Hand-powered crosscut saws long ago were supplanted by power saws and this is only a bare beginning of a recounting of the numerous changes that have been wrought in logging operations, sawmills, planer mills, plywood plants, etc. And all of them have resulted in vastly increased productivity.

Wage rates and benefits have increased also but employment in the industry has decreased. It is quite possible that—if the basic data were available—we would find in company after company that the percentage share workers receive from the value of the product they produce had declined. Studies of other industries have shown this to be true.

The economy, as a consequence, suffers because wealth and income become concentrated into fewer hands. The income of people who spend all, or nearly all, of their money on consumer goods fails to keep up with the ability to produce. The result is a relatively stagnant economy and a large number of chronically unemployed individuals and families. Employment of production and maintenance workers in the lumber and wood products industry in the United States in 1950 was 745,000. In 1972 it is less than 500,000. The decline was steady and steep over the 20-year period.

One possible way of solving this problem is a "production sharing" plan. . . . It can be applied companywide, plantwide, or departmentally.

The income derived from productivity sharing plans has been exempted from control by the Pay Board. The bonus does not, however, take the place of wage increases—a negotiated basic wage increase should also take effect every year. The "share of production bonus" would be in addition to the negotiated increase.

Experience indicates the plan would be viable for about ten years.

If a local union decides to investigate the possibility of installing a productivity sharing plan, there should first be a study made by a union economist. If the idea looks like it might be worthwhile, the union could sign an "engineering study memorandum." If this study showed enough potential advantages, the union then might include language in the collective bargaining agreement as a section, article, or addendum.

Another trend worth noting began in 1980 and started to pick up momentum in 1981. In 1980, Chrysler Corporation negotiated wage concessions with the UAW as a condition for obtaining government-guaranteed loans to keep the company out of bankruptcy. Part of the quid pro quo for the concessions were profit sharing and a UAW seat on the board of directors. As the 1981 recession deepened, more companies began to seek wage concessions. While labor's reactions to wage concessions were quite mixed, profit and productivity sharing began to be heard with some regularity in wage-concession discussions.

While the ideas suggested in the preceding documents do not follow all the guidelines proposed in this book, they do reflect some of the essential principles of gainsharing: workers and owners sharing productivity gains and greater employee involvement. The evidence points to a conclusion that gainsharing is acceptable in principle to organized labor. However, there is also ample evidence of workers' caution, skepticism, and resistance to the techniques and methods used to implement these principles.

It is not likely that a formal and uniform position regarding gainsharing will emerge from organized labor in the near future. However, it is likely that more and more unions will explore the possibilities in gainsharing and that some of them will become knowledgeable and willing partners in gainsharing programs.

A Recipe for Labor/Management Planning

In most cases, management is the first to consider gainsharing. As described in Chapter 8, management usually conducts a feasibility study, and if it favors the gainsharing idea, it approaches the union with an invitation. The invitation should be to begin a joint labor/management effort to explore the possibility of developing a mutually beneficial gainsharing program. Joint labor/management committees to explore productivity improvement and quality-of-work-life improvements are becoming more and more common. Batt and Weinberg provide a good description of the current status of joint labor/management cooperation in their article "Labor-Management Cooperation Today" (see Bibliography). It is doubtful that union leaders will have had any prior gainsharing experience, so they will need time and assistance to become familiar with the idea and their role in the joint effort.

The leadership of each local union will react to management's invitation according to what it perceives to be the best interests of its organization and membership. These perceptions will be strongly influenced by past experience and the nature of the invitation. With some precautions and sensitivity to the union position, management can present a proposal to the union that will result in a successful joint effort. There are several issues for management to consider in preparing to present a gainsharing proposal to the union.

THE UNION ORGANIZATION

The local union leaders are part of a large organization and must communicate up and down in the process of making decisions. Sometimes this process is slow, but it must run its course if effective decisions are to be made. If management becomes impatient or tries to force a decision, resistance and mistrust of management's motives will result. Unions are political organizations with frequent elections. Thus, local leaders must be cautious in approaching a joint labor/management project to prevent any appearance that they have compromised their trust in an effort to cooperate with management.

BONUSES

Bonuses over an adequate base pay and benefit level are clearly an advantage to union members and will be supported by union leaders. Any effort to trade a bonus for previously won wages and benefits or to offer a bonus in lieu of an increase in wages and benefits will be resisted by the union. Exceptions to this rule are possible only in the most adverse circumstances.

PARTICIPATION

Union leaders favor more influence for their members in the work situation. They can be expected to view participation as an advantage. However, unions have also seen participation programs turn into excessive peer pressure among their members, which they will not endorse. Union leaders will therefore approach the participation system with caution.

MANAGEMENT

Union leaders will not resist a proposal that includes "better management." But, on the basis of past experience, they can be expected to be skeptical and take the Missouri attitude of "Show me."

UNION SECURITY

The unions have experienced or heard of many examples of "new" programs being used by management to counter organizing efforts or to weaken an established union. The union will be protective of its status and its right to organize. A successful joint effort not only must avoid anything that threatens the union status but must also include a benefit for the union as an organization. The support of local union leaders is essential to the successful implementation and maintenance of a gainsharing program. They should therefore play a key role in developing and sustaining the program. Ex officio participation in feasibility studies and steering and policy committees is usually required.

CONTRACT SECURITY

Another cause for concern to the union will be that gainsharing may interfere with, or in some way weaken the strength of, the collective-bargaining agreement. Though productivity is not a negotiable issue, the integrity of the labor contract must be protected in any truly joint effort. In successful gainsharing programs, both labor and management carefully maintain a respectful distance between contract issues and gainsharing issues. Grievances are handled by the grievance procedure; suggestions go through the participation system; and neither overlaps.

One situation to avoid is starting a joint planning effort just prior to the expiration of one contract and negotiations for the next. It is virtually impossible for the union to view an invitation to consider gainsharing just prior to negotiations as anything but an attempt by management to influence the collective-bargaining process. When this has been tried, the union invariably reacts defensively to the invitation. This defensive posture makes it impossible for the union to engage in a cooperative joint effort. With negotiations on the horizon, the joint planning effort should wait until the contract has been negotiated and settled. The intention to engage in a joint labor/management planning effort can be discussed during negotiations and even noted in the signed agreement but should not become a bargaining issue.

In Appendix C are two examples of memorandums of agreement that have been used to identify the joint project and clarify its relationship to the labor contract. There is also an example of a memorandum pertaining to a joint feasibility study. A written agreement just to conduct a feasibility study is very rare, but the mere fact that a union would make such a formal request reflects the union's concern for protecting the collective-bargaining agreement.

EMPLOYMENT SECURITY

Increasing labor productivity by definition means reducing the labor cost content of goods and/or services produced by the organization. This means that some work will be eliminated. Because the union is committed to protecting jobs, this aspect of gainsharing is in conflict with one of its fundamental goals. Management should be prepared to deal with this issue early in any joint planning. Crucial to obtaining union support for any plan will be a provision for adequate employment security for union members. This issue is not insurmountable; employment security is one of the results of a successful gainsharing program. An increase in productivity makes a company more competitive and therefore more secure for employees and investors alike. Not to increase productivity in a competitive environment is a much greater risk to employment security. In the early 1980s, there were one million people out of work because of the productivity problems in the automobile industry.

As the company becomes more productive and more competitive, it is possible to increase market share, which provides new work to replace work that was eliminated. An increase in profit resulting from the company's gainshare provides more funds for advertising, new product development, and capital investment, all of which improve employment security.

Neither the company nor the union can provide employment security against recessions, declining markets, product obsolescence, or major technological advances. There can be no guarantees at the plant level against such uncontrollables as OPEC, the failure of a major customer, new inventions such as the integrated circuit, or government policy. The best any organization can do is to be as strong and flexible as possible and make quick strategic changes to react to such outside events.

But, under normal circumstances, a guarantee of no loss of employment due to gainsharing productivity improvements is not only necessary; it is quite feasible. Seldom will a gainsharing program result in job elimination greater than the company's attrition or turnover rate. An occasional major suggestion might result in some surplus people for a few months until they are absorbed by attrition, but this is a small price to pay for a major savings. This cost must be weighed against the potential savings and the possibility that the savings would not have occurred at all without the gainsharing program. A gainsharing program assumes that sooner or later an employee will come up with the ultimate suggestion: the elimination of his or her own job. Such a suggestion will be made only within the framework of a guarantee that the suggester does not go directly to the unemployment rolls.

Another feature of the employment-security provision is to give employees whose jobs have been eliminated preference in the bidding process and a temporary rate guarantee—usually six to nine months—until they can bid back to a job at or above their old rate. This issue will be a major obstacle for the union considering gainsharing, but experience has shown that a workable solution is entirely possible.

ACCURACY OF INFORMATION

Most unions feel that management is not completely honest in reporting costs, profit, and loss information. Accurate, honest, and reliable information is necessary to a successful gainsharing program. Practices such as reporting widget scrap at the $10 sales price rather than at the $3 actual cost at the time the widget was scrapped do not lead to confidence in management information. On the other hand, management does at times have a legitimate need to prevent competitors and customers from knowing certain cost information. Depending on past experiences and the business situation, management must be prepared to show how its gainsharing information will be accurate and reliable.

Summary

Unions have been brought into a cooperative and sustaining role in many gainsharing programs. Although data are unavailable, it can be safely assumed that unions have also rejected invitations to participate in joint gainsharing projects. Because productivity and organization development are properly the responsibility of management, it is appropriate that management initiate a gainsharing program. Experience has shown that considerably more progress can be made in improving productivity and organization effectiveness when all employees cooperate in a joint effort. Where employees are represented by a labor union, management must bring the union into a joint effort to develop and implement a successful gainsharing program. To create an effective joint labor/management gainsharing effort, management must be aware of and sensitive to the past experience, the caution, and the needs of the union.

Chapter 13

Gainsharing in the Service Sector

There is a myth circulating that gainsharing is applicable only in manufacturing plants, and small ones at that. The rumor is so persistent that organizations in the service sector—including retail, repairs, personal services, health, construction, education, finance, utilities, insurance, transportation, hotels, insurance, food services, and government—believe that gainsharing programs do not apply to them. Some service-sector organizations have been window shopping, but so far, very few have bought the idea. Service-sector personnel accounted for about 20 percent of the attendance at the 1980–81 gainsharing seminars conducted by the American Productivity Center.

The answer to "Does gainsharing apply in the service sector?" is that gainsharing applies in any organization where people work and where productivity is a concern. Many people work in the service sector, and productivity is a growing concern for these organizations.

The service sector now employs the bulk of our labor force and is the least productive. Some of the productivity lag in the service sector is due to a lack of capital equipment and tools to support the knowledge and service workers. Of the three major economic sectors in the United States, farming is the most productive; manufacturing is second; and the service sector is a distant third. As measured in dollar value, farm workers have 15 times more—and manufacturing workers have 10 times more—capital equipment and tools than service-sector workers to help them do their jobs. The electronic revolution will change this in the decade to come, but for now, the service sector is substantially behind in productivity-enhancing tools.

Readiness for Gainsharing

The service sector is very labor-intensive and, thus, is probably a better candidate for a gainsharing solution than the other sectors. Managers in the service sector are aware of the labor-intensive nature of their work and have been exploring human or organizational solutions to their problems for the past 20 years. Management development and organization development are just as prevalent in the service sector as in manufacturing. The military, led by our nuclear navy, has been a pioneer in the application of behavioral science to management practices and group processes. A few hospitals and secondary school systems have explored efforts to improve effectiveness by upgrading their management practices.

Employee participation seems to be almost second nature in the service sector. Knowledge workers, who make up a large percentage of service-sector employees, must interact with each other to a far greater extent than manual workers. Staff meetings, task forces, and committees are utilized in the service sector with much greater frequency and involve a larger percentage of the workforce than in manufacturing. Highly trained technical, scientific, and professional specialists are essential to decision making in many service-sector areas and therefore participate more actively in the process. Whereas participation is considered innovative in the manufacturing sector, it is normal in the service sector.

The only gainsharing element missing completely is the shared reward. If service-sector organizations are this close to gainsharing, why don't more of them try it? The answer is that the shared reward is a formidable obstacle for the service sector, and until it is overcome, it is not likely that many will attempt gainsharing programs.

For service-sector organizations to develop shared rewards, they will have to address the major management and organizational weakness in the service sector: performance. Service-sector organizations are activity-oriented rather than performance- or goal-oriented. Whereas industrial organizations are guided by entrepreneurial thinking, service organizations are dominated by professional, technical, and skilled-worker thinking. The work orientation in many service fields is more toward accuracy and correctness than toward productivity. How the work is done is seen as more important than the results of the work. Although this is normal in the evolution of work, it is still a problem: Productivity is low.

When new work is introduced in any sector, correct procedure is emphasized rather than results. The key to success is to first learn to do it right, then learn to do it more productively. Most service-sector work is relatively new and changing rapidly, which keeps it in a perpetual state of learning to do it right. The biggest danger in this situation is that the activity orientation can become habitual, and there are indications that this may be happening. There are signs that service-sector organizations are resisting efforts to increase productivity—that they want to maintain the activity focus and not be held accountable for results. Chief among these signs are resistance to productivity measurements and resistance to performance-reward practices.

Measuring the productivity of human work is not easy in any sector and is even more difficult in the service sector. The manufacturing sector, of course, is the leader in the field of measuring performance and productivity. However, there are two reasons why manufacturing is ahead of the service sector in this respect. First, manufacturing has been at it longer, and necessity produced the work-measurement techniques of Frederick Taylor and others long before the need existed in the service sector. Second, it is easier to measure the work of widget makers than the work of planners, analysts, and other service-sector knowledge workers. The problem in the service sector is that although the reasons for not measuring productivity were once valid, they are now being used as an excuse. Too many service-sector managers, finding it difficult to measure productivity, have interpreted difficult to mean impossible. They aren't even trying to do it.

Drucker devotes four chapters of his book *Management: Tasks, Responsibilities, Practices* to the issue of performance in the service sector and portions of other chapters to the performance and productivity of the knowledge worker. He states very clearly that if we want the service sector and the knowledge worker to be productive, we must make their jobs as specific as the job of the widget maker. We must define performance and contribution for these jobs and stop making excuses for not doing so.

The service sector could learn a great deal from the manufacturing sector, but the transfer of knowledge has been very slow. There is a tendency on the part of service organizations to view all manufacturing experience as not applicable, stemming from a type of arrogance that regards factory methods as out of place in the operating room or office. It is true that some experience does not transfer well from factory to office, but some experience does, and we must let this transfer occur when it is useful to do so. Techniques such as setting performance standards, work sampling, and work-flow analysis are just as applicable to service work as to the manufacturing sector and should be used.

Another sign of resistance to productivity measurement in the service sector is reward practices. Reward management is not a very well practiced art in any sector but is handled somewhat worse in the service sector. Salaries and wages are determined not by contribution or as a reward for performance but almost exclusively by competitive pressures. Every organization has a need to pay competitive wages in order to attract and retain its workforce. This practice results in a situation where every organization is following the pack, and no one is leading. It is a lemminglike activity. Manufacturers are just as competitive in their pay practices but include additional criteria in the process. They do a better job of matching performance to pay and of limiting pay to the organization's ability to pay. Because they do a better job of measuring performance, industrial organizations receive more performance from employees for each dollar of pay. And because competitive pricing limits the revenue of manufacturing companies, payroll costs tend to stay within the company's ability to pay. Many service-sector organizations are monopolies and are not controlled by any competitive pressures.

Every organization talks about pay for performance, and most have merit pay systems intended to implement that principle. However, most so-called merit pay systems are fictional. A close examination of actual pay practices shows that annual salary decisions are based on competitive pressure, tenure, and cost-of-living indexes. People ask for and are given raises because the organization next door got a raise, or because a year has passed, or because the cost of living has gone up. Rewards for performance or the withholding of rewards for nonperformance seldom actually occur.

Cost-of-living pay increases are the worst of the pay practices. Cost-of-living increases reward nothing, are not based on the organization's ability to pay, and send the employees a subtle message that productivity and performance are not necessary. Cost-of-living indexing makes sense only for programs like Social Security and for retirement benefits. Our contract with retired employees is to provide them with a benefit that will enable them to live at a certain standard of living as a reward for long years of productive service. Retired people can no longer influence productivity, so their reward should not be dependent on it. But people who are actively employed create the value that pays their wages, and they cannot receive more than they produce without doing great harm to the system.

Automatic annual adjustment makes no more sense than cost-of-living adjustments. The only ways an organization can obtain more money for annual salary adjustments are to increase output (revenue) or reduce inputs (costs), which means increasing productivity. Unless an organization can automatically increase productivity, it simply cannot afford automatic annual adjustments. Since increasing productivity means working harder or smarter, or both, annual increases should only come as a result of working harder or smarter, or both.

To make any serious progress with their productivity problems, service-sector organizations must significantly change their thinking about measuring performance and rewarding productivity.

The gainsharing bonus—properly constructed—is a reward for performance and cannot be otherwise. The introduction of such a bonus will begin the process of rewarding performance where and when it occurs. Once pay for performance is in place and fully understood by the organization, it could be extended to other reward practices. Gainsharing offers a practical way to introduce this principle in the service sector.

Prospects for Gainsharing

It would appear that the service sector has some of the elements for successful gainsharing. Management practices are at least as good as in manufacturing, and employee participation is already more advanced. Though service organizations lack specific performance and productivity measures, gainsharing may be more feasible in the service sector than it would seem to be at first glance. Gainsharing, to be successful, does not require individual performance and productivity measurements. The productivity measures necessary for gainsharing are organizationwide output/input measures, which are easier to develop than individual measures.

Many service-sector organizations already have the information necessary to determine a base productivity level. Commercial enterprises in the service sector, both profit and not-for-profit, can define output as sales or revenue. Cost data for labor, materials, supplies, and purchased services are available. The existing information is probably adequate for use in a gainsharing program. This is true at least for retail, food service, transportation, construction, and finance organizations as well as hospitals and utilities.

Government and schools face a more difficult challenge, because they lack a sales figure to define output. But even in these areas, some definition of output seems possible. Schools should be able to use student population (full-time equivalent) as an output measure. Government agencies should be able to define a level of service with a combination of statistical and qualitative statements as output. In both cases, historical or budgeted costs can be used as the input for a productivity measure. While some outputs and some costs may not be usable, the odds are quite good that enough of each are now available to provide a satisfactory measure of productivity for gainsharing.

Efforts are under way to develop more useful productivity measures in the service sector. Here are some studies now available:

"Research and Development Productivity" (1978)
Hughes Aircraft
Culver City, California

"Measuring Productivity in Physical Distribution" (1978)
National Council of Physical Distribution Management
Chicago, Illinois

"A National Strategy for Improving
  Productivity in Building and Construction" (1980)
National Academy of Sciences
Washington, D.C.

"Aetna/Loma Productivity Measurement Project" (1980)
James S. Devlin
Aetna Life Insurance Company
Hartford, Connecticut

"Work Sampling Program Handbook" (1979)
Auditing Department
Detroit Edison Comapny
Detroit, Michigan

"Dimensions of Productivity Research—
  Several Papers on Various Aspects of
  Service Sector Productivity" (1980)
American Productivity Center
Houston, Texas

Even though it has not been tried, gainsharing is as applicable in the service sector as it is in manufacturing. While it is true that there are virtually no models to guide this development in the service sector, it must be remembered that this was once true of manufacturing. Today we have a good deal of gainsharing experience in manufacturing due to the pioneering efforts of some early risk takers. Service-sector pioneers are now needed.

A final comment has to do with the principles of gainsharing. Gainsharing is a strategy, not a technique. Service-sector organizations should not try to copy manufacturing-sector techniques; they should explore the use of the principles of participative management, employee participation, and shared rewards and develop new techniques that are appropriate to their own situations.

Examples for Service Organizations

The following are a few somewhat speculative scenarios that might apply in the service sector.

RESTAURANT

Management practices:
- Clarify organization goals to provide clear direction for everyone.
- Provide cost, quality, and volume information for use in problem solving.
- Provide customer feedback information for recognition of good performance and for problem solving.
- Provide effective training and coaching for individual and group performance.
- Encourage employee participation and provide proper structure.

Employee participation:
First-, second-, or third-degree system to facilitate employee participation and problem solving.

Reward:

$$\frac{\text{Output}}{\text{Input}} \text{, namely } \frac{\text{Total sales } + \text{ a quality measurement}}{\text{Cost of labor, food, supplies}}$$

Share:
Variable, depending on inputs used in the productivity base.

HOSPITAL

Management practices:
- Clarify organization goals to provide clear direction for everyone.
- Provide cost, quality, and service information for use in problem solving.
- Provide patient and doctor feedback for recognition of good performance and for problem solving.
- Provide effective training and coaching for individual and group performance.
- Encourage employee participation and provide proper structure.

Employee participation:
First-, second-, or third-degree system to facilitate employee participation and problem solving. Second- or third-degree systems should be built around the multidisciplinary nature of patient care. Group problem solving may need to be two-dimensional: one dimension for specialties such as nursing, food service, and pharmacy and the second dimension comprised of all disciplines serving one wing, floor, or other patient group. Very large hospitals using a second-degree system may need a tri-level structure as described in Chapter 6, with an all-hospital senior committee and intermediate committees in major areas.

Reward:

$$\frac{\text{Output}}{\text{Input}} \text{ , namely } \frac{\text{Total revenue}}{\text{Cost of labor, materials, supplies}}$$

Where insurance companies reimburse for actual costs, it would be necessary to negotiate a standard reimbursement rate.

Share:
Variable, according to inputs used in the productivity base.

BANK

Management practices:
○ Clarify organization goals to provide clear direction for everyone.
○ Provide cost and revenue information for problem solving.
○ Provide customer-service feedback for recognition of good performance and for problem solving.
○ Provide effective training and coaching for individual and group performance.
○ Encourage employee participation and provide proper structure.

Employee participation:
First-, second-, or third-degree system to facilitate employee participation and problem solving. Branches and functional departments are ideally suited to a third-degree work-team structure.

Reward:

$$\frac{\text{Output}}{\text{Input}} \text{ , namely } \frac{\text{Total revenues (interest, fees, investments)}}{\text{Cost of labor, supplies, capital}}$$

Larger banks may treat commercial, individual, trust, and credit card operations as separate businesses, each with its own gainsharing program, provided there is little overlap and interdependence.

Share:
Variable, according to inputs used in the productivity base.

GOVERNMENT

Management practices:
○ Clarify organization goals to provide clear direction for everyone.
○ Provide cost and budget information for use in problem solving.
○ Γ ovide user feedback for recognition of good performance and for problem solving.

○ Provide effective training and coaching for individual and group performance.
○ Encourage employee participation and provide proper structure.

Employee participation:
○ First-, second-, or third-degree system to facilitate employee participation and problem solving.
○ Structure should consider frequent leadership changes among elected officials.
○ Structure may need to accommodate appointed boards, citizen advisory groups, and special-interest groups.

Reward:

$$\frac{\text{Output}}{\text{Input}} \text{, namely } \frac{\text{Specific quantity and quality of service valued at cost as budgeted}}{\text{Cost of labor, materials, supplies}}$$

Defining services for output measure may be difficult, but it is also extremely valuable for employee direction and for citizen support. Larger government bodies may need to define separate gainsharing units with different productivity measures, provided there is little or no interdependence or overlap. A large parks department may be an ideal gainsharing unit, especially if it has its own police and fire service. In a smaller jurisdiction, where the parks department receives service from separate police and fire departments, it may be better to have all in a single gainsharing program because of the need for collaboration and mutual influence.

Historical data may provide some productivity benchmarks, but the productivity base should probably be the budget.

Share:
Variable, according to inputs used in the productivity base. Organization share should be used to offset future costs, to reduce tax rates, to defer future tax increases, or as a refund to the taxpayers.

Note:
Because of the difficulty of obtaining voter approval for bonuses in the public sector, any effort to use gainsharing in government organizations should be very deliberate, use publicity extensively, and have visible citizen input to feasibility studies, design, and development.

Summary

Gainsharing is applicable wherever people work and productivity is important. It is not more or less difficult to apply gainsharing principles in either the manufacturing or service sector. The only difference is that there happen to be more examples of success and failure in the manufacturing sector. The service sector must become more productive, and gainsharing is one approach that should be explored in an effort to solve its productivity problems.

Twenty years ago the experts were asking whether gainsharing could be extended to larger manufacturing organizations and whether it was applicable in a variety of untested circumstances. (See Katz and Kahn in Bibliography, and also Shultz's chapter in *The Scanlon Plan* by Lesieur.) These questions have now been answered affirmatively, and the plan is being used in larger organizations today and under a variety of circumstances. The questions about applicability in the service sector will also be resolved in time.

Chapter 14

Why Gainsharing?

The technique of gainsharing has been explored, but what about the most important question: Why gainsharing? Is gainsharing just another in a long list of programs that have strutted their hour upon the industrial stage, to be heard no more? Are there reasons suggesting that gainsharing will be any better than the 25 other programs we have tried over the last 25 years? Is gainsharing any better than Theory Y or MBO or work simplification? Will it work any better than Quality Circles or cafeteria fringe benefits?

The answer to all these questions is that gainsharing is a better program. Gainsharing, properly applied, can solve the problems of lagging productivity and sagging quality of work life. Gainsharing is a truly innovative program, and the innovation is not in techniques. Gainsharing is innovative because it goes to the root of our organizational problems, whereas other programs have dealt with symptoms, secondary causes, or only part of the problem. The root cause to which gainsharing is directed is the fundamental relationship between labor and capital in an industrial society. We have inherited a value that labor and owners of capital are natural adversaries—which is absurd and also a very costly value to maintain. Tremendous damage, from hurt feelings to wars, has been done to people under the banners of the rights of capital and the rights of labor.

How absurd to hold that capital can produce anything without labor. How absurd to hold that labor can produce anything but wild roots and berries without capital. How absurd to have organizations in which small groups of employees receive security, information, and the right to influence what goes on, while the rest of the human resources are treated as things, only capable of manual labor, with much less security and very little influence.

We have a productivity problem in U.S. industry. The productivity of the American economy grew at a healthy 3 percent clip from 1945 to 1967. In 1967, the rate of increase began to slow until it turned negative in 1981. At the same time, the productivity of other industrialized nations continued to grow at rates faster than that of the United States. The experts tell us that U.S. productivity will be surpassed during the 1980s by Japan, France, Canada, and Germany. American companies in industries such as shoes, TV, steel, and automobiles have already been passed in the productivity race.

We have a quality-of-work-life problem in U.S. industry. The media have bombarded us with reports of blue collar blues; white collar woes; mechanics' malaise; burnout; stress; and general, all-around "don't give a damnism." National studies conducted over the past 12 years by the Institute for Social Research at the University of Michigan confirm this. Their conclusion, which has a stronger data base than most of the popular articles, is that there *is* a worker-alienation problem. And though it is not as severe as the media proclaim, it is getting worse.

Gainsharing is not proposed as a solution to these national problems. But for an organization with problems of productivity, motivation, or quality of work life, gainsharing is recommended as a strategy for dealing with them.

The three major gainsharing features—improved management practices, employee participation, and productivity-based shared rewards—are similar to features found in other programs. But gainsharing, unlike other approaches, combines these features into a single, comprehensive response to problems of productivity and quality of work life. This is another innovative aspect of gainsharing: the integration of all of the major factors of success and organizational excellence into one comprehensive package.

Labor/Management Cooperation

Labor/management cooperation is not a feature or an element of gainsharing; it is the essence; it is the tap root and value base from which all other features take their form and derive their strength.

Management, as used here, is synonymous with *owners* and *capital.* Although managers are also employees, their job is to represent the interests of owners. As such, managers are the visible signs of owners and capital in the relationship with labor. Today's generation of managers and employees have inherited the idea that management and labor are natural adversaries. We should not carry that notion into the future. There is no evidence in the nature of organizations that management and labor, employers and employees must be adversaries. In fact, the opposite is true. There is much in the nature of organizations to support the idea that management and labor must be, and in fact are, partners. Research by

Likert and by Blake and Mouton shows that adversarial organizations are low in productivity and quality of work life, and that the more cooperative, participative, and teamlike organizations are stronger, produce better, and enjoy a higher quality of work life.

John Bates Clark, an American economist, suggested early in this century that the struggle between labor and management would proceed through four stages: from competition, to arbitration, to sharing, to cooperation. It would appear in the United States that we are somewhat beyond competition, well into the arbitration stage, and starting into the sharing phase with programs such as gainsharing. Clark's model would also suggest that there is a further stage of cooperation to be realized. In gainsharing, this has been achieved by a few companies using an effective long-term development plan as suggested in Chapter 11.

M. Scott Myers, in *Managing with Unions* (see Bibliography), shows that management and labor are quick to abandon their traditional conflict when faced with a mutual crisis. He also describes a new program of the Federal Mediation and Conciliation Service, called Relationships by Objectives (RBO). He attributes the success of this program to its tapping a fundamental commonality of interest between management and labor that exists in every firm.

We must develop in our organizations a new spirit of cooperation based on the idea that labor and capital are natural partners, not natural enemies. People in organizations do not show any strong desire to deal with problems of this kind at the theoretical level. Gainsharing is useful because it offers a practical way to start doing things cooperatively. Theoretical understanding can follow at a respectable distance.

Management Practices

Early in 1982, *The Wall Street Journal* reported that 57 percent of the companies in a quick survey were continuing their management-training programs despite the severe recession of 1981–82. In past recessions, management-training programs were among the first to go as costs were cut to meet declining revenues. A percentage as high as 57 percent reflects a growing commitment by organizations to management training. This is a good sign that we are becoming more aware of the importance of effective management and more conscious of our shortcomings.

Millions are spent each year on management training; organizations providing such training are sprouting like weeds. Anyone involved in management training and development always has an in-basket full of brochures. The problem is how to sort through all of the available programs and select those that will meet the needs of the organization and its managers. Despite the pleas and warnings of training specialists to conduct a thorough analysis of training needs, it is seldom done. Too many decisions are made according to such criteria as the attractiveness of the brochure, the location of the training, and the date of the program.

We have decided that management training is good for organizations, but we have not taken the next step to any serious degree. We have not developed criteria to guide us in deciding who in management needs what training. As a result, at least half of the management training today is not effective. Some programs are good but are given to the wrong people; others are just plain poor programs. There is only one valid criterion for these management-training decisions: performance.

Gainsharing can help solve this problem by providing the focus of performance. The gainsharing program can help an organization make better decisions about management training and development. Gainsharing, to be effective, requires performance from management in the following areas:

- Strategic planning—in marketing, finance, technology, operations, and human resources.
- Analysis and diagnosis—what data to collect and how to use information in planning and decision making and for proper control.
- Effective communications—how to send the right information, how to get good feedback, how to facilitate communications between people and groups.
- Decision making—how to use all of the organization's resources to make the "best" decisions.
- Participative management—how to encourage and nurture participation of employees toward organizational excellence.
- Group problem solving—how to lead groups in identifying, analyzing, and solving problems.

Furthermore, gainsharing helps determine who in management needs what kind of training. First-line supervisors are expected to lead their work groups in finding new and better ways to do things and in solving known problems. To do this, they need information and skills about group problem solving. Top management needs to understand processes such as communications and decision making in organizations. Staff managers need skills in strategic planning, analysis and diagnosis, and communications. Training programs can be designed or selected to educate those managers who need a good understanding in some subject area and to provide skill training for those who need it. Gainsharing contributes a missing ingredient in our management-development efforts. It provides a better way to determine who needs training and what training they need. Because the gainsharing program also requires specific performance of managers, it is easy to evaluate the training to determine which training is useful in improving managerial performance, and which is ineffective.

For organizations that have not done much management training, this may represent an increased cost but one with an excellent ROI. For those already doing management training, this could very likely result in a reduction in management-training costs. In either event, gainsharing provides a focus for managerial performance and the prospect of more cost-effective management training.

Employee Participation

The quality, quantity, and effectiveness of employee participation in a successful gainsharing program will be much greater than in any other context. While the techniques used are no different than with suggestion systems, zero-defects programs, or Quality Circle programs, gainsharing provides a context and two support systems that result in more employee participation and a higher quality of participation.

A gainsharing program provides a context in which the entire organization participates in achieving organizational excellence. Gainsharing, especially as the organization moves closer to a third-degree system, makes participation a norm rather than an extra. Participation and commitment are expected from everyone in the organization. In fact, all of the job descriptions in an organization should be rewritten to show that every person is expected not only to do his or her job but to help find ways to do that job better. Other employee-participation programs treat participation as an extra. Other approaches provide the opportunity, but the expectation is missing. People are told: If you want to participate, here is your chance; if you don't, that's O.K., too. The context of other programs treats participation as an extra added attraction, peripheral to the organization's real work. In gainsharing, participation is expected from everyone as part of their job.

In addition to a different context, participation in gainsharing is supported by management practices that facilitate participation and a bonus that rewards it. Some participation efforts require little or nothing of management other than an occasional letter or pep talk. Others provide training to first-level supervisors in group methods and problem-solving techniques. No program, other than gainsharing, brings the entire management group into a supporting role. As a mainstream activity in a gainsharing program, participation is everyone's business. Line managers at all levels expect, encourage, and facilitate participation, and staff managers provide information and help to fuel the effort.

The information that people receive is the most important of the management practices in a gainsharing program. People are told about the organization's long-range goals and annual plans. They are given regular feedback about progress and problems as well as training in problem-solving techniques. People are encouraged to improve productivity by:

Saving time, materials, supplies, and energy.
Finding better methods and tools.
Making it right and avoiding scrap and rework.
Reducing down time by proper use of equipment.
Working safely and avoiding accidents.
Improving layout and work flow.
Reducing inventories.
Simplifying paperwork.
Communicating needed information to others.
Maintaining schedules to avoid late deliveries.
Substituting less costly materials and supplies.
Providing excellent service to customers.

In gainsharing programs, people do respond with ideas, cooperation, and enthusiasm. As a result, people find the work more interesting and satisfying, and the organization becomes more productive, which provides greater financial rewards for everyone.

Shared Reward

Finally, the gainsharing bonus provides support to participation by rewarding it to the extent that it is effective. Other programs provide financial rewards for specific suggestions; some include a sort of promise that if the business is more profitable, there will be something in it for everyone; some omit a financial reward completely.

In general, it can be said that in these other programs, the more successful the participation, the more dissatisfied people are with the rewards provided or the lack of rewards. In programs such as suggestions systems that provide an individual reward, the person receiving it often feels that the reward is not enough, and fellow employees who help implement a new idea feel left out. In situations where there is a promise of future rewards, such rewards seldom meet people's expectations. In situations where there is no reward, a feeling of inequity builds over time in direct proportion to the success of the program.

The source of this difficulty lies in the expectations of employees. When the organization asks employees for something more or extra, an expectation of reward is established in people's minds. When a reward is received that is equal to or better than the expectation, people are satisfied. However, the history of these efforts is that the expectations are seldom fulfilled.

In gainsharing, expectations are clarified in advance. Employees are told precisely how gains will be measured and how they will be shared. This allows employees to check the rewards against their expectations in advance. If this is found to be acceptable, the program is adopted, and there is little chance of rewards failing to measure up to expectations. People are still disappointed when they miss a bonus. But because they understand the system, they go to work to improve productivity rather than blaming management or the system for not giving them a handout.

Another important advantage to the gainsharing bonus system is that it rewards group performance. Other compensation—base pay and benefits—rewards only individual performance. Because the gainsharing bonus rewards group performance as such, group performance improves. Individuals and groups are rewarded for cooperative efforts. This feature in gainsharing provides a practical solution to such problems as intershift conflict, line and staff conflict, and the demolition derby that often exists between production, engineering, and sales.

Sharing the gain between employees and owners provides a realistic way to address the myth that owners and employers are natural enemies. Deciding to share forces us to take a practical look at this issue. Once the decision to share has been made, the basic problem has been solved, and the only remaining issue is to determine who gets what. But with sincerity and some experience, an equitable way to share can be found.

Conclusion

With gainsharing, we have a comprehensive approach to improving organizational effectiveness: *management practices* that facilitate *employee participation,* leading to improved performance that provides *rewards,* which are *shared* in a new spirit of partnership.

Other management-development and organization-development efforts use many of the same techniques and methods to improve management practices, encourage participation, and reward performance. None do these as well as gainsharing, nor do they achieve the results attained in successful gainsharing programs.

This is still no guarantee that a gainsharing program will be more successful than the other 25 programs tried in the past 25 years. Yet the potential is certainly present in the gainsharing idea. Whether Acme Widget can make it work depends on how diligently the people of Acme Widget work at it. There are very few conditions and forces *outside* of Acme Widget that can prevent a gainsharing program from working. However, there are many conditions and forces *inside* Acme Widget that are critical to the program's success.

Appendix A

Suggestion Forms and Records

Shown here are two examples of suggestion forms for use with any system of employee participation. The first is a form being used by Trans-Matic Manufacturing Company, Holland, Michigan. The second is a more involved form provided by The Eddy-Rucker-Nickels Company, Cambridge, Massachusetts. It includes a second page to record a more thorough investigation of the "biggies" and "toughies."

The suggestions log and record entitled "Idea and Problem Status" was also provided by The Eddy-Rucker-Nickels Company, courtesy of Robert C. Scott.

TRANS-MATIC MFG. CO.
EMPLOYEE SUGGESTION

HOW TO MAKE YOUR SUGGESTION:

DATE_____

USING THE FORM SIMILAR TO THE ONE
BELOW, WRITE YOUR SUGGESTION IN
THE SIMPLEST MANNER YOU CAN.

YOUR DEPT._____

SUGGESTION #_____

A.   (WHAT) MY SUGGESTION IS:
B.   (WHY) I BELIEVE IT SHOULD BE DONE BECAUSE:
C.   (HOW) IT IS DONE AS FOLLOWS.
D.   EXPECTED SAVINGS.

SUGGESTOR_____

I SUGGEST THAT:_____

_____

_____

_____

_____

_____

_____

PRODUCTION COMMITTEE ACTION_____

_____

_____

_____

_____

_____   _____
PRODUCTION   SUGGESTOR
REPRESENTATIVE

242

PRODUCTIVITY SHARING PLAN
IDEA AND PROBLEM IDENTIFICATION

TO BE FILLED OUT BY EMPLOYEE

? WHAT CAN BE IMPROVED?

? HOW CAN IT BE IMPROVED?

? WHERE ARE WE WASTING?

? WHERE IS THERE A SAFETY HAZARD?

☐ MATERIALS ☐ PEOPLE'S TIME

☐ SUPPLIES ☐ PEOPLE'S EFFORT

☐ ENERGY ☐ MACHINE TIME

☐ SAFETY ☐ QUALITY

MY THOUGHT IS:

BY   GROUP   DATE

TO BE FILLED OUT BY PRODUCTIVITY COMMITTEE REPRESENTATIVE AND SUPERVISOR

FIRST LEVEL REVIEW: (BUDGET LIMIT IS $200)

APPROXIMATE COST: _____ WILL QUALITY SUFFER? _____

FIRST YEAR SAVINGS: _____ DO WE HAVE THE AUTHORITY? _____

WHAT WILL HAPPEN: ☐ RETURN TO ORIGINATOR (100%)

☐ IMPLEMENT AND ADVISE COORDINATOR (100%)

☐ ROUTE TO _____ GROUP

☐ ROUTE TO COORDINATOR FOR FURTHER STUDY

DISCUSSION NOTES:

FURTHER STUDY:

THE INVESTIGATOR CONTACTED ME ON (DATE)

SIGNED (ORIGINATOR)

INVESTIGATION BY   REPORT DUE

TO BE FILLED OUT BY INVESTIGATOR

RESULTS OF STUDY:

COST OF CHANGE $ FIRST YEAR SAVINGS $

TO BE FILLED OUT BY COORDINATOR

DECISION:

ACTION: BY WHOM: BY WHEN:

PROBLEM NO.   COMPLETED ON

IDEA & PROBLEM STATUS

July 24, 1980

NO.	DATE	CONTRIBUTOR	DEPT.	DESCRIPTION	INVESTIGATION			DECISION	ADOPTION		
					WHO	TARGET	ACTUAL		WHO	TARGET	ACTUAL
CP312	06/03/80	Pat Garrett	FRONT SHOP	B250782 drill holes in end of slots on drill press	Harry Lindsley	06/10/80	06/03/80	ACCEPTED	Ron Bowering	06/10/80	07/01/80
CP313	06/03/80	Roger Crandell	ASMB	Make a cheap cart to hold rolls of paper used for masking	Dave Hable	06/10/80	06/09/80	REJECTED			
CP316	06/10/80	Pat Garrett	Shop	Do not penalize anyone whos work caught up after 40 hours	Ron Bowering	06/18/80	07/01/80	ACCEPTED	Ron Bowering	07/28/80	07/28/80
CP317	06/05/80	Pat Garrett	SHOP	C245718-C252940-C262388 change redimensioning	Harry Lindsley	06/06/80	06/05/80	ACCEPTED	Carl Wilcox	07/01/80	07/01/80
CP318	06/12/80	Robert Clark	FOREMAN	Eliminate c'bores in brg retainers for dr spindles	Rick Phillips	06/20/80		REJECTED			
CP319	06/12/80	Pete Viscome	FRONT SHOP	A164566-item #3 should be drilled before welding	Matt Miotla	06/20/80	06/16/80	ACCEPTED	Matt Miotla	06/24/80	06/24/80
CP320	06/12/80	Hal Smith	FRONT SHOP	Y5762-80-01-12/1, could use a carbide core 1.73 diameter	Fred St.Onge	06/20/80	06/17/80	REJECTED			
CP321	06/12/80	Kevin Gazeau	ROLL SHOP	Drill press (horizontal) be replaced	Ron Bowering	06/20/80	06/15/80	PARTIALLY ACCEPTED	Ron Bowering	06/16/80	06/16/80
CP322	06/12/80	Loren Darling	ASMB	Re-investigate CP286 -- Timestudy make up allowances	Mike Brubaker	06/20/80					
CP323	06/19/80	Randy Worden	ASMB	Safety cages should be put around the steps leading to the cranes	Tom Baker	07/09/80	07/11/80	REJECTED			
CP324	06/20/80	Jerry Stanitis	ROLL SHOP	Have two machine repair men	Ron Bowering	06/28/80		PARTIALLY ACCEPTED	Ron Bowering	06/26/80	06/27/80
CP325	06/20/80	Jerry Stanitis	ROLL SHOP	Have a de-magtitzer in crib	Jim Clark	07/24/80					
CP326	06/16/80	David Roosa	PRODUCT	B/M pages be referenced back to asmb page	Brian Pusey	06/28/80		ACCEPTED	Brian Pusey	06/20/80	06/30/80
CP327	06/16/80	Roger Crandell	ASMB	Use scotch tape instead of staples	Bob Clark	07/12/80	06/25/80	REJECTED			
CP328	06/19/80	Bob Bonoffskt	FRONT SHOP	Remove old heater unit at the stop at end of large budget hoist	Joe Slane	06/30/80		REJECTED			
CP329	06/19/80	Pete Viscome	FRONT SHOP	Do All 173 should have less work due to scrap and rework	Harry Lindsley	06/30/80	06/24/80	REJECTED			
CP330	07/02/80	Jerry Stanitis	ROLL SHOP	Need for more soft jaws for # 138 turret lathe	Fred St.Onge	07/15/80	07/12/80	ACCEPTED	Fred St.Onge	07/07/80	07/21/80
CP331	06/25/80	Ward Tarasek	FOREMAN	Order several pcs of 3"plate from Watn	Ron Bowering	07/15/80	07/08/80	ACCEPTED	Ward Tarasek	07/09/80	07/09/80

245

Appendix B

Corporate Policies and Guidelines

The following are two examples of the types of corporate policy/guideline statements that have been issued as a result of feasibility studies.

MULTINATIONAL CORPORATION:
GAINSHARING POLICY AND GUIDELINES

The following points constitute the corporation's policies with regard to gainsharing programs:

1. *Use.* Multinational Corporation encourages the use of gainsharing programs as an appropriate strategy for rewarding employees throughout the company. Although recommended, their use is not mandatory in any unit.

2. *Corporate approval.* Unit programs are to be developed locally to meet specific needs. Unit programs are expected to conform to the enclosed policies and others that may develop with experience. All programs require corporate approval prior to implementation. Details of the program—including general approach, objectives, method of measurement, funding, sharing, and payout—must be included with requests for approval.

3. *Involvement.* All employees should be involved in the unit's program in some way, since a major purpose of gainsharing is to tap our total human-resource capability. There are many options available to each unit, so plans for which approval is being sought should show how this policy will be accomplished.

4. *Commitment.* Gainsharing programs have a major impact on units and should not be approached casually. There must be a management commitment to properly use the tool in the management process. There must also be a commitment by the employees to support the unit's objectives through the gainsharing process.

5. *Program objectives.* Improved operating performance must be a primary objective in every plan. Performance improvements must be defined by local management and approved by corporate management, according to the needs of the unit, such as increased profit, reduced costs, lower unit costs, growth in

246

volume, improved quality, better service, or reduced time. Programs must also include as an objective increasing the commitment of employees to the goals of the local unit and the corporation.

6. *Interunit impact.* In addition to achieving the local unit's business and human-relations objectives, gainsharing programs should contribute to overall corporate efficiency and effectiveness. Therefore, during the design phase, changes in areas such as compensation or operations must be examined for their impact on other corporate units and steps taken to resolve adverse impacts. This is especially true for multiple-unit sites and for units that provide or receive services or materials from other Multinational Corporation units.

7. *Measurement.* Productivity measurements must be clearly established prior to any program start-up. With experience, a unit may discover a better measurement of productivity. Changing from one measurement to another because a better one is found is encouraged. However, to begin with an estimate or ambiguous productivity measurement in the hope of discovering a clearer one with experience is not acceptable.

8. *Sharing.* Programs must include a method for sharing the value of improved productivity with employees. The sharing method can take any form that provides a meaningful and equitable reward for those who create the improved productivity: employees and company.

9. *Bonus.* Bonus systems, if used, must be genuine. Bonuses must not be used to supplement noncompetitive base pay. Base pay must be internally equitable prior to the introduction of the bonus, since bonuses magnify inequities and create additional employee-relations problems.

10. *Compliance.* All programs must be in compliance with applicable laws regulating wages, hours, working conditions, and labor/management relations.

11. *Labor contracts.* In units with a labor contract, no provision of the gainsharing program can be in conflict with the current agreement, nor is the gainsharing program to become part of the labor contract.

12. *Trial period.* At the time of implementation, new programs should be presented to employees as trial projects with no guarantee of continuance. Continuation of a program will be based entirely upon results.

Recommended Program-Planning Guidelines

The following suggestions are offered to help operating units in planning gainsharing programs. These guidelines are important but are not required features, as are the preceding policies.

1. *Participation in planning.* While certain goals and procedures of any plan are specified by management, it can be very beneficial to solicit the participation of all employees in design and planning. This is best done by an elected representative committee. In units where employees are represented by a union, it is recommended that the union leadership be brought into the planning process at the earliest possible stage. When unions, and/or employee groups, are able to influence the design of a program, its acceptance and ultimate success are more easily achieved.

2. *Coordinator.* While all levels of management must provide active leader-

ship for the program, units may want to consider appointing an on-site coordinator, whose role will be the "care and feeding" of the program, especially in the design, implementation, and trial phases.

3. *Other programs.* Gainsharing programs should be integrated with, and supportive of, MBO plans, management development programs, and similar efforts.

4. *Communications/suggestions.* Gainsharing programs achieve performance improvements by soliciting ideas and improving employee motivation. An important element is a two-way communication system for soliciting, screening, and approving employee suggestions. The details of this system should be worked out before implementing a program. The results of any program are enhanced by an efficient employee-participation system.

5. *Measurements.* For all plans, there should be a clearly stated productivity level to be achieved before a gainshare is earned. It is highly desirable that the data be easy to grasp. Employees tend to mistrust complex performance reports and measurements they cannot understand. Simplicity is recommended.

This measurement should be established at the beginning of a measurement period and not changed. If experience shows the need for change, it should be done by mutual agreement and applied to the next period. After-the-fact adjustments based solely on management's judgment should be avoided.

Productivity factors that are measured and that form the basis for the gainshare should be costs or other factors that are within the control and/or influence of the employees. Among the programs in use today, some base their sharing on labor costs only; others include materials and other expenses in their base; and some use total profit as a base.

6. *Bonus frequency.* Where the gainshare takes the form of a cash bonus, monthly payouts seem to work best. A unit's ability to have a frequent payout depends on its ability to measure performance frequently. Some units may find it necessary to modify accounting procedures to permit frequent payouts.

7. *Bonus form.* Payout can take any form that meets the needs of the company and the participating employees. While cash is very common in United States plans, it is possible that stock or fringes could be acceptable here and in other countries. Earned time off has also been used effectively when production needs have been met. Local tax laws should be studied in designing this aspect of the plan.

8. *Sharing ratio.* There are several criteria to apply in determining a formula for sharing the gain between the company and the employees.

○ The employees' share should be sufficient to function as an incentive/reward.

○ The employees' share should equitably reflect the employees' overall contribution. A percentage of actual pay is most often used as base pay, and it should reflect differences between contributions made by different employees.

○ The company's share should provide an equitable return to the company.

○ The sharing formula will vary with the elements included in the base. In labor-only plans, a higher percentage of the measured improvement is returned to the employees. As more elements are added to the base, a smaller percentage of the total savings goes to the employee share.

UNITED WIDGET CORPORATION:
GAINSHARING POLICY STATEMENT

The corporation recommends consideration of gainsharing programs as a means to increase productivity and profitability, provided the following principles are fully understood and utilized.

Application

- Each program must be specifically designed to fit the needs of a division.
- A gainsharing program should not be used with another type of incentive program.
- A gainsharing program should include as participants all employees of the division, including managers.
- Gainsharing program consideration for a facility should be communicated in a manner that will enlist strong employee support.
- Installation of any new gainsharing program should be contingent upon an 80 percent affirmative vote of all employees.
- All new gainsharing programs should begin with a minimum one-year trial period, with continuation subject to an additional employee vote (80 percent favorable) and, thereafter, program cancellation subject to a 90-day notice by either party.
- Prior to the implementation of a gainsharing program, all management employees should be thoroughly educated about the program and its principles. Consideration should be given to special training programs for management.
- Although the gainsharing program embodies the principles of participative management, no participation system should be established to replace management's responsibilities.
- It is recommended that a third-party consultant be used in the development and installation of new gainsharing programs and that such a consultant be retained for a minimun of two years.
- When a plant manager is transferred from a nongainsharing plant to one with a gainsharing program, it is imperative that the manager fully understand and be committed to the principles and concepts of gainsharing. To assist the manager's education, it is recommended that he or she spend a short internship in a gainsharing plant prior to assignment.
- Plant managers, controllers, and personnel managers of gainsharing plants should meet twice each year to share experiences and problems to help assure the best possible gainsharing performance for the corporation.

Suggestion System

- Success of a gainsharing program will largely depend upon the dedication and enthusiasm of the plant management. Encouraging quality suggestions and open communications will help guarantee the continuing success of the program.
- All suggestions and minutes of the committee meetings should be posted to provide maximum employee recognition.

Bonus

- ○ Competitive wage and fringe programs should be in place prior to the installation of a gainsharing program.
- ○ All gainsharing programs should be designed to provide a 75 percent employee/25 percent company sharing ratio.
- ○ Gainsharing bonuses should be distributed to all employees as a percentage of pay.
- ○ Gainsharing bonus programs should provide a monthly 25 percent reserve to cover possible deficit months.
- ○ When a gainsharing program is being installed to replace an existing incentive plan, and red-circle rates are required, special provision should be made to insure that minimum productivity levels are maintained. Provision should also be made for the most practical and rapid termination of all red-circle rates.
- ○ The basic computation of the gainsharing bonus should be kept as simple as possible (sales dollars divided by payroll dollars).
- ○ The gainsharing bonus ratio must be monitored regularly and carefully to insure equity for all parties. The effect of product-mix changes, labor increases and/or price increases, and so forth may dictate a change in the formula.

Labor Contracts

- ○ It should be understood by all employees at union facilities that the company does not intend to negotiate any of the elements of a gainsharing program.
- ○ Gainsharing program years should be kept out of phase with labor contract termination dates.
- ○ Discussions of labor contract and fringe benefit provisions should be avoided at all gainsharing meetings.

Appendix C

Memorandums of Agreement

Where a labor union is involved in the gainsharing program, it is necessary to describe the program in some detail to show that it will not in any way interfere with the labor contract. A memorandum of agreement is fairly often used when the parties wish to enter an agreement separate from the formal labor contract, and in many organizations, the union and management have a format for such agreements. This appendix contains two examples of gainsharing memorandums of agreement and one example of a memorandum specifically agreeing to conduct a joint feasibility study.

The first memorandum was prepared by Roy A. Ockert, research director for the International Woodworkers of America. Although the example specifies Rucker Plans, it could be used as a model for any gainsharing program.

The second is the actual agreement used at American Valve & Hydrant Manufacturing Company in Beaumont, Texas. It refers to a Scanlon Plan but could also be used with any gainsharing program.

The third example is an agreement to conduct a joint feasibility study. This type of memorandum has been used only infrequently, but it is a good example of the kind of documentation that may be requested by unions in their effort to protect their collective bargaining position. This example, like the first one, was prepared by Roy A. Ockert of the IWA.

SAMPLE MEMORANDUM OF AGREEMENT

The Company and the union agree that there shall be an Economic Productivity Sharing Plan in the [company], according to the following provisions:

A. *Group Productivity Earnings Plan*

This Agreement establishes a plantwide incentive plan designed to enable all bargaining unit employees of the Company to benefit from their increased economic productivity. In order to assure full participation in the benefits of the increased economic productivity which should result from the plan, the copyrighted economic productivity sharing program known as the "Rucker Share of Production Plan" shall be applied to remain in full force and effect subject to the terms and conditions of termination stated in the final section of this Agreement.

B. *Definition of Terms*

Terms used in this Agreement as applied to the Share of Production Plan are defined as follows:

1. Sales Value of Production—The realized or realizable competitive market value of all saleable products manufactured during a bonus period.
2. Production Value—Sales Value of Production minus the actual cost of Materials, Supplies, and Purchased Services consumed in the same bonus period.
3. Materials, Supplies, and Purchased Services—Include raw material used for production; small tools, factory supplies; boiler fuel, power and water used in manufacturing; electrical maintenance supplies, janitor and watchman supplies; materials and supplies used in repairs to machinery, equipment, molds, and dies; truck expense; shipping supplies; solvents used; outside mold and repair work; and outside work on machinery and equipment.
4. Eligible Payroll Costs—Include the aggregate costs to the Company of the contractually-specified compensation paid to or on behalf of the members of the bargaining unit, except that it shall *not* include:
   (a) Non-contractual payments made voluntarily to or on behalf of employees by the Company;
   (b) Legally required deductions such as Social Security (OASI), Unemployment Insurance, and Workmen's Compensation now in effect or which are enacted in the future;
   (c) The earnings of new employees who have not yet been in the employ of the Company for more than 30 days;
   (d) Payments to or on behalf of former employees on retirement, except for work performed while in the bargaining unit;
   (e) Any subsequent contractually-specified payments mutually excluded by the parties.

C. *The Standard*

Records for the _____ year period ending _____ were used in determining labor's annual standard share of Production Value in the plant. This standard share was found to be _____ per cent during the base period.

1. In each Bonus accounting period _____ per cent of the Production Value will represent the Standard Workers' Share.
2. Only a *major* change in product, process, or plant facilities will be cause for restudy of the Standard.
3. In the event of a restudy of the Standard the Company may temporarily suspend the Plan until the Study has been completed, provided that the Company pays the eligible members of the bargaining unit the average earned Hourly Bonus Rate of the preceding 9-month period, less the proration of any negotiated base rate increase granted during the 9-month period, until a new standard is established.
4. If the composition of the bargaining unit as defined in the Recognition Article of the Labor Agreement is changed, the Standard Workers' Share shall be changed accordingly.
5. In the event of war or other national emergency this Agreement may be amended or suspended by mutual agreement.

D. *The Productivity Bonus*

Whenever the Eligible Payroll Costs for a Bonus accounting period are less than the Stardard Workers' Share, the difference will constitute the Productivity Bonus Earnings. In each of the twelve months of the fiscal year the Company will calculate the Bonus Earnings in the most accurate manner possible following generally accepted accounting practices. The final year-end audit and inventory will be the basis for calculating total Bonus Earnings for the fiscal year.

E. *Distribution of the Productivity Bonus*

1. The Productivity Bonus Earnings shall be distributed to eligible members of the bargaining unit according to the following terms:
   (a) Eligibility—Only those employees who are members of the current bargaining unit, including those on layoff, leave, or retirement who worked during the accounting period and the estate of those who died during the accounting period after establishing eligibility through work, shall participate in the distribution of the Workers' Share of the Productivity Bonus, except that no one who has been in the employ of the Company for thirty (30) days or less, who resigned during the period, or who has been terminated for just cause shall share in the distribution of the Bonus. Exceptions to the above rule may be made only by mutual agreement between the Union and the Company.
   (b) Share of Production Adjustment Account—Twenty per cent (20%) of the Productivity Bonus Earnings for the monthly accounting period shall be placed in a reserve fund to provide for possible overpayments

in the monthly Bonus distribution which might be revealed by the annual productivity bonus calculation after the fiscal year-end inventories and audit. The cumulative amount in this account shall be posted with each month's Productivity Bonus calculations for the information of the employees.

(c) Monthly Bonus Accounting Periods—The monthly accounting period shall be the period of one calendar month, or such alternative period of approximately one month, normally used by the Company.

(d) Method of Monthly Distribution:*

  (i) The Bonus Earnings available for distribution shall be divided by the cash base rate payroll (including statutory overtime premium pay, but excluding individual incentive, Vacation and Holiday Pay) which has been paid to the eligible members of the bargaining unit during the monthly accounting period (Distribution Payroll) to arrive at the Productivity Bonus percentage, carried to the fourth decimal place. The Bonus percentage shall be applied to the total cash base rate payroll (including overtime premium pay, but excluding individual incentive, Vacation and Holiday Pay) of each eligible employee to determine gross Productivity Bonus Earnings for the monthly accounting period. See example in box.

  (ii) In any given monthly accounting period should an accounting factor be discovered which is properly assignable to prior periods and which would substantially alter the values and costs used in the calculation of the current monthly Bonus Earnings, that factor shall be apportioned to the remaining calculations in the fiscal year in such manner as not to seriously distort a single month's earnings and the matter shall be discussed by the Productivity Coordinating Committee prior to distribution of the Bonus.

  (iii) The monthly Productivity Bonus shall be distributed not later than the end of the third week after the conclusion of the monthly accounting period during which it was earned, except in circumstances in which the Productivity Coordinating Committee determines otherwise for good and sufficient reasons.

(e) Year-End Bonus—At the end of the Company's fiscal year, after physical inventories have been taken and the audit of the books completed, a final calculation of the Share of Production Bonus Earnings for the fiscal year shall be made. From the total annual Bonus Earnings shall be deducted all monthly Bonus payments made during the year and the remaining amount shall be distributed to the eligible members of the bargaining unit on the basis of the total payroll earnings (including overtime premium pay, but excluding individual incentive, Vacation and Holiday Pay) of the fiscal year. If the deductions are greater than the Adjustment Account, such deficit shall be ab-

*See substitute paragraphs and examples at the end of this document for two other ways of calculating and distributing the bonus.

Example. Calculation and distribution of bonus as a percentage of base pay.

In the five-year base period it was found that the Workers' Share of Production Value is 40.000% which includes certain fringe benefits. This is labor's standard share of Production Value for the XYZ plant against which to measure your performance each month.

1. Assume that this month the *sales value of shipments* comes to $900,000
2. Because of the build-up of inventory, however, the *sales value of production* is $975,000
3. Materials, supplies, and purchased services cost........ $225,000
4. Leaving a Production Value of...................... $750,000
5. The Workers' Share of this Production Value is 40.000% or $300,000
6. Eligible Payroll Costs during the month were $250,000
7. Leaving a Bonus of .... $ 50,000
8. From this Bonus is set aside 20%, or .... $ 10,000 which will be put into a Reserve Account to be distributed at the end of the fiscal year after the physical inventory and final audit have been made.
9. This leaves for Bonus distribution this month .... $ 40,000
10. The productivity Bonus percentage is calculated by dividing the Distribution Bonus ($40,000) by the Base Distribution Payroll ($217,852) 18.3611%
11. Your own pay record for the month might look like this:

Total Hours Worked	Including Overtime Hours × 1½	Hourly Base Rate	Total Base Pay	Bonus Per Cent	Total Bonus	Individual Incentive Earnings	Gross Earnings
185	15	$2.50	$462.50	18.3611%	$84.92	$138.75	$686.17

sorbed by the Company and not charged against Bonus Earnings of a succeeding year. The distribution of the Year-End Bonus shall take place not later than the first day of _____ each year, except by agreement with the Union.

2. At the time of the distribution of the Year-End Bonus the Company shall:
   (a) Cause the President of the Local Union to be furnished with a statement from The Eddy-Rucker-Nickels Company, or other mutually acceptable Certified Public Accountant, attesting whether the provisions of this agreement have been followed in determining the Workers' Share of Production Value and describing any discrepancies in detail. The Union shall have the right to call on The Eddy-Rucker-Nickels Company at any time to investigate possible discrepancies. If the in-

vestigation indicates that the Company is at fault, the Company shall pay the expenses of the investigation. If it is found that the Company is not at fault the Union shall pay the fees and expenses.

(b) Furnish the President of the Local Union, copies to the Regional Council and the International Union, with an analysis of the plant's average hourly cost per bargaining unit manhour worked of each individual fringe benefit included in Eligible Payroll during the fiscal year, with average straight-time hourly earnings for men, women, and combined bargaining unit employees, total manhours worked during the fiscal year, average working enrollment, average total enrollment and net seniority enrollment of bargaining unit members.

(c) Supply the President of the Local Union, copies to the Regional Council and the International Union, with a statement of the fiscal year's accrued sales value of shipments, net inventory, sales value of production, costs of materials, supplies and purchased services, production value, eligible payroll costs, and wage, bonus, and supplemental benefit payments for the plant. This information shall be held confidential by the Union.

3. Disputes over the interpretation or application of this Plan which cannot be settled between the Company and the Union shall first be submitted to The Eddy-Rucker-Nickels Company for analysis and decision, which must be rendered within a two-week period. If agreement is not reached within two weeks thereafter the dispute shall be handled according to the grievance procedure established in the basic collective bargaining agreement, commencing at Step 3. A Board of Arbitration shall not have the power to add to, subtract from, or modify this Agreement. The Eddy-Rucker-Nickels Company or _____ shall be informed of the results of any negotiations or grievance awards concerning this Plan.

F. *Administration of the Plan*

The heart of this plantwide incentive plan is participation, implemented by the creation of joint committees of employees and management to promote increased productive efficiency. The committee structure includes departmental Production Committees and a Productivity Coordinating Committee.

1. Production Committees—There shall be a Production Committee established for each of the following plant departments or units: [List the departments and/or units]

(a) Composition—Production Committees shall be composed of _____ (____) Union and _____ (____) Management representatives. The Management group shall include a top Management official of the department or plant unit. Union representatives chosen in the first election shall serve for one year, by the end of which term the Union shall establish a definite elective period.

(b) Functions—The Production Committees shall meet in their departments or units once each month, or more often if deemed necessary, for the specific purpose of discussing ways and means of reducing waste and increasing productive efficiency. In advance of each meeting every effort will be made to schedule specific production problems which will be placed on the agenda for discussion. Committee members may call upon those employees in their departments who are most familiar with the specific problems outlined to participate in the scheduled meetings. In no event, however, may a committeeman call in more than two employees. It shall be the responsibility of the Committee members to record and explain all suggestions intended to increase productive efficiency or reduce waste together with the disposition of each. An approved copy of the minutes shall be transmitted immediately to the Productivity Coordinating Committee. The functions of the Production Committees shall in no way conflict with the responsibilities and duties of the duly elected union grievance committees or stewards.

2. The Productivity Coordinating Committee
   (a) Composition—The Productivity Coordinating Committee shall consist of four Union representatives and a like number of top Management officials. The members are to be chosen in the manner prescribed by their constituents. A representative chosen by the Regional Council shall be an ex officio member of the Productivity Coordinating Committee. A maximum of three Union members of Production Committees may be invited to attend sessions of the Productivity Coordinating Committee.
   (b) Functions—The Productivity Coordinating Committee shall meet at least once each month and shall, through joint discussion, screen out all suggestions that are designed to increase productive efficiency or reduce waste, including all suggestions made at meetings of the Production Committees. Those that have been placed in effect at the Production Committee level shall be placed in the record and recommendations shall be made concerning the remaining suggestions. It will also be the function of the Productivity Coordinating Committee to review the facts and figures used in the calculation of the bonus before the bonus is announced. At each meeting of the Committee the Company shall be prepared to present graphs and figures concerning individual items that affect the calculated results. The productivity bonus will be announced within two weeks after the end of the accounting period and will represent the bonus for that accounting period.

G. *Duration and Termination*
   1. This Economic Productivity Sharing Plan shall become effective on the date signed subject to approval of the Local Union and the Regional Council, and shall continue in effect for the duration of the current Agreement of which this Plan is a part.
   2. In the event the company holding the copyright to the "Rucker Share of Production Plan," or its agent, withdraws the copyright privileges, this Plan shall be immediately terminated and the Local Union shall be notified

concerning the reason and shall have the right to terminate the collective bargaining agreement upon a sixty-day prior written notice.

3. In the event this Plan is terminated, the Company shall have the option of either distributing the entire accumulated Reserve Account to the members of the bargaining unit within one week of the date of termination, or of conducting the necessary inventory and audit to determine the audited Reserve Account balance which shall then be distributed within forty-five days of the date of termination.

Substitute Paragraphs and Examples

There are three basic methods of distributing the bonus. The one shown within the preceding sample memorandum uses the bonus as a percentage of base pay (*excluding* individual incentive earnings). The second method uses a flat hourly bonus, and the third uses a percentage of total pay (*including* individual incentive earnings). If either of these two other methods will be used in your organization, changes will be required in paragraph E-1(d)(i) and in the boxed example that accompanies it.

Bonus as a Flat Hourly Rate

(i) The Bonus Earnings available for distribution shall be divided by the hours worked (including overtime hours times the applicable factor) for which the eligible members of the bargaining unit have been paid during the monthly accounting period (Distribution Hours) to arrive at the Productivity Hourly Bonus, carried to the nearest one-tenth of one cent. The Hourly Bonus shall be applied to the total hours worked (including overtime hours times the applicable factor) of each eligible employee to determine his Productivity Bonus Earnings for the monthly accounting period. See example in box. [Use Substitute example 1.]

Bonus as a Percentage of Total Pay

(i) The Bonus Earnings available for distribution shall be divided by the cash payroll (including statutory overtime premium pay, but excluding Vacation and Holiday Pay) which has been paid to the eligible members of the bargaining unit during the monthly accounting period (Distribution Payroll) to arrive at the Productivity Bonus percentage, carried to the fourth decimal place. The Bonus percentage shall be applied to the total cash payroll (including overtime premium pay, but excluding Vacation and Holiday Pay) of each eligible employee to determine gross Productivity Bonus Earnings for the monthly accounting period. See example in box. [Use Substitute example 2.]

Substitute example 1. Calculation and distribution of bonus as a flat hourly rate.

In the five-year base period it was found that the Workers' Share of Production Value is 40.000%, which includes certain fringe benefits. This is labor's standard share of Production Value for the XYZ plant against which to measure your performance each month.

1. Assume that this month the *sales value of shipments* comes to $900,000
2. Because of the build-up of inventory, however, the *sales value of production* is $975,000
3. Materials, supplies, and purchased services cost $225,000
4. Leaving a Production Value of $750,000
5. The Workers' Share of this Production Value is 40.000% or $300,000
6. Eligible Payroll Costs during the month were $250,000
7. Leaving a Bonus of .... $ 50,000
8. From this Bonus is set aside 20%, or .... $ 10,000 which will be put into a Reserve Account to be distributed at the end of the fiscal year after the physical inventory and final audit have been made.
9. This leaves for Bonus distribution this month .... $ 40,000
10. The Hourly Bonus Rate is calculated by dividing the Distribution Bonus ($40,000) by the Distribution Hours, which in the month were 87,146 hours $0.459
11. Your own pay record for the month might look like this:

Total Hours Worked	Including Overtime Hours × 1½	Average Hourly Rate	Total Pay	Bonus Per Hour	Total Bonus	Gross Earnings
185	15	$3.25	$601.25	$.459	$84.92	$686.17

Substitute example 2. Calculation and distribution of bonus as a percentage of total pay.

In the five-year base period it was found that the Workers' Share of Production Value is 40.000%, which includes certain fringe benefits. This is labor's standard share of Production Value for the XYZ plant against which to measure your performance each month.

1. Assume that this month the *sales value of shipments* comes to $900,00
2. Because of the build-up of inventory, however, the *sales value of production* is $975,000
3. Materials, supplies, and purchased services cost $225,000
4. Leaving a Production Value of $750,000
5. The Workers' Share of this Production Value is 40.000% or $300,000
6. Eligible Payroll Costs during the month were $250,000
7. Leaving a Bonus of .... $ 50,000
8. From this Bonus is set aside 20%, or .... $ 10,000 which will be put into the Adjustment Account to be distributed at the end of the fiscal year after the physical inventory and final audit have been made.
9. This leaves for distribution this month .... $ 40,000
10. The productivity Bonus percentage is calculated by dividing the Distribution Bonus ($40,000) by the Distribution Payroll ($283,208) 14.1239%
11. Your own pay record for the month might look like this:

Total Hours Worked	Including Overtime Hours × 1½	Average Hourly Rate	Total Pay	Bonus Per Cent	Total Bonus	Gross Earnings
185	15	$3.25	$601.25	14.1239%	$84.92	$686.17

SCANLON BONUS PLAN AGREEMENT

The following is an agreement between American Value & Hydrant Manufacturing Company, Beaumont, Texas, and its employees, both hourly paid and salaried, to establish and participate in the Scanlon Plan.

This plan is not a part of the basic labor agreement between the Company and the Union, and can in no way invalidate or conflict with any of the provisions therein.

The Scanlon Plan was initiated at American Value & Hydrant on March 1, 1978. After the first nine months, a renewal vote was taken and over 90% of the employees approved continuation of the plan. The Scanlon year begins on December 1 of each year and ends November 30 of each year.

I. Bonus Plan

This bonus plan is designed to enable the following employees of American Valve & Hydrant Manufacturing Company, Beaumont, Texas, to benefit from their increased cooperation and efforts as reflected in increased productivity and the reduction of costs. All AV&H employees (shop hourly, company hourly, and salaried) shall participate in the plan.

In order to assure full participation in the benefits of increased productivity and cost savings, which should result from union-employee-management cooperation, a monthly bonus plan based on the relationship between wages and production was established. This was revised in December, 1979 to include total plant costs. The costs do not include ACIPCO allocated expenses, sales expense, interest, etc.

The bonus percent shall be applicable for all employees (full-time and permanent part-time, shop and company hourly, and salaried) who have been in the employment of the Company for the full working month and shall be applied based on gross pay for actual hours worked. It will not be applied to sick pay, pay for personal time, holiday pay, jury duty pay, or bereavement pay. The employee must be on the payroll the day the bonus is distributed in order to receive any bonus check for the previous month.

The plan shall remain in effect on a continuing basis under the provisions herein described, subject to discontinuance upon a six (6) months prior notice by either the Company or the employees. If the employees elect to discontinue the plan, discontinuance must be based on a majority vote by the employees.

II. Basis for Plan

The basis used for calculating the participating efficiency bonus each month is the ratio of total cost to sales, plus or minus any inventory change at cost. This ratio was developed from records for the full year of 1978 and shows 87.393 cents in total costs allowed for each dollar of sales value of production.

The sales figures which were used in developing this ratio were made by gross sales less returns and allowances—plus or minus the change in inventory at cost. The total costs which were used in developing this ratio were the actual total costs during the above mentioned period.

When bonus calculations are made each month under the plan, sales will be compiled in the same way as the base period as well as the actual total expense for the month used. Any difference will go into the bonus pool. (See Example 1.)

III. Employee/Company Split

Whenever the actual costs are less than 87.393%, the gross bonus pool is distributed on the basis of 32% being paid to the employees and 68% being retained by the Company.

IV. Reserve

Twenty-five (25) percent of the total gross bonus earned by the employees will be reserved. This has been established to protect the Company's interest in any deficit month (that is, a month in which the total actual cost as related to sales value of production exceeds the base period cost). This reserve also serves as a yearly accumulated bonus if it remains on the positive side. (See Example 2.)

V. Year-End Bonus

If the reserve that is set up in bonus months is in excess of the sum necessary to restore the ratio to the established norm in the deficit months, this total excess shall be distributed as a year-end bonus. However, quits and terminations will not participate in this payout. In order to be eligible for the year-end bonus, an

Example 1. Multicost calculation for Scanlon bonus.

Sales Value of Production (Gross Sales—plus or minus—Inventory, Less Freight and Returns)		$2,000,000
Cost Margin % for Current Month (Total Costs as percent of Total Sales)	84.893%	
Standard Margin % from Base Period 1978	87.393%	
% Better or Worse than Base Period	2.50 %	
Total Bonus Pool Available		$ 50,000
Distribution at 32% Level (32% was used to equate prior cost improvements to current improvements)		$ 16,000
Actual Distribution:		
75% Actual Bonus Paid Current Month		$ 12,000
25% Actual Bonus Reserves for Year End		4,000
100%		$ 16,000

Example 2. Reserve in bonus calculation.

	September	October	November
Bonus Pool	$30,000	($100,000)	$35,000
Employees Share 32%	9,600	(32,000)	11,200
Reserve for Deficit			
Months (Employees) 25%	2,400	(32,000)	2,800
Total Payable Bonus	$ 7,200	-0-	$ 8,400
Employee Reserve:			
Balance Previous Month	$2,000	$ 4,400	($27,600)
This Month	2,400	(32,000)	2,800
Total	$4,400	($27,600)	($24,800)

Note: A monthly bonus was paid to employees in November although a year-end bonus was not paid.

employee must be employed the day the Screening Committee meets in December. At this time, the November bonus figures will be reviewed and both the November check and year-end check will be distributed. If the deficits for the year are in excess of this reserve, this deficit shall be terminated at the end of the period and shall not be charged against bonus earnings of the next year.

VI. Conditions Which May Necessitate a Change of Ratio
Substantial changes in the conditions or objectives which prevailed in establishing the ratio norm may necessitate a changing of this ratio for the purpose of protecting the equity of either party in the benefits of the plan.

The plan is designed to compensate all employees for their ideas and efforts. Pay increase, technological change, capital expenditure, etc. should automatically be considered but may necessitate some adjustment in the future.

VII. The Committee Structure
The heart of this bonus plan is participation, implemented by the creation of joint committees of management and employees to promote increased productive efficiency, cost reduction, and a suggestion system. The committee structure consists of production committees and a screening committee. There are 14 production committees:

1. *Finance/Purchasing/Inventory Control*
   Three (3) unit representatives and one (1) management representative. One (1) of the unit representatives will be elected out of each area.
2. *Production Control/Plant Office/Employee Relations*
   Two (2) unit representatives from combined areas and one (1) management representative.

3. *Pattern Shop*
   Two (2) hourly rate employees and one (1) management representative.
4. *Loop*
   Two (2) hourly rate employees and one (1) management representative.
5. *Hunters*
   Two (2) hourly rate employees and one (1) management representative.
6. *Core Room*
   Two (2) hourly rate employees and one (1) management representative.
7. *Melting (Day Shift)*
   Two (2) hourly rate employees and one (1) management representative.
8. *Core Room and Melting (Night)*
   Two (2) hourly rate employees and one (1) management representative.
9. *Cleaning Room*
   Three (3) hourly rate employees and one (1) management representative.
10. *Assembly Lines (Hydrant, Valve, Spare Parts, and Inspection)*
    Three (3) hourly rate employees and one (1) management representative.
11. *Maintenance and Construction*
    Three (3) hourly rate employees and one (1) management representative.
12. *Machine Shop (Evening and Midnight)/Maintenance (Evening)*
    Three (3) hourly rate employees and one (1) management representative.
13. *Machine Shop (Day)*
    Three (3) hourly rate employees and one (1) management representative.
14. *Materials Handling/Shipping/Plant Protection*
    Three (3) hourly rate employees and one (1) management representative.

A. Elections

The hourly rate employees of each committee shall be elected by the group they represent. Representatives elected in December 1979 will serve an eighteen (18) month term. Beginning December 1980 and thereafter, each newly elected representative will serve a one-year term. When an elected representative leaves the group which he represents, the remainder of his term shall be filled by an election of the group. The management representatives for each group will be appointed by the Scanlon Coordinator.

Ballots distributed by the Scanlon Coordinator will be used in the December election. The work force members of that group will vote for three employees of their choice. The three employees receiving the highest number of votes will be placed on nomination for the Screening Committee position. A run-off election will be held by the group to elect the person who will represent that group on the Screening Committee. If positions of both Screening Committee representative and Production Committee representative are open, the person receiving the highest vote in the run-off will serve as Screening Committee representative and the person receiving second highest will serve the term of Production Committee representative.

B. Production Committees

The Production Committees shall meet in their respective groups the first week of each month, or more often if deemed necessary, for the specific purpose of discussing ways and means of reducing costs and increasing productivity. All Production Committee representatives must be present at each meeting. In the event a Production Committee representative cannot be present, an alternate person designated by the committee chairperson shall serve at the meeting. It will be the responsibility of the Production chairperson to record and explain all suggestions (intended to increase productivity, reduce waste, and reduce costs) which are made to them by the employees of their group.

The Production Committees shall keep accurate minutes of their meetings on a common minute form. An approved copy of the minutes and a copy of the new suggestions shall be transmitted to the Scanlon Coordinator by the 10th of the month in order that he may compile an agenda for the Screening Committee Meeting.

The Production Committee has the authority to spend up to $200 per suggestion with the approval of the committee. Any suggestion the Committee cannot agree on, or any suggestion that exceeds the $200 limit, shall be forwarded to the Screening Committee.

The functions of a Production Committee shall in no way conflict with the responsibilities and duties of the duly elected bargaining committee.

C. The Screening Committee

The Screening Committee shall consist of the three (3) Union committeemen and the chairman, one representative of each of the fourteen (14) Production Committees and twelve (12) management employees appointed by the Plant President. The term of the elected Screening Committee members shall be one (1) year. The Screening Committee shall be elected as outlined in Section A—Elections.

The Screening Committee shall meet once a month, with all members present and the Scanlon Coordinator as chairman. If a member of the Screening Committee cannot be present, he/she shall appoint a representative to take his/her place for that meeting.

At the monthly meetings, the Screening Committee shall review all suggestions made the month before designed to increase productivity, reduce scrap, and reduce costs. The Committee shall also review and make a final decision on any suggestions that exceed the $200 limit and suggestions that Production Committees could not agree upon.

During this meeting, management will inform the people on the Company's backlog and economic outlook on the business market. Any problems or changes will also be discussed.

It will also be the function of this Committee to go over the facts and figures used in the calculation of the bonus earned for the previous month in order to establish the greatest degree of faith and confidence in the calculated results.

The bonus percent earned the previous month will then be announced. A separate bonus check will be issued to all participating employees as soon as the necessary paperwork can be processed and the checks can be printed.

Revised March 31, 1980.

ECONOMIC ENGINEERING STUDY MEMORANDUM

Whereas the _____ Company and Local Union No. _____ desire to explore the nature and possible implementation of an economic productivity sharing program in the _____ plant in order to promote the welfare of both the workers in the bargaining unit and the Company; now therefore:

I. The Company does hereby agree to have an economic engineering study made of the records of the plant, at its expense, in order to determine the feasibility and the advisability of installing the "Rucker Share of Production Plan."

II. The economic engineering study shall begin within 60 days from the date of this Memorandum and shall cover not less than the most recent five fiscal years of the plant, and shall include wherever possible data concerning the costs of the following:

    A. Legally required payments by the Company, such as Social Security (OASI), Unemployment Compensation, and Workmen's Compensation;

    B. Earnings of new employees with 30 days or less of service;

    C. Payments to or on behalf of former employees while on retirement;

    D. Severance or other payments required by the displacement of workers which result from the installation of new or improved machinery or equipment.

III. The economic engineering study shall be made by The Eddy-Rucker-Nickels Company of Cambridge, Massachusetts
and/or _____
of _____
or other individual firm or consultant now or hereafter legally licensed by The Eddy-Rucker-Nickels Company to apply its principles and practices, such to be mutually acceptable to the Union and the Company.

IV. At the conclusion of the economic engineering study, the consultants shall furnish the Union and the Company with sufficient information such that both parties will be able to determine whether to proceed with negotiating the "Rucker Share of Production Plan."

V. It is the intent of the Union and the Company to limit their commitment in this Memorandum to exploring the possibilities of the application of the "Rucker Share of Production Plan" to the specified plant and to receive and review the recommendations of the specified consulting engineers concerning its detailed application to the local conditions of the plant for possible future negotiations.

VI. Within 60 days after receipt of the results of the economic engineering study, representatives of the Union and the Company shall meet to decide whether:

    A. To proceed with such negotiations and to prepare an Economic Productivity Sharing Agreement which shall outline the terms and conditions under which the program shall be operated; or

B. Not to proceed with negotiations on the basis of the "Rucker Share of Production Plan"; in which case the Union and the Company hereby agree to discuss and seriously consider possible alternative plans.

In witness whereof the parties hereto have set their hands this __day of _____,
19__.

FOR THE LOCAL UNION   FOR THE COMPANY

_____   _____

Resources

Consultants:

R. J. Bullock
Psychology Department
University of Houston
Houston, Texas 77004
(713) 749-1835

Robert J. Doyle
2660 S.W. Garden View Avenue
Portland, Oregon 97225
(503) 292-9377

Mitchell Fein (Improshare)
202 Saddlewood Drive
Hillsdale, New Jersey 07642
(201) 664-2055

Frost, Greenwood and Associates
217 N. Clippert Street
Lansing, Michigan 48912
(517) 332-8927

Edward E. Lawler III
Center for Effective Organizations
University of Southern California
Bridge Hall 200
Los Angeles, California 90007
(213) 743-8765

Fred G. Lesieur
110 Fairway Drive
Novato, California 94947
(415) 883-7514

Timothy L. Ross
Bowling Green Productivity & Gain-
    sharing Institute
Bowling Green State University
Bowling Green, Ohio 43403
(419) 372-0016

M. Peter Scontrino
21832 S.E. 28th
Issaquah, Washington 98027
(206) 392-5694

Robert C. Scott (Rucker Plan)
The Eddy-Rucker-Nickels Company
4 Brattle Street, Harvard Square
Cambridge, Massachusetts 02138
(617) 864-9300

Organizations:

American Center for the Quality of
    Work Life
Ted Mills, Director
3301 New Mexico Avenue, N.W.
Suite 202
Washington, D.C. 20016
(202) 338-2933

American Productivity Center, Inc.
C. Jackson Grayson, Jr., Chairman
123 North Post Oak Lane
Houston, Texas 77024
(713) 681-4020

Center for the Quality of Working Life
Louis Davis, Chairman
Institute of Industrial Relations
University of California
405 Hilgard Avenue
Los Angeles, California 90024
(213) 825-1095

Illinois Quality of Working Life
Program
Institute of Labor and Industrial
Relations
University of Illinois at Urbana-
Champaign
540 East Armory Avenue
Champaign, Illinois 61820
(217) 333-1480

Maryland Center for Productivity and
Quality of Working Life
Thomas C. Tuttle, Director
College of Business and Management
University of Maryland
College Park, Maryland 20742
(301) 454-6688

Massachusetts Quality of Working Life
Center
Michael J. Brower, Director
14 Beacon Street
Boston, Massachusetts 02108
(617) 227-6266

Ohio Quality of Working Life Program
Center for Human Resource Research
The Ohio State University
1375 Perry Street, Suite 585
Columbus, Ohio 43201
(614) 422-3390

Oklahoma Productivity Center
Scott Sink, Director of R&D
School of Industrial Engineering and
Management
Oklahoma State University
Stillwater, Oklahoma 74074
(405) 624-6055

Oregon Productivity Center
James L. Riggs, P.E.
Oregon State University
Corvallis, Oregon 97331
(503) 754-3249

Profit Sharing Research Foundation
Bert Metzger, President
1718 Sherman Avenue
Evanston, Illinois 60201
(312) 869-8787

Texas Center for Productivity and
Quality of Work Life
Barry A. Macy, Director
College of Business Administration
Post Office Box 4320
Lubbock, Texas 79409
(806) 742-1537

Work in America Institute, Inc.
Jerome M. Rosow, President
700 White Plains Road
Scarsdale, New York 10583
(914) 472-9600
(212) 823-5144

Bibliography

Ashburn, Anderson, "Devising Real Incentives for Productivity." *American Machinist,* June 1978, pp. 116–130.

Batt, William L., Jr., and Edgar Weinberg, "Labor-Management Cooperation Today." *Harvard Business Review,* January–February 1978, pp. 96–104.

Blake, Robert, and Jane Mouton, *The Managerial Grid.* Austin, Tex.: Gulf Publishing, 1964.

Bowers, David G., and Jerome L. Franklin, *Survey Guided Development I: Data-Based Organizational Change.* San Diego, Calif.: University Associates, 1977.

Davenport, Robert, "Enterprise for Everyman." *Fortune,* January 1950, pp. 50–58.

Donnelly, John, "Participative Management at Work," interview. *Harvard Business Review,* January–February 1977, pp. 117–127.

Doyle, Michael, and David Straus, *How to Make Meetings Work.* Chicago: Playboy Press, 1976.

Doyle, Robert J., "A New Look at the Scanlon Plan." *Management Accounting,* September 1970, pp. 48–52.

———, "Gainsharing—A Total Productivity Approach." *Journal of Contemporary Business,* Vol. II, No. 2, 1982, pp. 57–70.

Driscoll, J.W., "Working Creatively with a Union: Lessons from the Scanlon Plan." *Organizational Dynamics,* Summer 1979, pp. 61–80.

Drucker, Peter, *The Practice of Management.* New York: Harper & Row, 1954.

———, *Management: Tasks, Responsibilities, Practices.* New York: Harper & Row, 1973.

Frost, Carl F., John H. Wakeley, and Robert A. Ruh, *The Scanlon Plan for Organization Development: Identity, Participation and Equity.* East Lansing: Michigan State University Press, 1974.

Golembiewski, Robert T., *Men, Management and Morality.* New York: McGraw-Hill, 1965.

Gooding, J., "It Pays to Wake Up the Blue Collar Worker." *Fortune,* September 1970, pp. 133–135, 158–168.

Judson, A.S., "The Awkward Truth About Productivity." *Harvard Business Review,* September–October 1982, pp. 93–97.

Katz, Daniel, and Robert L. Kahn, *The Social Psychology of Organizations.* New York: Wiley, 1966.

Katzell, R., D. Yankelovich, et al., *Work, Productivity, and Job Satisfaction.* New York: The Psychological Corporation, 1975.

Lawler, Edward E., III, *Pay and Organization Development.* Reading, Mass.: Addison-Wesley, 1981.

Lesieur, Fred G., ed., *The Scanlon Plan: A Frontier in Labor-Management Cooperation.* Cambridge, Mass.: The MIT Press, 1958.

———, and Elbridge S. Puckett, "The Scanlon Plan Has Proved Itself." *Harvard Business Review,* September–October 1969, pp. 109–118.

Likert, Rensis, *New Patterns of Management.* New York: McGraw-Hill, 1961.

———, *The Human Organization: Its Management and Values.* New York: McGraw-Hill, 1967.

McGregor, Douglas, *The Human Side of Enterprise.* New York: McGraw-Hill, 1960.

Moore, Brian E., and Timothy L. Ross, *The Scanlon Way to Improved Productivity.* New York: Wiley, 1978.

Myers, M. Scott, *Every Employee a Manager.* New York: McGraw-Hill, 1970.

———, *Managing with Unions.* Reading, Mass.: Addison-Wesley, 1978.

Nadler, David A., *Feedback and Organization Development.* Reading, Mass.: Addison-Wesley, 1977.

O'Dell, Carla S., *Gainsharing: Involvement, Incentives, and Productivity.* AMA Management Briefing, 1981.

Odiorne, George S., *MBO II: A System of Managerial Leadership for the 80s.* Belmont, Calif.: Fearon Pitman, 1979.

Ouchi, William, *Theory Z: How American Business Can Meet the Japanese Challenge.* Reading, Mass.: Addison-Wesley, 1981.

Pascale, Richard T., and Anthony G. Athos, *The Art of Japanese Management.* New York: Simon & Schuster, 1981.

Productivity Sharing Programs: Can They Contribute to Productivity Improvement? Staff report, United States General Accounting Office, 1981.

Quinn, Robert P., and Graham L. Staines, *The 1977 Quality of Employment Survey.* Ann Arbor: The Institute for Social Research, The University of Michigan, 1979.

Riggs, J.L., and G.H. Felix, *Productivity by Objectives.* Englewood Cliffs, N.J.: Prentice-Hall, 1983.

Torbert, Frances, "Making Incentives Work." *Harvard Business Review,* September–October 1959, pp. 81–92.

Workers' Attitudes Toward Productivity. Survey results, Chamber of Commerce of the United States, 1980.

Index